Tim Rowse is one of the most thoughtful, informative and widely respected commentators on government policies relating to Indigenous Australians. These essays explore the differences between thinking about Indigenous Australians as peoples or as populations, by way of historical and contemporary episodes in this ongoing debate. They are essential reading for anyone interested in thinking about what might be the conditions of a just relationship.

Professor Paul Patton, University of New South Wales

A thought-provoking set of essays that explore through key public intellectual figures and at different historical junctures a vexed and complex question: if Indigenous Australians can be politically and ethically recognized only as a collective, then the question of how this collective is conceived arises. Rowse shows that such conception is rooted in settler liberalism, both colonial and postcolonial, that it is contested, and that it operates in terms of two distinct ideas of the collective as either a people or a population. How justice for Indigenous Australians is thought about depends on which of these ideas guides such thinking. A must-have resource for all students and practitioners in Indigenous affairs.

Anna Yeatman, Professorial Research Fellow, Whitlam Institute, University of Western Sydney

This publication has been printed on paper certified by the Programme for the Endorsement of Forest Certification (PEFC). PEFC is committed to sustainable forest management through third party forest certification of responsibly managed forests. For more info: www.pefc.org

RETHINKING SOCIAL JUSTICE

FROM 'PEOPLES' TO 'POPULATIONS'

TIM ROWSE

Aboriginal Studies Press

First published in 2012
by Aboriginal Studies Press

© Timothy Rowse 2012

All rights reserved. No part of this book may be reproduced or transmitted in any form or by any means, electronic or mechanical, including photocopying, recording or by any information storage and retrieval system, without prior permission in writing from the publisher. The Australian *Copyright Act 1968* (the Act) allows a maximum of one chapter or 10 per cent of this book, whichever is the greater, to be photocopied by any educational institution for its education purposes provided that the educational institution (or body that administers it) has given a remuneration notice to Copyright Agency Limited (CAL) under the Act.

Aboriginal Studies Press
is the publishing arm of the
Australian Institute of Aboriginal
and Torres Strait Islander Studies.
GPO Box 553, Canberra, ACT 2601
Phone: (61 2) 6246 1183
Fax: (61 2) 6261 4288
Email: asp@aiatsis.gov.au
Web: www.aiatsis.gov.au/asp/welcome.html

National Library of Australia Cataloguing-in-Publication entry

Author: Rowse, Tim, 1951-

Title: Rethinking social justice: from 'peoples' to 'populations'/Tim Rowse.

ISBN: 9781922059161 (pbk.)

ISBN: 9781922059192 (ebook: Kindle)

ISBN: 9781922059185 (ebook: epub)

ISBN: 9781922059178 (ebook: pdf)

Notes: Includes bibliographical references and index.

Subjects: Aboriginal Australians — Civil rights. Aboriginal Australians — Social conditions. Social justice — Australia Reparations for historical injustices — Australia. Australia — Government policy.

Dewey Number: 342.940872

Printed in Australia by Opus Print Group

Front cover: *Op Phase*, Ruth Waller, 2009, oil and acrylic on linen, courtesy Watters Gallery

Cover design by Greg Nelson, Upside Creative

This project has been assisted by the Australian Government through the Australia Council, its arts funding and advisory body.

Contents

Foreword by Fr Frank Brennan	vii
Acronyms and Abbreviations	xiii
Introduction	xv
Part I: Recognising 'Populations' and 'Peoples'	**1**
1. Recognising 'Peoples' and 'Populations'	3
Part II: Evoking People-hood	**29**
2. Hasluck and Elkin	31
3. Strehlow Damns Coombs	45
4. 'The Whole Aboriginal Problem in Microcosm': The South Australian Land Rights Debate of 1966	62
5. The Politics of Enumerating the Stolen Generations	80
Part III: Critical Reflections on Political Capacity	**99**
6. The Changing Cultural Constitution of the Indigenous Sector	101
7. The Ambivalence of Helen Hughes	128
Part IV: Thinking Historically About 1967–76	**141**
8. 'If We are to Survive as a People ...': Noel Pearson's Economic History	143
9. Peter Sutton and the Historical Roots of Suffering	160
10. The Coombs Experiment	173
Part V: The Appeal of Quantification	**199**
11. The Australian Reconciliation Barometer and the Indigenous Imaginery	201
Notes	217
References	235
Index	245

For useful suggestions while I was writing this book, I thank: Bob Boughton, Julie Finlayson, David Martin, Elizabeth Watt, Ed Wensing and Anna Yeatman. My intellectual debts to the researchers in the Centre for Aboriginal Economic Policy Research will be evident in my endnotes and references. And thanks to Murray Goot for encouraging critical recycling.

Foreword

This year, we Australians have marked the fortieth anniversary of the establishment of the Aboriginal tent embassy erected without a permit in front of the old Parliament House in Canberra, and the twentieth anniversary of the High Court's *Mabo* decision putting right the long term failure to recognise native title to lands. Back in 1972, Aboriginal Australians were campaigning for 'land rights', taking to the streets because they had no voice within the national decision making processes. It was only five years before that the Australian people voted to amend the Constitution giving the Australian Parliament the power to make laws with respect to Aborigines. By 1992, Aborigines and Torres Strait Islanders were celebrating the High Court's recognition of native title, and preparing to negotiate the *Native Title Act* with the Keating Government and with the conflicting parties in the Australian Parliament.

Prime Minister Paul Keating in his 1992 Redfern Park Address said: '*Mabo* is an historic decision — we can make it an historic turning point, the basis of a new relationship between indigenous and non-Aboriginal Australians. The message should be that there is nothing to fear or to lose in the recognition of historical truth, or the extension of social justice, or the deepening of Australian social democracy to include indigenous Australians.'

During these last twenty years, social justice for Indigenous Australians has been very contested political territory. The Liberal Party led by long time Prime Minister John Howard was wary of the term 'social justice'. It therefore came to be seen as the policy preserve of the Labor Party and the minor parties including the Democrats and the Greens. Whatever the prevailing political fashions and orthodoxies, we cannot give an adequate account of justice in philosophical terms if we simply restrict ourselves to commutative and distributive justice. Commutative justice relates to just outcomes for all participants in economic transactions, contracts and promises, including the just recognition of prior land titles. Distributive justice focuses on the necessary distribution of income, wealth and power in society so that everyone's basic needs might be met, including the provision of land for those in need under arrangements such as post-war soldier resettlement schemes. Social justice is concerned with the conditions for persons to participate in community and in society enjoying those things and relationships necessary for them to achieve their full human flourishing. Social justice may work in tandem with the redistribution of wealth and resources. But social justice is not to be equated with wealth redistribution. Those who exclude social justice tend to view Indigenous Australians as poor, disadvantaged individuals who simply need better economic, health and education outcomes. Those who include a social justice perspective do not decry initiatives founded on distributive justice but they also see a need for political processes and state structures facilitating Indigenous participation in decisions affecting Indigenous communities, service delivery, and negotiation of the relationship between the Indigenous polity and the nation state.

Tim Rowse neatly posits that those who focus primarily or exclusively on distributive justice see Indigenous Australians as populations whereas those who emphasise a social justice perspective see them as peoples. The same observer might oscillate their primary focus from distributive justice to social justice, thereby changing their description from 'Indigenous populations' to 'Indigenous peoples'. When attending to commutative justice, we are not much concerned about outcomes, being focused on pre-existing entitlements, even if, as was the case for the first land rights legislation in South Australia, the vast North West Reserve of the state was being made available for only 300 persons — 91 per cent of the Aboriginal reserve land being dedicated to just 4 per cent of the Aboriginal population. When attending to social justice, we are focused on outcomes or consequences, seeking measurable improvements in health, education, housing and employment for all people.

Twenty-five years ago, I was meeting with a group of Aboriginal teachers, teacher aides and welfare workers in Bourke, western New South Wales. I made the point that most Aboriginal people at that time were poor, disadvantaged, dispossessed and Indigenous. I invited them to imagine the scene of an Aboriginal person in later years driving a Rolls Royce down the main street of Bourke. What would they think? One woman immediately answered, 'It's stolen.' I was shocked but everyone else in the room enjoyed the humour. I wondered what might their situation look like in years to come were they no longer poor, disadvantaged and dispossessed. For many of my listeners, this was unimaginable. Would their situation, their worldview, their way of life be the same as other Australians? Or would there still be something distinctive? Should there be maintenance of distinctive entitlements or possibilities?

Rowse offers us 'a series of historical observations' traversing the terrain between *terra nullius* and land rights, and the years between assimilation and self-determination — 'a perplexing matter for historians to narrate because the meanings of these terms of political art have always been contestable'. Self-determination includes self-determination for the individual, for the extended family and for the Aboriginal community whether viewed as a population or as a people — any or all of which might be somewhat dysfunctional.

It is never easy for a non-Indigenous writer to delve into this dysfunctionality, its causes and possible remedies. Rowse engages with a series of Indigenous and non-Indigenous intellectuals who have wrestled with these questions. Paul Hasluck had a dream, that Aborigines would be able 'to live like us'. In 1959, he spoke of Aboriginal people being 'tangled in their own distressed situation like flies on sticky paper. They could fly if only they could get clear of their surroundings, lift themselves free of their past, leaving behind them their present life'. Contemporary non-Indigenous thinkers as diverse as Peter Sutton and Helen Hughes agree; so too do Indigenous leaders like Noel Pearson and Marcia Langton if 'living like us' is taken to include the finest opportunities for human flourishing, including the enjoyment of just land entitlements, cultural integrity, respect and due acknowledgment from the State and from one's fellow citizens. These contemporary thinkers continue to wrestle with the question posed by Hasluck in 1959: 'How do you make sure that the staging camp does not become the end of the road?'

Though he is very tough on Helen Hughes, Rowse is refreshing in not impugning the moral integrity of those who propose policy solutions different from his own preferences. As the biographer of H C Coombs, he rightly takes to task those who speak in sneering terms about the Coombs experiment in Aboriginal policy during his chairmanship of the Council for Aboriginal Affairs from 1967 to 1976. All governments are experimenting when it comes to seeking policy which produces right results in commutative, distributive and social justice for Indigenous Australians. Rowse warns against the 'juridical liberalism' which treats Indigenous persons as 'citizen-isolates'. No man is an island. Not even the non-Indigenous Australian is an atomistic individual who can achieve her full human flourishing without life in community. The anthropologist Elkin who provided Hasluck with the anthropological underpinnings for the assimilation policy still espoused that missions and government settlements should preserve 'Aboriginal group life with its social and ceremonial aspects, thus aiding the development and integration of the individual personality'. He saw that everyone needed to belong to a community, not just being a hanger on or survivor.

When land rights policies were first being enacted in Australia, the unwilling Bjelke-Petersen government in Queensland fought a strong rearguard action against the outstation movement which encouraged, or at least provided the opportunity for, Aboriginal groups to return to their traditional lands. Petersen and his departmental head, Pat Killoran, were adamant that people should remain in large communities where the State could efficiently deliver health, education, and police services together with local government infrastructure necessary to augment housing. Two generations on, Rowse asks dispassionately: 'Can small units of Aboriginal self-determination deliver the infrastructure and services to which Aborigines are entitled? Is it necessary to make remote and rural units of government larger as a means to make them better?' When considering social justice, rather than commutative justice, we have to consider these consequences. An Aboriginal community may have the right to live on their traditional country. The State is not obliged to provide the full suite of health, education and police services regardless of the remoteness, smallness and peripatetic nature of a community. What's essential is a relationship between the Aboriginal community and the State facilitating acceptance and ownership of decisions about resource allocation for the well being of all citizens, including those living in the remotest parts of the country and those who may have to travel to those parts to deliver services.

Even though both sides of the political fence have put their stamp on the *Native Title Act* and on the Intervention in the Northern Territory, it's not as if there are no contested issues. In his book *Up from the mission*, Noel Pearson says that 'both black and white Australians have struggled for two centuries for that elusive ideal: a moral community in the Antipodes'. A moral community would be founded on trusting relationships permitting the dialogue necessary to determine the limits of social justice in addition to the commutative and distributive justice available to Indigenous Australians. In the first enthusiasm for self-determination, big mistakes were made. Long-time bureaucrats Mike Dillon and Neil Westbury note: 'The rationale for substantive non-engagement [by governments] has been that self-determination and self-management by definition, exclude the need for government involvement (apart from the ongoing funding arrangements).' Noel Pearson recalls his own service on the Hope Vale Aboriginal Community Council in the 1980s when the community was cutting its links with the Lutheran Church which had administered the community: 'We cut these last ties with a relishing sense of historic reckoning. The awful truth is that we threw the baby out with the bathwater: the role of the church in the secular and spiritual life of our community was conflated; both the church and our people should have found a way to move beyond the paternalism of the past without destroying the moral and cultural order which had been such a strong quality of our community'. In secular Australia, this is very difficult and barren terrain for government and for the academy. Peter Sutton has made a valiant effort in his *The politics of suffering* affirming 'a child's basic human right to have love, wellbeing and safety'. He espouses not politics and law, but the personal. Governments don't do love well, even when there are no issues of cultural difference and historic injustice.

Rowse is upset that Sutton's book contains 'so many scornfully worded pages' about the 'liberal consensus' of the Coombs era which presumed that land rights and self-determination would provide Aborigines with a new parousia, curtailing the racist pressure to assimilate and lifting people's self-respect and pride, enabling them 'to embark on a new era in which the quality of their lives would improve'. But those who never saw the 'liberal consensus' as the answer for Aboriginal existential angst about life and change — any more than it was the answer for other Australians — have little problem with his change of heart.

Rowse provides us with a constructive challenge: 'agree that the government of remote Australia is an ongoing project of exploratory testing of the relative significance of human sameness and cultural difference between Aboriginal and non-Aboriginal Australia'. As the admiring Coombs biographer, he notes that 'Coombs sought to slow things down, to give time and space for Indigenous Australians to make choices about which elements of European-Australian culture to embrace and how quickly they would embrace them'. Land rights have given some the space; but time may be running out. We need to recommit to the relationship affirming Indigenous agency, ensuring that 'reconciliation' is more than a project to overcome Indigenous socio-economic disadvantage and to enhance non-Indigenous Australians' negative perceptions of Indigenous Australians. We need to build trust so that having addressed the claims of commutative justice through land rights measures, having aligned the Aboriginal claims for distributive justice in a racially non-discriminatory way with those of the general Australian community, we might then negotiate the compromises and experiment with the new possibilities for social justice. Social justice for indigenous peoples in a post-colonial context requires recognition of and respect for their continuing differences from the 'mainstream' society, and procedures for negotiating the ongoing accommodation of difference even once we have succeeded in 'closing the gap'.

The test will be whether each night in the privacy of the family home, Aboriginal parents will urge their children to give life in contemporary Australia their best shot because, after all that has gone on, Australia now gives them a fair go. We are still a long way from that, given that the latest Reconciliation Barometer from Reconciliation Australia finds that more than 80 per cent of us (whether Indigenous or not) think that we have a low or very low level of trust across the Indigenous–Non-Indigenous divide. The tent embassy still has a place in the national psyche forty years on, and the commutative justice of land rights is no substitute for the social justice which needs to be negotiated through Indigenous agency twenty years after *Mabo*.

Fr Frank Brennan SJ AO

Acronyms and Abbreviations

ABS	Australian Bureau of Statistics
ACCHO	Aboriginal Community Controlled Health Organisations
AIAS	Australian Institute of Aboriginal Studies
AIATSIS	Australian Institute of Aboriginal and Torres Strait Islander Studies
ANU	Australian National University
ANZAAS	Australian and New Zealand Association for the Advancement of Science
ASIC	Australian Securities and Investments Commission
ATSIC	Aboriginal and Torres Strait Islander Commission
ATSISJC	Aboriginal and Torres Strait Islander Social Justice Commissioner
AusAID	Australian Government Overseas Aid Program
BAC	Bawaninga Aboriginal Corporation
CAA	Council for Aboriginal Affairs
CAEPR	Centre for Aboriginal Economic Policy Research
CDEP	Community Development Employment Projects
CHIP	Community Housing and Infrastructure Program
COAG	Council of Australian Governments
FCAATSI	Federal Council for the Advancement of Aborigines and Torres Strait Islanders
HREOC	Human Rights and Equal Opportunity Commission
ICC	Indigenous Coordination Centre
ILO	International Labour Organization
ILUA	Indigenous Land Use Agreement
MP	Member of Parliament
NGO	Non-government organisation
NTRB	Native Title Representative Body

ABBREVIATIONS AND ACRONYMS

OAA	Office of Aboriginal Affairs
OPAL	One People of Australia League
ORAC	Office of the Registrar of Aboriginal Corporations
ORIC	Office of the Regulator of Indigenous Corporations
QCAATSI	Queensland Council for the Advancement of Aborigines and Torres Strait Islanders
SAC	Society for Aboriginal Civilisation
SCRGSP	Steering Committee for the Review of Government Service Provision
SRA	Shared Responsibility Agreement
WCARA	Western Central Arnhem Regional Authority

Introduction

This book is a series of historical observations, not a work of policy advocacy. My intention is to investigate recent ways of thinking of Indigenous Australians as different and as deserving of more just treatment.

In my first chapter, I set up a framework for thinking about Australian public reasoning about social justice for Indigenous Australians. I suggest that one way to understand Australian policy towards, and debate about, Indigenous Australians since the late 1950s is to see it as mingling two ways of recognising them: as 'peoples' and as 'populations'. We think of Indigenous Australians as 'peoples' (the Aborigines and the Torres Strait Islanders) who have rights (to land and self-government); in seeing them as 'peoples', we attribute to them self-governing capacities — whether recently acquired or arising from their heritage (their customary law). At the same time, we see them as 'populations', defined sub-sets of the 'Australian population', quantified in terms of socio-economic characteristics and comparable to the 'Australian population'. Each of these recognitions carries with it a notion of social justice. Between 'peoples' there can be negotiated political relationships; between populations there can be measured statistical (dis)parity, in respect to this or that socio-economic variable. The dissonance between these recognitions and these two conceptions of social justice animates and at times confuses the rhetorical landscape of contemporary Indigenous affairs policy. In Chapter 1, I point to some of the problems that arise in both recognitions. Although I do not advocate one over the other, this book is an invitation to reflection on the ways that these two concepts of Indigenous collectivity shape understandings of the past and the future, and thus help us to consider what is owed to Indigenous Australians in the name of social justice.

The recognition of Indigenous Australians as 'peoples' had to overcome a firm conviction that Aboriginal 'society' had disappeared or would very soon be gone. Paul Hasluck — with characteristic lucidity — argued in the

1950s that a policy of 'assimilation' was the right response to this decline; with the public's help, governments would manage Indigenous Australians' transition humanely. In Chapters 2 and 3, I highlight the critiques that two anthropologists mounted against 'assimilation'. AP Elkin and TGH Strehlow argued that 'assimilation' as practised by the governments of Australia had become a program for the destruction of Aboriginal culture.

Chapter 2 contrasts two conceptions of 'assimilation' that competed for the endorsement of liberal intellectuals in the 1950s and 1960s: Hasluck's 'juridical' individualism that sought to raise the individual from the mire of a decadent Aboriginal milieu versus Elkin's Durkheimian respect for Aboriginal 'group life'. Warning Hasluck not to overlook the historical and cultural necessity of the 'group', Elkin addressed the ambivalence of Hasluck's social policy: was Aborigines' sense of solidarity with one another entirely a handicap, or was it in some ways a strength? Arguments by anthropologists such as Elkin helped to awaken policy intellectuals to the value of Aborigines' unextinguished capacities for collective action.[1] When invited to advise the Australian government on policy, HC Coombs endorsed that affirmation of Indigenous capacity.

As I show in Chapter 3, Coombs was unable to enlist the support of anthropologist TGH Strehlow, even though Strehlow had been criticising the cultural coerciveness of 'assimilation'. While Strehlow's reasons for distancing himself from Coombs' faith in Aboriginal capacity had much to do with his sense of his own responsibility as a trustee of Indigenous knowledge, his alienation from Coombs also points to a genuine dilemma for the advocates of 'people-hood': in what terms should a distinctive Indigenous modernity be imagined? Is the mobilisation of Indigenous political capacity possible? And do the unprecedented projects of 'self-determination' turn Indigenous heritage into something that is alien to Indigenous people?[2]

When legislators sought reform, they reasoned publicly about social justice. In South Australia's 1966 legislation to vest land in Aboriginal bodies, the Dunstan government was the first in Australia to establish contemporary forms of legislated title and to postulate Aborigines (at least those in that State) as a 'people'. Why and how did this government do this? In Chapter 4, I elucidate the notion of 'people-hood' evinced in South Australia's parliamentary debates about the 1966 Aboriginal Land Trust Bill. Unlike later legislators of land rights in the Northern Territory, the South Australians did not draw on knowledge of Aborigines' classical culture when evoking Aboriginal entitlement and capacity; rather, 'people-hood' was an implication of the government's desires to complete a truncated jurisdiction and to appease alienated (and potentially alienated) clients of government 'advancement' programs.

The 'Stolen Generations' has emerged as a 'people-hood' identity — particularly for those excluded from 'land rights'. In the public validation of that identity, it has been important to demonstrate that many were 'stolen'. Chapter 5 reviews attempts to quantify the Stolen Generations. I argue that this is not possible, because the meaning of key terms remains in dispute, government records are defective, and the definition and size of the base 'Aboriginal population' are, arguably, unknown. An alternative to recognising the Stolen Generations as a proportion of a population is to honour them as an 'ethical category' — one way to think about Aborigines as a wronged 'people'.

When the Whitlam and Fraser governments took Indigenous Australians' capacity for collective action seriously, the Commonwealth legislated in 1976 to enable the formation of Indigenous organisations; the Howard government rewrote this statute thirty years later, intending to make it less punitive and more tutelary in its mode of regulation. The Indigenous organisation has now emerged as a focus for anthropologists' research. Chapter 6 reviews this body of work, arguing that 'cultural authenticity' has become less credible as a criterion for judging the effectiveness of the Indigenous organisation. The chapter hails the emergent Indigenous middle class, sketches its ethic and points to changes in the structure of Australian government that compel this class's further acculturation to norms of good governance.[3]

The very idea of Indigenous corporate capacity has continued to attract scepticism in some quarters. There are commentators who label it 'separatism' or 'exceptionalism'; in their writing, organised Indigenous self-assertion — along with the other entailments of 'people-hood' such as collective land title — are held up to populist ridicule and policy-maker suspicion. When these insinuations circulate in the idiom of social science, the results can be potent. Chapter 7 examines Helen Hughes' *Lands of shame*; the publication of this book in 2007 helped to legitimise the Howard government's Northern Territory Emergency Intervention. I argue that in presenting Aboriginal leaders as 'big men', while urging Aborigines to seize opportunities for advancement, Hughes appears to be undecided in her evaluation of Indigenous people who have flourished in the era of self-determination. Her ambivalence about Indigenous success is matched by her vagueness about the population geography of remote and very remote Australia and her unwillingness to acknowledge the experimental character of her policy proposals. Her stentorian iconoclasm was the scaffolding of shoddy reasoning.[4]

In Chapters 8, 9 and 10, I consider a crucial period in Indigenous affairs policy — 1967–76 — through the arguments and actions of three policy intellectuals who, for different reasons, have felt compelled to interpret it. First, I draw out the historical arguments that Noel Pearson has presented: about his home community Hope Vale, about colonisation and about the formation of Australia's wider political culture. Part of the novelty of Pearson's work is his historical self-consciousness and his challenge to a historiography of 1967–76 that has given too much weight to the story of formal entitlement and too little to the story of Aborigines' economic adjustment. I argue that the effects of Pearson's account of the travails of 'people-hood' are to re-pose the 'people-hood' question in terms that are more 'economic' than 'cultural', and to question whether 'difference' should be assumed to be primarily a matter of 'culture'.

Peter Sutton's *The politics of suffering* presents the late 1960s/early 1970s as the moment when 'the liberal consensus' won political and cultural authority. Having named and dated this ideological formation, Sutton then takes it to task for its blindness to Indigenous suffering and its refusal to examine the deeper Aboriginal determinants of that condition. Taking Sutton seriously as a revisionist historian, I suggest amendments to his formulation of the 'liberal consensus', going on to argue that while his thesis of cultural pathology is plausible, its policy implications are unclear. In his disaffection for the categories 'Indigenous'/'non-Indigenous', Sutton harks back to a period before governments recognised 'people-hood', and affirmed and institutionalised Indigenous culture; in those times (the gestation of Sutton as ethnographic witness), difference could be accommodated, informally, through personal relationships of caring and respect. However, this critique-by-memoir does not give rise to an alternative conceptual scheme: Sutton remains analytically committed, by default, to a notion of Indigenous people-hood — albeit viewing it in a firmly anti-romantic light.

The years 1967–76 were the zenith of HC Coombs' influence, and for some recent policy revisionists he has become iconic of dangerously misplaced faith in Indigenous Australians' ability to advance on their own terms to a condition of 'autonomy' within Australia. In Chapter 10, I restate the case in favour of Coombs as a policy intellectual — not by reaffirming the 1970s optimism about Indigenous capacities but by taking seriously the phrase (used pejoratively by Coombs' critics) the 'Coombs experiment'. To do so, I draw attention to Coombs' least-known essay — a 1969 piece in which he presented the colonial encounter, and his own times in particular, in the deep time perspective of human evolution. A corollary of his Darwinian hypothesis of historically differentiated human nature is that policy-making is best understood as continuing experimental adaptation. The pejorative resonance of the phrase the 'Coombs experiment' vanishes to the extent that the reader accepts this argument. I illustrate with examples Coombs' intelligent uncertainty about the project of Indigenous self-determination, and I conclude by commenting on the ways that contemporary statistics — the 'evidence' in policy experiments — embody debatable assumptions about Indigenous sameness and difference.

One of the ideological moves of the Howard government — discussed in Chapter 1 — was to distinguish 'practical' from 'symbolic' reconciliation. To give priority to 'practical' was to elevate the representation of Indigenous Australians as 'populations' and to set aside as 'symbolic' the claims that Indigenous Australians make in the name of 'peoplehood'. In my final chapter, I examine the terms in which Reconciliation Australia has presented 'reconciliation' in its biennial public opinion study, the Australian Reconciliation Barometer. In its attempt to measure 'reconciliation', Reconciliation Australia's questions imply that 'reconciliation' requires the abatement of prejudice and of Indigenous socio-economic 'disadvantage'. The data generated by the Barometer show that the assignment of responsibility for Indigenous disadvantage remains contentious — in particular, government actions to remedy disadvantage are viewed both as disastrous (in the past) and essential (now). The Barometer's questions subtly elide the possibility that reconciliation could be about a new political relationship between peoples, and it does not envisage that Indigenous actions towards non-Indigenous Australians could be of any consequence. The unfortunate result is that Reconciliation Australia seems, at least in its Barometer, to be captive to a conception of Indigenous Australians as both disadvantaged and lacking in agency. The Barometer, if it is continued, will help to reproduce the ascendancy of 'population' over 'people' in public reasoning about social justice.[5]

In working on the chapters in this book, two conclusions have crystallised for me. One is that while public reasoning about social justice for Indigenous Australians should continue to be conducted in both the 'population' and the 'people' idioms, we need to become better at reflecting on the implications and the limitations of each. Currently, the 'population' way of thinking is too much in the ascendancy. This is illustrated by the way that Reconciliation Australia has unthinkingly (I assume) left out of its Barometer any question that invites us to imagine the collective and individual political agency of Indigenous Australians. The current weakness of 'people-hood' is also evident in the ways in which the Northern Territory Intervention has been conceived and justified in a political climate in which 'closing the gaps' seems to exhaust our notions of social justice. My second conclusion is that for 'people-hood' to be persuasive, it needs to be detached from our habitual assumptions about 'cultural difference'. James Weiner, an anthropologist who has worked in both theatres of contemporary Australian colonialism — northern Australia and Papua New Guinea — has argued that the habit of asserting the Indigenous/non-Indigenous difference in cultural terms is a legacy of a certain politics of representation with which anthropology has been complicit. One of the achievements of that politics — I would present Elkin, Strehlow and Coombs as exemplars — was that we as Australians questioned the social and historical analysis on which 'assimilation' rested. However, in the resulting political landscape, as Weiner argues, the preoccupation with cultural difference is more and more misleading of the total social facts of Indigenous/non-Indigenous relationships, which he evokes as 'the tremendous burgeoning of the institutional relationships, buttressing, laws, procedures, and so on, between any indigenous community and the governments, companies, non-government organisations (NGOs), claimant Aboriginal corporations and other organisations … that give any single, rarefied "cultural group" a "place"'.[6] Weiner's paper is one item in a wider intellectual movement within anthropology (a discipline to which this book is indebted) that not only historicises the elements of 'culture' but historicises the very research programs and public rhetoric that make 'cultural difference' our object. In this book, there is one political activist — Don Dunstan — who prefigures what we might call this 'post-cultural' evocation of Indigenous people-hood; there is another — Noel Pearson — who is currently reinforcing it and controversially drawing policy lessons from it.

RECOGNISING 'POPULATIONS' AND 'PEOPLES'

CHAPTER 1

Recognising 'Peoples' and 'Populations'

Are Indigenous Australians — that is, Aborigines and Torres Strait Islanders — 'peoples' or 'populations'? Perhaps the reader is puzzled by this question: what's the difference? As long as we acknowledge Indigenous Australians as people — that is, as human beings — why does it matter whether we refer to them as peoples or as populations? In this commonsense view, the phrases 'Aboriginal people of Australia' and 'Aboriginal population of Australia' mean the same thing. In this chapter, however, I want to argue that 'peoples' and 'populations' are significantly different *concepts*, and that when we refer to Aborigines (or Torres Strait Islanders) as a 'people', we are thinking about them in a specific way that is not the same as referring to Indigenous people as a 'population'. In this 'people'/'population' distinction, we find a subtle but important struggle in the politics of recognition.

Recognition

Recognition matters, and it is political. In the emergence of Indigenous peoples as a global political presence, 'recognition' by others is complementary to Indigenous peoples' declarations of their own survival and ongoing needs and rights. For much of the twentieth century, non-Indigenous Australians recognised Indigenous Australians in ways that diminished them. Aborigines (a term often used as if it included Torres Strait Islanders) were not only a tiny minority; they were also a fading presence — demographically and culturally — in an ethnically 'white' nation. For much of the twentieth century, to the extent that they were 'recognised' it was as objects of humane solicitude, soon to be gone, 'absorbed' or assimilated. In the 1960s, that confident and sometimes regretful scenario lost credibility among thoughtful non-Indigenous Australians. They began to realise that Aborigines were not dying out; that even those with some 'white blood' identified as Aborigines; that they were aggrieved about how they had been treated; and that they were proud of their heritage. In a series of shifts in public perception — recently narrated with scholarly detail by Russell McGregor — non-Indigenous Australians began in the 1950s and 1960s to recognise Indigenous Australia in new terms.[1] Starting in the late 1960s, reformed Indigenous affairs policy encouraged Aborigines and Torres Strait Islanders to maintain separate identity and to establish or maintain certain institutions; in the 1970s, they were allowed to own (according to Australian law) some of the land that they regarded as belonging to them by custom and tradition, and the Australian government initiated several inquiries into the possibility and desirability of recognising 'Aboriginal customary law'.[2] One way to understand this transformation in non-Indigenous perspectives and practices is to see it as amounting to 'recognition' of Aboriginal and Torres Strait Islanders as 'peoples' with their own legal and governmental heritage.

Recognition is multiply constructed. The recogniser sets certain terms in which the recognised can become visible, and the recognised have an incentive to present themselves in these terms, resulting perhaps in changes to the ways in which they act and view themselves. Recognition is a more or less collaborative construction of new political subjects (it can be tense and agonistic). Recognition is multiple because states are complex assemblages of diverse practices of knowing and governing. When a settler colonial state such as Australia begins to 'recognise' Aborigines, it has more than one way to go about it. Elizabeth Povinelli has shown how the state's 'recognition' of the Northern Territory's Indigenous population as people with rights to land has turned out to be not necessarily a coherent ensemble of processes. Povinelli writes of the state's multiple production of Aboriginal subject positions — that is, laws and policies open up more than one way for Aborigines to present themselves as people with a plausible claim. 'We have here ... a set of incommensurate, though often mutually referring, state regimes sitting alongside a set of incommensurate, though often mutually referring, local social regimes.'[3] Povinelli has investigated some 'local social regimes' in the Northern Territory. My task is to work at a more 'macro' level, tracing the history of two modes of recognition that have emerged in Australian public policy since the late 1960s. I will highlight the distinction between being recognised as an Indigenous 'population' and being recognised as an Indigenous 'people'.

The significance of the people/population distinction

The International Labour Organization (ILO) has published two covenants on the rights of the Indigenous: Covenant 107 (1957), known as the Indigenous and Tribal Populations Convention and Covenant 169 (1989), known as the Convention on Indigenous and Tribal Peoples. The replacement of 'populations' by 'peoples' is understood to signify a shift in political vision. In 1957, the vision was 'assimilationist': the authors of Convention 107 assumed that eventually the Indigenous would be absorbed peacefully and equitably into the nation that ratified the Convention. In 1989, the authors of the Convention assumed that the Indigenous would remain indefinitely a distinct collective agent within the nation. The dimensions of that abiding distinction between nation-state and Indigenous people were to be some mixture of the cultural, the political, the territorial and the economic. Whereas an Indigenous *population* would one day disappear, as its individuals and households assimilated into the wider society and were counted as part of the national population, an Indigenous *people* would remain a lasting interlocutor of and within the nation — with a distinct identity, heritage, institutions and land base. Indigenous leaders have insisted to international forums that the key term in the discussion is 'peoples' and not 'populations'. In the 1994 session of the UN's Subcommission on Prevention of Discrimination and Protection of Minorities, a Native American delegate protested at a US government official's use of 'population'; 'people' without an 's', 'tribes' and 'tribal': 'We are not populations, people or tribes or bands. We are not gaggles of geese or packs of wild dogs. We are peoples and nations.'[4]

The rhetoric of Prime Minister John Howard (1996–2007) made me think again about the significance of this distinction between being a 'people' and being a 'population'. Howard contrasted 'practical' reconciliation with 'symbolic' reconciliation, and for a while he used these terms as if one had to choose between them — or at least to prioritise them. Howard insisted that his goal was 'practical' reconciliation: the equalisation of the Indigenous and non-Indigenous populations in respect of a suite of socio-economic indicators of employment, health and educational achievement. As each Indigenous individual or household improved in terms of certain socio-economic indicators, the gap between the average (or mean or median) Indigenous individual and the average (or mean or median) non-Indigenous individual would close, until the Indigenous and non-Indigenous populations had the same rates of mortality, employment, formal schooling, and so on. By offering this vision of a just society, Howard disdained — or gave a distant second place to — what he called 'symbolic' reconciliation, meaning that he dismissed or treated as relatively unimportant all those claims that Indigenous Australians were making about their rights *as a people* — such as their right to govern and represent themselves and to own land collectively.

When Howard spelled out what 'practical' reconciliation meant, he drew on statistical representations of Indigenous Australians — the statistics of their socio-economic disadvantage; that is, he was referring to Indigenous Australians as a population. In his distinction between 'practical' and 'symbolic', he gave priority to thinking of Indigenous people in terms of their population characteristics, and he discounted their collective rights as the Aboriginal and the Torres Strait Islander 'peoples'. It is one thing to represent the Indigenous as a population — as a category of individuals and households enumerated in a Census or survey — it is quite another thing to represent the Indigenous as a 'people' (or as two 'peoples'). A 'people' can plausibly be represented as a rights-bearing entity defined by its self-conscious organs of collective agency; a 'population' is merely a category within a nation's official statistical account of millions of individuals and households. An Indigenous population will be made up of rights-bearing individuals (citizens), but a 'population' is not a bearer of a collective right; a population is not even a collective agent, just an artefact of the administrative imagination.

We might suppose that an Indigenous people that aspired to self-determination would insist on representing itself as a people and be wary of being represented as a mere population. However, in Australia and New Zealand, Indigenous intellectuals represent Indigenous collectivity in both the idiom of people-hood and the idiom of population. For example, Indigenous and other intellectuals use official statistics to give persuasive accounts of a recurring pattern of socio-economic disadvantage; this descriptive account of social injustice informs the 'Closing the Gaps' policy. Many Indigenous intellectuals who want the various gaps to close also want to present Aborigines as a 'people' with collective rights. Noel Pearson wrote in 2007: 'The Indigenous Australian struggle is for socio-economic advancement and equality, but it is also about the recognition of status and rights as a people. The goal here is to preserve and win legal recognition of cultural distinctness as well as citizenship. Indigenous Australian political issues are "peoplehood issues".[5] In his 2012 Gandhi Lecture, Patrick Dodson, while regretting that Indigenous Australians were being 'defined in the language of disadvantage and gaps, portrayed in the media as impoverished welfare mendicants who were incapable of uplifting ourselves from a state of disadvantage, dependency and social malaise', affirmed that 'parity' should still be one goal of policy; thus he lamented that Australia had been 'incapable of lifting the vast majority of Indigenous people in this country to anywhere near parity on any social indicator with non Indigenous Australians'. However, Dodson called for reconciliation to be pursued in both 'practical' and 'symbolic' terms. The 'symbolic' politics to which he devoted much of his Gandhi Lecture focused on changing the vocabulary by which the Australian Constitution refers to Indigenous Australians — as he put it, 'how to recognise Aboriginal and Torres Islander people and their unique place in the nation, and provide the Commonwealth with the power to pass laws for us without resorting to outmoded identifiers such as race'.[6]

Indigenous intellectuals are not inconsistent if they use both the idiom of population and the idiom of people-hood. However, one argument of this book is that the effect of employing two idioms of representation — 'population' and 'people' — has been to install within Australian political culture (and Indigenous political discourse) two distinguishable notions of social justice. The idiom of 'people-hood' implies that social justice comes from a resolution of differences between political entities, between peoples; in the idiom of 'population', there are not two (or three) peoples, there are many individuals and households within an Australian population categorised by self-assigned 'race' or 'ethnic identity', and the task of social justice is to ensure that the inequalities among those individuals and households do not correspond to such characteristics as their self-identified 'ethnicity'. The social justice agenda of relations between peoples is about their respecting, via a political negotiation, each other's standing (operationalised in laws and institutions); the social justice agenda of relations within a national population is to realise the liberal ideal that socio-economic inequality should not be the result of some kind of discrimination, such as racial discrimination.

Thus we have two modes of recognitions, two notions of social justice and two distinct perspectives in the politics of Indigenous affairs. Both 'people' and 'population' are important and necessary idioms of Indigenous self-representation and state recognition, but we will understand the politics of our times better if we bear their difference in mind. In the remainder of this chapter, I will sketch the history of the recognition of Indigenous Australians as 'populations' and as 'peoples'. While 'population' is an inadequate idiom in which to encompass all the things that make Aborigines and Torres Strait Islanders 'peoples', the 'people' idiom also has problems that make it vulnerable to the rival cognitive authority — official statistics — of the 'population' idiom.

Population

The 'recognition' of Indigenous Australians as a 'population' could easily be taken for granted as merely a technical achievement. To grasp the significance of this 'recognition', we must first concede that an Indigenous population is not a natural fact that the colonists *must* recognise; colonial authorities have choices about whether to count 'Indigenous' people and about how to define them as sub-groups of the national population. Because the Australian colonies passed special laws to control Aborigines, it was legally necessary to define 'Aborigine' and it was administratively rational to count them. By the third quarter of the nineteenth century, most Australian jurisdictions were recording what they thought to be the absolute size and the sex composition of the Aboriginal population. The colonies began to record the ages of Aborigines in different years (Victoria from 1871, New South Wales and Western Australia from 1891, Queensland from 1901, and South Australia, Tasmania and the Northern Territory from 1911).[7] From 1860 to 1905, as each colony began to form a specialised administration and statutory regime through which to govern its Indigenous population, two other features were noted: the racial character of Indigenous people (differentiating 'full-bloods' from 'others' who were of mixed Aboriginal and European parentage) and their relationship to administrative control. There were two variables within 'administrative control', and each jurisdiction made use of at least one of them. The Indigenous population could be recognised as subject to enumeration or imagined as living beyond enumeration — a distinction sometimes conveyed by the distinction between 'settled districts' and regions that were beyond colonial settlement and administrative reach. The other 'administrative control' variable had to do with differentiated institutional authority: whether or not Aborigines were 'in employ', or 'under the Act', or living within reserves and government institutions.

When the Commonwealth government began to standardise the six Australian colonies' Indigenous statistical archives in the 1911 Census, it adopted the practice of the Western Australian 1901 Census of enumerating Aborigines if they were accessible to ordinary enumeration procedures; assuming those not enumerated to be 'full-bloods' and estimating their number; including 'half-castes' (but not 'full-bloods') in the general Australian Census population; and publishing separate figures on 'full-bloods' and 'half-castes' as two components of the 'Aboriginal population'.[8]

The 1966 Census was the last to use fractional racial terms: the government allowed respondents to distinguish 'one-quarter' Aboriginal descent from 'half'. From 1971, the Census ceased to ask respondents to distinguish such fractions of 'racial' descent. The 1971 question asked each head of the household about each member:

> What is this person's racial origin? (If of mixed origin, indicate the one to which he considers himself to belong. Tick one box only or give one origin only): 1. European origin; 2. Aboriginal origin; 3. Torres Strait Islander origin; 4. Other origin (give only one).[9]

This transition from a fractional to a unitary conception of descent (in later Censuses 'origin') was important, but it has overshadowed another innovation that preceded it.[10] Although the statisticians were not confident of the technical adequacy of the 1966 enumeration, on 16 April 1969 the government published, for the first time, tables that compared the 'Aboriginal' with the 'Australian' populations in respect of occupation and level of education. The measurement of what we now call 'gaps' began with *The Aboriginal population of Australia: summary of characteristics* (ABS, cat. no. 2.23). Social scientists in the late 1960s had complained of Indigenous Australians' statistical invisibility. These comparative tables on occupation and education were the beginnings of a remedy; they seemed to advance the scientific grasp of the difficulties of assimilating Aborigines. Appreciative social scientists and public servants argued that Australia should continue to measure a distinct 'Aboriginal population' so that such comparisons could gauge progress (or a lack of it) and inform policy. In 1975, Australia's leading demographer, Professor W Borrie, welcomed the decision by the Whitlam government that the National

Population Inquiry should 'include the Aboriginal population not only in the total situation, but also as a separate sub-study'.[11]

Since 1971, the Census has continued to enable social scientists and governments to compare Indigenous and non-Indigenous Australians in terms of their income, education and labour market status. Other administrative databases have been reformed, so that we can now distinguish Indigenous fertility, rates of arrest and imprisonment and dimensions of health. The Productivity Commission's biennial *Overcoming Indigenous disadvantage: key indicators* reports since 2003 have enabled the Australian government to institutionalise a simple but rhetorically powerful question: are we closing the gaps? The depth and persistence of the structural inequality in Australian society have become painfully clear. By casting the enriched statistical visibility of Indigenous Australians into a comparative framework, Australia's statisticians and social scientists have operationalised 'social justice' as parity.

Do statistics distort Indigenous realities?

There is justifiable concern that in the remote regions of Australia, Aborigines and Islanders are difficult to enumerate. To deploy trained officials to interview remote Aboriginal people is an enormous task. The problems are both technical and conceptual. Population geographer John Taylor has listed the factors that bear on the 'accuracy and reliability of census data':

> The wording of census questions ... the design of census questionnaires ... field procedures for administering questionnaires ... the level of respondent acceptance of the census ... the nature of the response to the questions, and ... the efficacy of the processes for translating census information to appropriate and meaningful data categories.[12]

Technical improvements have been possible: the redesign of forms (separating the 'household' form from the 'personal' form for recording data on individual members of the household); collecting data over several weeks in remote Australia, rather than on one night; and avoiding collection of data during predictable aggregations of Aboriginal people in festivals and ceremonies (to minimise misrepresenting spatial dispersion). In the 1976 Census, the Bureau trialled enumeration by interview in the Northern Territory and then extended this technique to parts of

South Australia and Western Australia in 1981. The Australian Bureau of Statistics (ABS) has recruited and trained casual Aboriginal staff as Census collectors, replacing local police. The ABS has also sometimes welcomed administrative partnership with local Aboriginal organisations such as the Tangentyere Council.[13] When John Taylor describes what went wrong with counting at Wadeye (NT) in 2006, the remedies he proposes are dependent, in his view, on the ABS cultivating working relationships with Aboriginal organisations in that region. In his opinion, 'a dwelling-count approach to capturing a mobile population' is too difficult for Census collectors who lack the local knowledge that such organisations would bring to the task.[14] In remote Aboriginal Australia, he argues, the Census is doomed to inaccuracy if it remains a 'direct encounter between the ABS and individual householders'.[15] Thorburn's account of the 2006 Census in Fitzroy Crossing also highlights administrative deficiencies that a determined and well-resourced ABS could remedy if it drew on the contextual population knowledge possessed by 'local NGOs'.[16]

When Taylor refers to 'wording' and 'translation', he touches on problems that require more than administrative solutions: conceptual issues such as the understanding of 'family' and of 'productive activity'. He complains elsewhere about a lack of ' cross-cultural fit' between the way the Census models social processes and how Aborigines really live.[17]

Domestic processes among remote Aborigines work differently from those most Australians would take for granted as 'normal'. Taylor warns against assuming that a 'household' is a space for the coincidence of co-residence, commensality, family relations and domestic economy: for remote Aborigines, these four processes frequently are dissociated, the work of different — if overlapping — ensembles whose locus is not necessarily a single dwelling. An Aboriginal family, in the sense of frequently interacting blood relatives, may extend across two or more dwellings that are close to each other. A remote Aboriginal household is unlikely to be an economic isolate (as the Census seems to imply): 'Clusters of households … commonly form the basic units of sociality and consumption in remote Aboriginal communities'.[18]

One way to get better 'cross-cultural fit' is for Aboriginal social processes to change so that they are more like the models implicit in the Census. After all, as Taylor reminds us, the complete administrative coverage of Aborigines by 1966 was made possible not only by the spatial extension of the state apparatus, but also by the spatial reorientation of the Aborigines themselves as they became more sedentary and centralised in government settlements and missions, in apparent cooperation with government welfare policies.[19] It is less a misrepresentation of Aboriginal sociality and more a change in Aboriginal sociality if the processes and forms of Aboriginal social life approximate the categories of the Census. The Census categories 'family' and 'household' might well become more true over time. Perhaps the co-residents of a dwelling will come to be more and more commensal, recruited to household membership primarily by genealogically close kin ties, their individual expenditures coordinated in an agreed household budget.[20] When Taylor and his colleagues from the Centre for Aboriginal Economic Policy Research (CAEPR) raise 'cross-cultural fit' as an unsolved problem of Census accuracy, they hover between saying that the state should not promote social changes among Indigenous Australians that would bring about a better fit, and saying that the state is simply unable to promote such changes in the short term.

From the point of view of the Aboriginal respondents to the Census, the problems of 'cross-cultural fit' would seem to be, first, that their deficits of well-being (for example, the unevenness and unpredictability of their cash incomes, the overcrowding of their houses, the numbers of school-age children) may be under-reported, so that they do not get the help that they need; and second, that features of their existence which do not seem to them to be problems may be recorded as problems, warranting the state's intervention in order to 'help' them. The Census itself thus could become — in both ways — an instrument of social injustice.

David Martin and Frances Morphy have illustrated further the lack of 'cross-cultural fit' in the portrayal of domestic processes. Martin reports that in the Census at Aurukun it was very difficult to state each householder's relationship to 'Person One' because the relationship terms allowed by the form did not match the system of relationship terms used by Aborigines there: 'At most, one could deduce [from the Census returns] that almost all households involved complex extended family structures.'[21] At a Northern Territory outstation in 2001, Morphy watched Census collectors struggle to translate kin relationships into the kin categories that the Census forms assumed to be universal. The resulting data were either meaningless or misleading. If misleading, then the systematically generated misrepresentation is that Aboriginal households recruit members according to the same nuclear family principles that most Australians find 'normal'. Note that the Census is not so rigid as to assume that every household consists of one nuclear family: that is demonstrably not so, even in the non-Indigenous population. But the Census does model the concepts 'family' and 'household' in a certain way. A family is defined as 'Two or more persons, one of whom is at least fifteen years of age, who are related by blood, marriage (registered or de facto), adoption, step, or fostering, and who are usually resident in the same household.'[22] A household may consist of up to three such 'families'. Even such flexible definitions of family and household do not capture the actual composition of many remote Aboriginal domestic groups, Morphy points out. Census form data from some regions thus have to be coded to fit the terms of these definitions, as she observed when she did fieldwork within the Indigenous Processing Team in the Melbourne Data Processing Centre. The Census assumption that all households are composed of nuclear families, or of fragments and adaptations of nuclear families, is a systematic source of misrepresentation of the variety of forms taken by Australian domestic groups.

Does that misrepresentation matter? In a related paper, Morphy explores how a Census representation might be not only misleading but subtly prescriptive: the Census could give social policy-makers confidence in certain schemes of socio-economic betterment. She warns that when we use genealogical data elicited by anthropologists to flesh out a definition of 'family', and note the practical extension of 'family' beyond the conjugal or nuclear family, we can see 'that it will not be a simple matter to socially engineer people from homeland communities ... into the mainstream by "encouraging" them to migrate as individuals, or as conjugal units "normalized" under the term "nuclear family", to populations centres where there is a mainstream labour market'.[23] Social engineering programs will not necessarily be dissuaded by the difficulty of disembedding putative wage-labourers from their kin networks, however. Public policy may create powerful incentives for people to modify their behaviour, legitimised by a vision of the normal that the Census helps to uphold. Martin and his co-authors suggest that, to the extent that the social justice ideal is to 'close the gaps', 'there are enormous political and social pressures for the retention of standard questions' in the Census, even though 'many standard questions seem of little social relevance to circumstances in traditionally oriented communities', and such questions yield data 'which [are] close to nonsensical'.[24]

This critique is an interesting combination of insisting on both fidelity to the facts and the existence of a plurality of ways of life. In this vein,

Morphy invokes 'the reality of Yolngu co-residence patterns' in order to criticise the Census-based representation of Yolngu society as if its basic unit were 'the self-contained nuclear family'.[25] However, it is not 'reality' that grounds Morphy's critical observation, but rather a Yolngu construction of reality to which she feels loyal. As an anthropologist with a long history of respectful and friendly association with Aboriginal people in Arnhem Land, Morphy has made an effort (which I admire unreservedly) to understand Yolngu social processes as Yolngu represent and enact them. Her research has interrogated the Census's demographic portrait of Yolngu by questioning 'the degree to which it was commensurable with: (a) the Yolngu view of themselves, and (b) a depiction informed by anthropologically derived categories'.[26] Assuming for a moment that (b) is an exhaustive replication of (a), what are the practical implications of her critical deployment of the Yolngu construction of reality? In representing (in this double sense) Yolngu, does Morphy wish to *displace* Census data with data assembled in Yolngu terms? Or would it be best to see Yolngu households and families through both Census and ethnographic lenses, to appreciate the ways in which Yolngu terms differ from those of other Australians? Her critique is salutary insofar as users of the Census would not otherwise appreciate that the domestic processes of remote Aboriginal people are different. However, there is a danger here of simply equating 'the Yolngu view of themselves' with the 'depiction informed by anthropologically defined categories'. Perhaps the Yolngu view of themselves is more multiple and opportunistic — sometimes making sense of social processes in the terms elucidated by anthropologists such as Morphy and at other times assenting to and putting into practice the categories assumed to be real in the Census. We should pause before we 'regret' the latter.

To return this discussion to the theme of this chapter, perhaps the difference between the idiom of 'people' (exemplified here by Morphy's insistence on the Yolngu/anthropology account) and the idiom of 'population' (the questionable representations given in the Census) is not only scientific and ethical, but also pragmatic and strategic.

When deployed to represent remote Australia, the Census also tendentiously represents 'productive activity', as we can see from its treatment of the Community Development Employment Projects (CDEP) program. Commenting on the 2001 Census's Special Indigenous Personal Form, Martin and colleagues comment that the questions about employment and about looking for work were constructed on the premise that labour market conditions in these regions are comparable to those in other parts of Australia. CDEP schemes were treated as if their sole purpose [were] to provide 'real' jobs, and all CDEP participants were deemed to have a job. The design of the questions rested, therefore, on two fictions: firstly, that there is a local labour market in which employment can be sought, and secondly that all CDEP participants are in paid employment. This is another example of the dilemma faced in trying to reconcile local Indigenous reality with comparability across the board ... If the principle of comparability is to be preserved, some thought needs to be given to how the level, or degree of fiction can be reduced, both in the forms of the questions and in the likely responses.[27]

Morphy and her colleagues report some adaptations in coding of these questions in the 2006 Census. When a respondent was a participant in a CDEP scheme, that person's answers were coded using a special CDEP 'pick list' of occupations. This list of CDEP-specific occupations is subject to revision between Censuses, however, as the Commonwealth goes to great effort to think of CDEP jobs in the normal nomenclature of occupations in the wider workforce. Nonetheless, the CDEP pick list was not easy to apply to the new forms of employment made possible by the growth of the ranger programs of the Indigenous Protected Areas scheme. In short, the Census vocabulary for classifying occupations has difficulty encompassing the publicly funded economic institutions that have been devised for remote Indigenous Australia. Other problems also remain, on which I can do no better than quote Morphy:

> The questions on the Census form are designed with mainstream employment situations in mind, and do not have salience for people who are not employed in the mainstream ... There is nowhere in the Census form where people are encouraged to record [subsistence hunting and gathering] — not even in the questions on unpaid domestic work ... Despite the inclusion of 'artist' in the list of suggestions for occupations ... only one or two people [where Morphy observed Census responses] put this down as their occupation ... [T]he majority of people do not really think of art production as a job, and the emphasis in the Census questions on sources of regular income — as opposed to intermittent and somewhat unpredictable income — conspires with this attitude to

render an important source of income and economic engagement essentially invisible.[28]

Although people see community leadership as 'work' that consumes a lot of their time, within the terminology for describing CDEP 'work', there is no category that allows individuals of political importance to nominate this as their 'work'. And the concept of 'voluntary work' (Question 54) seems foreign to Yolngu.[29]

The Census is the single most important instrument for representing Indigenous Australians as a 'population' whose comparative socio-economic deficits warrant a social justice politics of 'closing the gaps'. The critical studies of the Census that I have discussed show how a state project of representation can also be part of a wider program of prescription, deploying normal/normative models of society and economy. However, once we are sensitised to the fact that official population data are a 'way of seeing' complicit with certain projects of social change, should we then avoid this 'population' account, and adhere exclusively to representations of Indigenous Australians as 'peoples'? I believe not, for three reasons. First, official data (including the Census) can tell us a lot that is useful. Second, as the ABS has shown, there is much potential for the collection of population data to be undertaken jointly by Indigenous organisations and state agencies, with benefits to each.[30] Third, I will illustrate below some difficulties that arise when we use the 'people' idiom.

Peoples

It is abundantly possible, and very often ethically compelling, to think of Indigenous Australians — Aborigines and the Torres Strait Islanders — as 'peoples'. We variously honour 'heritage', an attribute of a 'people': in the organisation of art curatorship, in the recognition of the Aboriginal flag and the Torres Strait Islander flag as official flags of Australia, in the grounding of certain land titles in 'Aboriginal custom', and in many other ways. Russell McGregor describes the growing willingness of the Australian public in the 1960s to value features of Aboriginal heritage and to welcome the survival of these traits after Aborigines had been, in other respects, 'assimilated'. He quotes Minister for Territories CE Barnes explaining in 1967 that assimilation policy included recognition of 'the value to Aborigines and to the enrichment of Australian cultural life of encouraging pride and participation in elements of traditional Aboriginal culture in such forms as legend, music, dance and art'. Barnes went on to defend welfare administration from the misunderstanding that it sought to 'destroy such cultural elements'; the aim, rather, was to 'encourage them'.[31]

There was a limit to such positive valuations, however. The government had issued a booklet in 1960 titled *The skills of our Aborigines*, which noted what was missing from Aboriginal heritage: political capacity. The booklet asserted: 'There are no suitable aboriginal [sic] institutions that can easily be used as a basis for community growth.'[32] If Aborigines were to be effective in 'community growth', the booklet implied, they would have to be trained to it. Indeed, in welfare settlements of the Northern Territory, the administration soon began to do just this — setting up municipal councils as embryonic organs of community government.[33] Over the next fifteen years, without necessarily discounting the need for training, policy intellectuals challenged this presumption that Aboriginal people had no political traditions that might inform their 'community growth'. Documented customs of social organisation, leadership, authority and collective action remained available to be harnessed to Aborigines' own goals, if only public policy would recognise their potential. The transition from 'assimilation' to 'self-determination' is a perplexing matter for historians to narrate because the meanings of these terms of political art have always been contestable. However, if there is one feature of policy discourse to which we can point that enables us to think 'self-determination', it is the invitation — around 1970 — to recognise Aborigines' customary political capacity. In later chapters, I will detail some of the authors of and episodes in that recognition.

In public policy, the presumption that Aborigines are a 'people' with customary bases for collective action became influential in at least three ways that I will discuss here: in land law, the recognition of a customary basis for land entitlement; in corporations law and public administration, the recognition of Aboriginal groups; and in law reform, the ongoing debate about the contribution of 'customary law' to social order.

Land rights and native title

Although Justice Blackburn in 1971 ruled against the Yolngu plaintiffs in the case of *Milirrpum* by saying that their customs did not include the proprietary right to alienate land from others, he nonetheless recognised 'the system revealed by the evidence as a system of law'.[34] It had been possible to legislate for Aboriginal title without sourcing proprietary rights to 'Aboriginal law'. This was the South Australian government's position in 1966. 'While *they did not have a system of land tenure*,' Don Dunstan told a Select Committee of the Legislative Council on 28 September 1966, 'nevertheless they realized that there were lands over which they roamed and which they are now deprived of.'[35] Blackburn's judgment made it implausible to deny that there had been, and still was, an Indigenous 'system of land tenure'. In designing a land rights statute for the Northern Territory in 1973–74, Justice Woodward could build on Blackburn's recognition; he drew on anthropological research in recognising that identifiable Aboriginal groups owned identifiable areas. In Julie Finlayson's words: 'Woodward intended the Act to establish legal constructs which were congruent with the ethnographic reality of contemporary Aboriginal land practices.'[36] By legislation, certain Aborigines soon became 'traditional owners' in Australian law; their ownership was recognised as having a customary basis. This legislative recognition of 'custom' can be seen in retrospect to have prepared a judicial mindset conducive to rectifying the common law. In 1992, a six-to-one majority of the High Court recognised the customary basis of Aboriginal land-ownership throughout Australia when it articulated the doctrine of 'native title' as a doctrine of the common law. The court declared that there were two sources of law in Australia: British legal traditions (adapted by Australians courts and legislatures) and Indigenous customs. While the court held that British law was indisputably sovereign, the mere arrival of sovereign British power did not necessarily extinguish 'native title'. However, 'native title' is subject to Australian legislation. Native title can be either extinguished or recognised by Australian law, on terms decided by Australian judges and legislators. Australian parliaments, in 1993 and 1994, passed laws to recognise and regulate the property rights that Indigenous Australians enjoy as their 'native title'.

Between Woodward's inquiry and the High Court's judgment, however, there came an important warning from the Australian Law Reform Commission about the difficulties of recognising Indigenous customary law: how to come to a precise definition of 'Aboriginal customary laws'; how to avoid infringing basic human rights, including 'equality before the law'; how to allow Aboriginal customary law to change, including changes arising from the influence of other legal traditions; how to recognise that 'customary laws vary both in strength and content from community to community'; and how to ensure that Aboriginal people remain in control of their own customary law.[37] The commissioners questioned whether 'recognition' of customary law was empowering: rather than the Australian state 'recognising' or not recognising a given feature of Indigenous 'custom', would it not be better to concede power to Indigenous governing bodies over certain matters, in certain regions? To delegate jurisdiction to Indigenous authorities would leave 'custom' in Aboriginal hands, whereas 'recognition' effectively would transfer control over 'custom' to non-Indigenous legislators and administrators. Subsequent experiments in the recognition of Indigenous customary law have shown the wisdom of the ALRC's reservations, as I will illustrate.

The Law Reform Commission's questions appreciated a nuance in the meaning of 'recognition'. Australian governments could recognise Indigenous Australian customs as including owning and governing capacities, and invite Indigenous Australians to build upon those capacities in adapted practices of owning and governing. Or they could not only recognise these owning and governing customs, but also seek to articulate them — in statute and policy — as the content of title and as the shapes of organised authority.

Native title

In the grand compromise that is Australian land law, a version of 'Aboriginal custom' is articulated, for native title holders, by the state.[38] To be recognised by the Federal Court as holders of native title, the claimants must demonstrate that they are the descendants of those who, at the time Britain acquired sovereignty, inhabited and possessed rights (according to their own customs) to the claimed territory; that they have continued to enjoy those rights (a judge might allow for some historical change in the rights exercised); that the Crown has not extinguished these rights; that they have not surrendered their rights; and that their rights are not repugnant to the wider body of Australian law. 'If these conditions are met,' wrote Justice McHugh in an important formulation, 'the common law will recognize and enforce the particular native title rights and interests claimed in respect of land in a given case.'[39]

What guides the court (which may be the High Court if a Federal Court ruling is appealed) when saying what these rights and interests are? According to Noel Pearson, if the Federal and High Courts followed the High Court's 1992 *Mabo* decision, they would scan the evolving common law in nations such as Canada, New Zealand and the United States for models of 'native title' possession that could be applied — in the interests of justice — to Australia. However, as Pearson and other critics have pointed out, the developing practice of Australian judges has been to look for guidance to the *Native Title Act* — in particular, to its preamble and to section 223. The preamble says that native title reflects 'the entitlement of the indigenous inhabitants of Australia, *in accordance with their laws and customs,* to their traditional lands'.[40] Section 223 (1)(a) says that 'the rights and interests are possessed under the traditional laws acknowledged, and the traditional customs observed, by the Aboriginal peoples or Torres Strait Islanders'. Pearson has criticised the now-established judicial practice of assuming that 'native titles are *entirely* constituted by reference to traditional laws and customs adduced as a matter of proof'.[41] He writes: 'Australian law has misconceived native title by focusing on the traditional laws and customs of the indigenous people.'[42] Pearson argues that the details of traditional laws and customs — recognised by the court — make a poor basis for defining what Indigenous owners now have a right to do with their land. He maintains that their rights of possession should be full ownership as defined by reference to the evolving standards of common law. In an analysis consistent with that of Pearson, Lisa Strelein points out that the rights conferred in Australia's 'native title' regime will vary from determination to determination, as each case brings to light its own account of what the 'traditional laws and customs' of the claimants have been. When judges have articulated 'what rights and activities are expected to be carried out on native title land', they have tended to formulate a bundle of certain rights attested in anthropological research (such as the right to hunt and fish); each right in the bundle is vulnerable to legal extinguishment.[43] What some claimants have 'won' is often 'at odds with the view of country that many Indigenous Australians continue to hold: that the country is not in some sense external to them; they *are* instantiations of country, which is consequently inalienable from them'.[44] Native title is less than the 'full ownership' rights granted in other Australian laws, and to which they — as modern peoples — might aspire.

That judicial recognition of Aboriginal customary law in the native title regime can produce such antiquarian results is an instance of contemporary liberal statecraft described in general terms by Francesca Merlan. States now demand of Indigenous people that they demonstrate continuing difference from those who colonised them. In this mode of recognition, Indigenous people must present themselves as deprived 'of what was indigenously theirs' so that it can be 'restored to them in what are construed as their own mytho-religious (that is, non-market) terms'. The liberal state has developed a way 'to imagine a domain of the indigenous. Around this is formulated and contested a currency of indigeneity, and "tradition" is its coin.'[45] Merlan contrasts this way of recognising 'tradition' with a more historical understanding of Indigenous people that allows them to have been reflexive — that is, to have modified their way of life and their sense of continuity with the past in response to the demands of colonisation. She argues that the contemporary 'liberal project of recognition' seeks to determine and to 'bound' the 'Indigenous'; such a liberalism cannot tolerate a reflexive and historical concept of Indigenous tradition.[46]

Merlan may have stated too definitely what the contemporary liberal state can or cannot do. Even within the native title regime, it is possible for native title claimants to loosen the straitjacket of someone else's idea of their 'tradition'. David Martin has pointed out that without getting a court's 'determination' of the content of their title, people can assert native title and invite another party to negotiate an Indigenous Land Use Agreement (ILUA). ILUAs 'offer possibilities for Aboriginal people to construct their futures through explicitly transformative processes' without having their interests and rights 'refracted through the distorting lens of traditionalism. That is, in contrast to native title claims, agreements [i.e. ILUAs] are potentially privately resourced and optional projects of modernism.'[47]

Some of the problems of recognising 'native title' were anticipated — at least in general terms — by the Australian Law Reform Commission in 1986, when it pointed out that governments that *recognised* Indigenous customary law would *gain effective powers* over it. The legislative and subsequent judicial response to the High Court's recognition of native title may have produced some dispiriting acts of 'recognition', but it has also reinforced the idea that Aborigines and Torres Strait Islanders are *peoples* with long traditions of self-government that have been suppressed by colonial authority and that persist, dormant, until enlightened governance unbridles their capacities. The postulate that there is an Indigenous jurisdiction with roots in a viable, continuing normative system is the ground of much contemporary critique of public policy. In the next two sections, I will show more instances of this idea(l) — in the imagining of Indigenous capacities for collective action.

The customary basis for corporate action

The idea that Aboriginal people could act collectively through voluntary associations is not new, and its advocates need not believe that Aboriginal capacities for collective action derive from ancient tradition. Loos and Keast describe the Australian Board of Missions' attempt in the 1950s to use cooperatives 'to give Aboriginal and Torres Strait Islander people the confidence, education, and skills to develop profitable industries on their missions, employing Aboriginal or Islander people from the mission and controlled by an Aboriginal or Islander Board elected by the members of each cooperative'.[48] Assimilation policy encouraged Indigenous participation in voluntary associations. Governments were better disposed towards organisations that assisted church and government welfare efforts — particularly city-based agencies that helped an Aboriginal person or a household to move from country town or reserve to the cities. However, governments could not easily prevent such organisations from becoming vehicles for the assertion of Aboriginal or Torres Strait Islander rights and identity. In the 1950s and 1960s, relationships were sometimes tense between governments and such organisations as the Coolbaroo League (and its successor, the Aboriginal Advancement Council (WA)), several state-based 'Aborigines Advancement Leagues', the Federal Council for the Advancement of Aborigines and Torres Strait Islanders (FCAATSI) and the Foundation for Aboriginal Affairs. In Queensland, the government favoured the One People of Australia League (OPAL) as the 'apolitical' alternative to the feisty Queensland Council for the Advancement of Aborigines and Torres Strait Islanders (QCAATSI).

However, assimilation — when thoroughly pursued — required governments to risk empowering Indigenous Australians. Having been constituted as full citizens, they were entitled to mobilise — and were certainly capable of mobilising — associations that asserted Aboriginal or Islander identity and that criticised the cultural assumptions under which citizenship had been conceded. The maturing of this contradiction between officially encouraged *individual* citizenship and persistent senses of *collective* identity and grievance gave rise to 'self-determination' policy in the early 1970s.

Charles Rowley criticised government policy for trying too hard to individuate the Aboriginal client. 'A program involving social change must deal with the social group,' he insisted.[49] If 'community development' was an advanced tool for the promotion of social change, then it became possible and necessary to evoke, in positive and hopeful terms, the Indigenous capacity for community. In the late 1960s and early 1970s, some policy intellectuals evoked 'community' as drawing fruitfully on the customary law to which anthropologists attested, and that Justice Blackburn recognised in April 1971. In July 1971, the Council for Aboriginal Affairs pointed to the potential continuities between Indigenous traditions of collective action and the emergent Indigenous associations:

> Often when corporate action has been successful the element of traditional continuity has been important. To regard such continuity as always working against adaptation is mistaken. Often the breach of this continuity has led to demoralisation and disintegration.[50]

Land rights and grants to Indigenous organisations seemed to mobilise Indigenous Australians' previously ignored and/or suppressed customary capacities for self-government.

The observation that many remote Aboriginal communities have not, in fact, been governing themselves effectively has undermined a sense of progress. When this observation comes from Indigenous Australians themselves, it is all the more credible. At a 2002 conference at Murdoch University discussing the possibility of a treaty and affirming the principle of Indigenous sovereignty, I heard Eddie Mabo Jnr (introduced with reverence) urge us to be realistic: with many Indigenous communities in uproar, not yet controlling their own unruly members, it was premature to project 'Indigenous sovereignty'. In the same year, the Northern Territory Aboriginal MP John Ah Kit, in a widely reported speech, declared that few Aboriginal communities in the Northern Territory could yet control anti-social behaviour. He referred to petrol-sniffing, truancy, illiteracy, drunkenness, domestic violence, sexual assault, a heavy burden of illness and premature mortality. He embraced all these social pathologies within one word: 'dysfunction'. He referred in particular to the failure of local government to work for the benefit of Northern Territory Aborigines. Community Councils were politicised, over-burdened with responsibilities, and under-funded and lacking in human resources. Ah Kit's term — 'dysfunctional' — has acquired currency, referring to the apparent incapacity of certain individuals, combinations of individuals and even whole communities to provide the domestic security within which a woman can feel safe and a child can flourish.[51]

Another kind of argument about 'custom' and government comes from David Ritter's account of the native title regime. Ritter argues that while the common law doctrine of native title encouraged Indigenous Australians to expect much of their customary law, the operational forms of native title have proved to be a more mundane and flawed ensemble of ownership and representation devices. Native Title Representative Bodies (NTRBs) are responsible for helping native title claimants to represent themselves. Although claimants are not obliged to use their regional NTRB, many do. Ritter argues that NTRBs are torn between the imperative to honour customary tradition and the imperative of bureaucratic accountability. A temptation awaits NTRBs: 'The fact that native title involves the recognition of collective identity bonded to territory through a system of laws meant that NTRBs had just the hint of being emerging regional polities.'[52] He elsewhere explains: 'Native title applications resemble nationalist claims to the extent that they are assertions of dominion over territory by a group that asserts itself as bonded by a common myth of origins, law and custom, ethnicity, language and historical tradition.'[53] However, the native title statute and inadequate public funds combine to constrain what NTRBs can do to shape their cultural identity: 'NTRBs were always an unhappy hybrid of community organisation and professional service provider with the tendency inexorably shifting towards the latter …'[54] Notwithstanding some NTRBs' rhetoric about being 'representative' of the culture of those whose entitlement they pursue, the native title process is not an 'Indigenous process', Ritter insists; to practise it effectively requires the mobilisation of skills and outlooks without precedent in Aboriginal custom.

The promotion of Indigenous organisations as vehicles for people-hood has often highlighted, in a hopeful way, the potential contribution of 'custom' to Indigenous Australians' collective mobilisation. Anthropological descriptions of Aborigines and Torres Strait Islanders as peoples with 'law' have informed critiques of 'assimilation', and emerging Indigenous leaders have invoked 'custom' to legitimise themselves. However, the experience of, and research into, formal Indigenous institutions (corporations and councils) has generated scepticism about the operational relevance of customary law, as I will discuss further in Chapter 6.

Customary law as social discipline

Nonetheless, the impulse remains strong to look to 'customary law' for solutions to Indigenous Australians' problems. The morbid (and sometimes lethal) disorder of some communities has attracted increasing attention since the Royal Commission into Aboriginal Deaths in Custody illuminated psycho-social disorder as a proximate contributor to high rates of Indigenous incarceration. While criminologists rightly continue to scrutinise the colonising agencies of law and order, they do not shy away from acknowledging that 'many Aboriginal communities, in urban, rural and remote regions of Australia exist in conditions of *endemic* crisis'.[55] Harry Blagg refers in particular to male violence against women and children. However, he warns that 'in our haste to resolve the problem of violence, we should not abandon belief in Aboriginal agency as a necessary component of strategies to improve governance within Aboriginal communities'.[56] His reaffirmation of Aboriginal agency postulates 'Aboriginal law' as a continuing source of good governance. I now want to examine closely how Blagg reasons his case.

Noting a series of inquiries into the recognition of Aboriginal customary law at the national level in 1986, in Western Australia in 2006, in the Northern Territory in 2004, in New South Wales in 2000 and in Queensland in 2001, Blagg writes that 'there can be little doubt that Aboriginal law exists' and that 'giving recognition to Aboriginal forms of law requires acknowledging the existence of Aboriginal society as a distinctive functioning social system, rather than simply [as an] ethnic subset of mainstream Australia'. The issue for him is 'the relationship between Indigenous and non-Indigenous forms of law'.[57]

Blagg understands Aboriginal law to be a 'holistic tapestry of values and beliefs';[58] however, he also sees 'general agreement' that there is 'no formal code of customary laws' and that 'definitions of law may shift from place to place and over time'.[59] He agrees with the Australian Law Reform Commission and with subsequent inquiries that there should be no codification. For example, while he urges authorities to concede that spearing and other forms of physical punishment have a reintegrating effect on the men on whom they are inflicted, he stops short of advocating recognition of this mode of punishment. Aboriginal penalties must be taken into account on a case-by-case basis.[60] The elements of 'Aboriginal law' that he most wishes to affirm are those invoked by women as their mandate to assert themselves in Aboriginal governance: 'many of the positive initiatives taking place on Aboriginal communities have been driven by Aboriginal women, and many of these would argue that they derive their authority to act from within the very law and culture many white activists believe oppresses them'.[61] Thus he turns his critical attention to accounts of Aboriginal customary law that present women as customary law's victims, rather than as its effective agents.

In particular, he is critical of Joan Kimm's *A fatal conjunction: two laws, two cultures* (2004). According to Blagg, the book seems to give 'factual support for the proposition that Aboriginal men legitimate patriarchal violence against Aboriginal women through Aboriginal law'.[62] Rejecting this way of describing and invoking Aboriginal customary law, Blagg summarises (with apparent sympathy) 'Aboriginal narratives on violence' that present violence not as an operational effect of Aboriginal customary law but as a symptom of 'the breakdown of law, the impact of colonialism and the destruction of Aboriginal community structures through alcohol abuse, the multiple and cumulative effects of government policy, the theft of land and the crushing effects of removal policies'.[63] He describes these phenomena as 'the landscape against which communal violence needs to be set'.[64] If Aboriginal customary law were not so vitiated by these factors, what would it be like? To answer this question, Blagg points to representations of Aboriginal law authored by several women: Catherine Wohlan, Hannah McGlade and Kyllie Cripps. In their accounts, Aboriginal law is the context of the effective agency of Aboriginal women. Unfortunately, he notes, there are well-established ways of not noticing women's agency — a misperception reinforced by Kimm's book. In Blagg's view, we must make a choice between two competing representations of Aboriginal customary law: one (critical) has focused on Aboriginal law's empowerment of men and has implicitly demoted women to victim; the other (favourable) presents women as the effective agents of customary law. To recognise the relevance of Aboriginal customary law to social order is, in Blagg's view, to recognise Aboriginal women.

There are tensions within Blagg's account of Aboriginal customary law: between a 'holistic tapestry of values and beliefs'[65] and 'definitions of law [that] may shift from place to place and over time';[66] between acknowledging that women are vulnerable to violent men and exhorting us to recognise their agency; between evoking Aboriginal customary law as a living tradition and contextualising it as corrupted by historical trauma. I suggest that what his account shows is that the phrase 'Aboriginal customary law' has become a contested signifier, a blank screen on to which competing social interests and political visions project the historical narratives and ethnographic descriptions that suit their schemes for the management of what all sides agree to be a terrible problem: domestic violence.

Conclusion

Recognising Indigenous 'peoples' is not the same as recognising Indigenous 'populations': they generate different models of social justice. In Australia, as I will illustrate in the rest of this book, we have acquired the ability to see Aborigines and Islanders both as 'peoples' and as 'populations'. This chapter has begun to illustrate that the 'people' idiom and the 'population' idiom both have problems. The 'population' idiom models social processes in terms that imply cultural convergence; and it encourages a notion of social justice that begs the question of the political relationship between peoples. The 'people' discourse is tempted to model 'indigeneity' within a traditionalist straitjacket: it can beg the question of how much Indigenous Australians might benefit from learning new political technologies; and it can imply a customary substance that it fails to elucidate and that is open to critical description, drawn credibly from the anthropological record. To the extent that people-hood is evoked in terms of cultural difference, then historicising 'culture' makes trouble for the people-hood discourse. Both 'population' and 'people' are problematic concepts within Indigenous discourse, as the following chapters will show.

EVOKING PEOPLE-HOOD

CHAPTER 2

Hasluck and Elkin

Paul Hasluck (Minister for Territories, 1951–63) was an intellectually and politically influential exponent of the idea that Aborigines had ceased to be a people. Towards the end of his time as minister, his account of Aborigines and their future came under attack by academic anthropologists who argued that he had under-estimated not only the strength but also the value of the fabric of Aboriginal society. The anthropologists' critique contributed to the hopeful revaluation of Aboriginal political capacity that, in my view, enabled the transition from 'assimilation' to 'self-determination'.

The juridical, individualist tendency within Paul Hasluck's liberalism made him apprehensive about the persistence of Aboriginal peoples' sense of identity and togetherness. At times, this apprehension took the form of revulsion. In 1959, he spoke of Aboriginal people being 'tangled in their own distressed situation like flies on sticky paper. They could fly if only they could get clear of their surroundings, lift themselves free of their past, leaving behind them their present life.'[1] Even when the flies soar free, the image is hardly alluring to any Australian who has been on a picnic. However, we should not assume that Hasluck's account of 'assimilation' was about only the susceptibility and resistance of Aborigines. For him, 'assimilation' also required a certain relationship between the government and non-Aboriginal Australians.

By examining two unpublished speeches delivered by Hasluck in 1959, I will show his exploration of both problems. The first address was to the 'Pleasant Sunday Afternoons' gathering at the Lyceum in Sydney on 12 July; the second was Hasluck's presidential address to the Anthropology section of the August 1959 conference of the Australian and New Zealand Association for the Advancement of Science (ANZAAS) in Perth.

In 1959, Hasluck told the anthropologists: 'The policy of assimilation was not the result of someone in government having a bright idea but was the result of recognising what was happening to the aborigines and responding to the changes in their condition.'[2] If 'they are to live like us' — Hasluck's most succinct formulation of 'assimilation' policy — then it was not going to be government so much as 'society' itself that would do the transformative work. Hasluck sketched for the anthropologists the situation of Aborigines as he now saw it:

> Here and there throughout the continent there are crumbling groups of aboriginal people bound together by ancient tradition and kinship and living under a fading discipline ... the tattered threads of kinship ... None of these can be identified as a society in the same way as the rest of the people in Australia can be identified as a society.[3]

He also reminded the anthropologists that the policy of assimilation 'owed a good deal to the observation by anthropologists of the crumbling away of aboriginal society and culture'.[4] He offered the anthropologists the following justifying account of the pressures that Australian society was now placing on those who were emerging from the ruins of Aboriginal society:

> Societies come into being and they flourish through the similarity of outlook and habit among the members. A society has to impose some measure of conformity with its requirements as a society and its strongest sanctions are not — most certainly are not — the penalties imposed by its statutes but the customs and conventions according to which a person is accepted or rejected, considered worthy or considered unfit. Society will not change very much just to accommodate the person who is described as a 'social misfit' or as having 'anti-social tendencies'; nor, in the long run, will it tolerate him if he tries to live separately in his own way in the midst of society. He is expected to make a change. He is only accepted if he does make a change.[5]

It was an 'error' characteristic of the 'thinking of some champions of aboriginal rights', argued Hasluck, to assume that 'governments or administrative officers decide these matters. They do not.' Society has its own preferences, customs, habits, exclusiveness, censorship and cruelty.[6]

Hasluck chided his audiences to recall that Australian 'society' bore the major burden of assimilating those who no longer had a society of their own. In his Lyceum address, he made frequent use of the second-person pronouns 'you' and 'your' in order to accuse the 'general community' of being so distracted by the remote Aborigines' conspicuous (and only apparent) deprivation that it did not notice 'the fringe-dwellers':

> It would be your neglect if you let the fallen man lie in the dust. In the same way it is your neglect if you pass over the plight of the aboriginal with the remark that he is a poor type anyhow and will not try to better himself.[7]

'[T]he general community' had not helped these people to 'take advantage of the opportunities before them as citizens of Australia'.[8] In the same speech Hasluck cited an Aboriginal speaker's point that 'it is not governments but God who changes the hearts of the people': 'My parallel point is that it is not governments but the community that touches the feelings of these outcasts about the way they live.'[9] Hasluck's denial that government is pre-eminently responsible for 'assimilation' could be interpreted as a professional politician's evasion. His remarks may have had that pertinence, but there is more to his denials than that. Hasluck gave a number of examples of the inherent difficulty of the part played by governments.

Though statements about 'assimilation' often postulated a sequence of stages through which Aborigines would pass, it proved difficult, Hasluck reported to the anthropologists, for governments to know how to help to bring one stage to a close in order not to stifle the emergence of the next:

> Perhaps the most difficult decision to be made by anyone engaged in native welfare administration is a decision whether one form of help is no longer needed and when another form of help should be given, and this question is allied with another problem of how far the guardian should go in making decisions for the aboriginal. There is the danger of going on too long and impeding the development of the aboriginal's own character and sense of responsibility.[10]

Some people accused the government of tardiness in making legislative and administrative changes, he noted, while others complained of its crude haste in lifting restrictions. Hasluck nominated both haste and tardiness as dangers. 'Many of the problems today are often not problems of neglect but of the results of forcing the pace of change,' he said of the remote Aboriginal people of the 1950s, when speaking to the Lyceum audience.[11]

Yet Hasluck also believed that Aboriginal society was so irreversibly compromised by its contact with non-Aboriginal society that it had no future. Implicit in this view is the idea that governments have a certain responsibility not to let Aboriginal people linger, in an incapacitated condition, over their transitions to a better life. To the anthropologists, he presented his conviction that Aborigines should no longer be considered a 'society':

> Today, most groups of aborigines have passed the stage when they might make adjustments as a society and, in those few places where there might be something that could be described as an aboriginal society *the innovations are being forced upon the people* so purposefully that it is doubtful whether the aboriginal society can make those adjustments which, in slower days, marked their acceptance of an innovation and their attempt to accommodate their life to it.[12]

Of course, this was precisely what worried some anthropologists: external pressures forcing the pace of Aboriginal adaptation. Hasluck referred to such pressures as if they were beyond his responsibility as minister, but rather the work of larger social processes.

A second and related problem that preoccupied Hasluck in his address to the anthropologists was the 'administrative dilemma' of the institutional means at governments' disposal: the government or mission settlements. He was concerned with how to prevent a settlement

> which was designed for protection or education in a period of transition, from turning into a fixed community of its own? How do you make sure that the staging camp does not become the end of the road? At this ultimate stage of transition the aboriginal may also hold most devotedly to his own associations with people of his own kin and colour, rejecting of his own will the opportunity to 'become an Australian'.[13]

A third set of dilemmas is more deeply implicit in some of Hasluck's speaking and writing. Though he often evoked Aboriginal people as individuals, governments acted upon Indigenous Australians as categories of persons with common, disabling characteristics. Not all social administration in the assimilation era took the form of individual casework; the government inevitably had to act upon Aboriginal people in categorised aggregates, stimulating solidarities among those so categorised — senses of ethnic solidarity that would later be asserted as 'people-hood'. Since governments could not completely avoid categorically nominating such objects, Hasluck went to extraordinary lengths to find categorical terms that did not require entrenching criteria of 'aboriginality'. In attempting to reduce the salience of racial difference in Australia's public culture, Hasluck was also thinning out the terminology of people-hood and making a space that eventually would be filled by the comparative consideration of Indigenous Australians as a 'population'.[14]

The statement issued by the 1951 Commonwealth and States Conference on Native Welfare explained that the various populations to be given special treatment were not, in the eyes of government, 'Aborigines' or 'natives'. Rather, they were 'wards of the State who, for the time being, stand in need of guardianship': This view could be given clear expression by amendments of existing legislation where necessary, so that in place of attempts to define a 'native' or an 'Aboriginal', the legislation would be made to apply only to those persons deemed to need the provisions of such legislation for their guardianship and tutelage.[15]

Only in the Northern Territory was the term 'ward' written into legislation and the language of administration. The governing of the Aboriginal population in the States otherwise perpetuated one of the historic conditions of an emerging, politicised Aboriginal identity — the very terms 'Aboriginal', 'Torres Strait Islander' and 'native'. Even had Hasluck's wish that these terms disappear from the vocabulary of statute and administration been granted, the modalities of government action would have remained aggregative and segregative. This unavoidably categorical approach ill-suited Hasluck's vision for Indigenous Australians as socially mobile individuals and households.

The 'displaced individual' was now the most important phenomenon with which native welfare needed to come to terms, Hasluck told the anthropologists:

> I feel reasonably sure that, more and more, we will have to think in our native welfare administration of individual persons of aboriginal descent ... The behaviour of the individual, the response of the individual, the aspiration or the effort of the individual, the heart and mind of the individual are at the core of our problem.[16]

Not to revise the modalities of social administration would militate against the realisation of one of Hasluck's great hopes: that Aboriginal people would cease to think of themselves as members of a labelled category — 'Aborigines' — and start to regard themselves primarily as individuals and as households within Australian society. However, as the inheritor of an administrative practice that featured a number of discrete Aboriginal 'communities', Hasluck had to deal with social realities adverse to his ambition to individualise Indigenous Australians. He had no choice but to work within an institutional order whose segregative structure tended to create enclaves: the Ordinances and the administrative nomination of 'wards' preserved an Aboriginal 'commonality'. Hasluck might well argue that, as Aboriginal 'society' disappeared, the categorical constitution of Aborigines as collective objects of government was inappropriate and counter-productive; however, there was little that he could do about it, as this was the institutional legacy of 'protection' initiatives that had been in place since the 1860s.[17] The gap between Hasluck's cherished doctrine — the primacy of individuals — and these administrative realities gave him excellent grounds to write effacingly of government. Executive pathos is the sub-text of writings that otherwise exude cultural confidence.

Hasluck's 1959 speeches were preoccupied with the problem of the persistence of senses of difference between Aboriginal and non-Aboriginal Australians. In fact, he spoke about the persistence of difference as two different kinds of problem: the social psychology of Aboriginal people in transition and the problem of political representation. Let me deal with the second problem first.

In his Lyceum speech, Hasluck characterised criticism of governments as ostentation, as the gratuitous flaunting of difference. He opened his speech by referring to the kind of speech he was not going to make — a 'speech that is easy to make about aborigines', about their 'neglect' by governments: '[I]t is both easy and noisy — like kicking a can along the street ... I do not want to make that easy and noisy speech this afternoon.' And 'it is easy to paint a lurid and dramatic picture of primitive men and women crouching in crude bush shelters'. He contrasted the conspicuous behaviour of reformers and critics with the unostentatious work of good government: '[W]e are supposed to do good by stealth but there is not half the attraction in doing good by stealth as doing it in the full light of television cameras or popping up where someone is bound to take a picture of us.'

Hasluck was making a point not merely about the demeanour of public life, the virtue of modesty and the vulgarity of flaunted concern. He believed that the ostentation of some critics' approaches to public policy on Aborigines militated against the gradual reduction in the visibility of Aboriginality itself. For example, he warned against the kind of concern that has the 'effect of making everyone regard the aboriginal as something that ought to be in a side-show rather than as a human being' and that 'has the effect of heightening race consciousness on both sides'. He went on to say that:

> Any heightening of race consciousness becomes an obstacle to the process of assimilation ... we do not want to become more and more conscious of their differences from us but of their likenesses to us ... When we see them taking themselves naturally and escaping notice for heaven's sake keep their privacy sacred.[18]

Six weeks later, addressing the anthropologists, Hasluck again turned on the critics of 'assimilation', accusing them of selfishness and of a lack of genuine heed for the welfare of those they championed:

> The besetting folly of persons eager for reform is in forcing issues that need not be forced without regard to what happens to unfortunate parties. How many poor wretches have been dragged into the arena of social controversy and butchered to make a reformer's triumph or a prize-winning newspaper story?[19]

Again he contrasted such ostentation with the humility of effective government — the 'sheltering, protecting, guiding, teaching and helping and eventually, as the final and most difficult act of native welfare, quietly withdrawing without any proud fuss when the aboriginal enters the community'.[20] However, he admitted to being uncertain about one aspect of that scenario, saying it was 'reasonably clear what happens to aboriginal society', but 'rather more difficult to trace the expiring influence of aboriginal culture'. If the 'influence of his cultural past may still be felt by the individual', then some of the blame must be apportioned to certain unnamed critics of government policy, because 'the aboriginal ... is the victim of the Cult of the Aboriginal that is fostered in Australia today'. That 'cult' flourished partly because Aboriginal people whose society was gone or was doomed to expire were in a condition of psychological jeopardy:

'It appears that there has to be a breakdown of the aboriginal society and a loosening of the compulsions and emotional links with aboriginal life before there is any real chance of entry into Australian society.' It was therefore possible to take different views of the resulting vulnerability of Aboriginal people:

> Looked at from one point of view, the weakness of the old aboriginal society and of the present-day groups of aborigines is an advantage. The more it crumbles the more readily may its fragments be mingled with the rest of the people living in Australia. Looked at from another point of view, the disappearance of aboriginal society leaves the aboriginal person with limited capacity to assert himself or to serve his own interests.

Hasluck was conscious that Australian society was not necessarily sympathetic to Aborigines' transitional vulnerability. He hoped that Australian society would be 'capable of looking tolerantly at some departure from its usual standards'. As he ruminated, 'the complexity and fluidity of our society add to the difficulty and uncertainty of assimilation'.[21]

The interaction of the 'Cult of the Aboriginal' with the genuine problems experienced by Aboriginal people in their transitional state made it 'hard to disentangle the real from the spurious'. A sense of Aboriginal identity based in a mixture of the 'spurious' (political ostentation) and the 'real' (the emotional stresses of transition) posed a challenge to Hasluck. He met it by asserting a role for government as an inconspicuous support for troubled individuals. Without such protection as native welfare bureaucracies could offer, the Aboriginal person

> may seek his own shelter and protection within a group composed of persons like himself and these groups have a tendency to harden and become less penetrable than the individual ... the grouping together of Aboriginal people may become one of the most serious obstacles to social change.[22]

In short, it was Hasluck's view that 'grouping together' was doubly pathological — both an artefact of inappropriate political advocacy and a symptom of genuine Aboriginal distress.

According to Tigger Wise, Hasluck was stepping into a trap laid by Elkin when he made these points to the Anthropology section of ANZAAS. Elkin had been exchanging horrified letters with Ronald and Catherine

Berndt about some of the things Hasluck recently had been heard to say about 'assimilation'. Hasluck was giving 'unfortunate connotations of force' to a term over which Elkin felt some proprietorial responsibility. Elkin and the Berndts wondered whether Hasluck any longer read what anthropologists were saying. The Perth meeting of ANZAAS would honour Hasluck by allowing him the presidential address, but it would also call 'assimilation' to account to anthropology.[23]

As the discussant of Hasluck's paper, Elkin insisted that Aborigines' social solidarity was much more robust than Hasluck had allowed:

> [Although] full-blood Aborigines will become literate and educated, skilled and more fitted to play parts in our economic life, they will remain in the foreseeable future Aborigines in their social and kin relationships and in their appreciation of values. They will earn money, but their use of it and of what is obtained with it will be determined by their kinship ties, NOT by our concept of individual ownership, just as their houses will in many cases be shelters for relations, not for the exclusive use as a home for an individual family, and probably too, work will be regarded not as a responsible relationship to an employer, but as an inescapable food gathering activity when cash is low.[24]

Elkin asked Hasluck to accept that Aboriginal people 'will observe a partial and voluntary segregation — an apartness for an unpredictable period' because 'group life' and 'continuity with the past' were 'essential principles for a people's well being'. He reformulated 'our task' as being 'to see that the phase of apartness does not become apartheid, but that the Aboriginal integers are truly integrated ... in a plural society — Australia'.[25]

Over the next few years, other prominent anthropologists voiced similar concerns about Hasluck's application of the doctrine of assimilation. Catherine Berndt's point went further than Elkin's defence of the group life of 'full-bloods'. Her critique questioned the assumed individualisation even of people of mixed descent. She observed that Aborigines were evidently not making the move 'from an environment of warm, secure, primary relations to a world where the "citizen-isolate" stands alone and unprotected'.[26] Nor should they be expected or forced to make such a move. She referred to arguments within recent social theory maintaining that the family was a better site of care than the institution. In this perspective, welfare clients' relationships were considered more significant to his or her well-being than their 'material and physical environment'.[27] Berndt argued that in all industrial societies, the solidity of 'primary group relations' had become problematic — not only for those whose lives were a 'social problem', but for all. The dilemma facing administrators of Aboriginal welfare was thus universal — although particularly sharp in the Aboriginal case — since 'assimilation' had been trying to detach young Aboriginal people from their families — emotionally, culturally and sometimes physically. 'Assimilation' also sought to detach 'nuclear' families from the wider kin network:

> The principal dilemma here is an intergenerational one, hinging on the nature of the bond between parents and children: should the social and emotional aspects of this relationship be stressed at the expense of the achievement aspect? Or does prolonged separation, breaking up the family as a co-resident unit, have long-run advantages which counterbalance its apparent demerits?[28]

Berndt was inviting authorities such as Hasluck to recognise that what she termed the 'citizen-isolate' was an abstraction — an undesirable working hypothesis for social policy to the extent that it ignored the social constitution of individuality.

There is a discursive tradition in which it makes sense to imagine that people can be 'citizen-isolates'. I propose that we call this tradition 'juridical liberalism', and that we distinguish it from a strand of liberalism on which Berndt and Elkin were drawing — a sociological liberalism, which highlights the social relationships that make effective individuality possible. Programmatic statements about the desirability of 'assimilation' were phrased in terms of either of these two versions of liberalism.[29] The sociological theory of Emile Durkheim (1858–1917) is helpful here. Durkheim was a liberal who explored the possibilities of new forms of social order that were appropriate to modern differentiated societies. Durkheim argued that if modern democratic nation-states were to be held together, it would be by cultivating new moral ideals — such as respect for the individual. Durkheim was highly critical of the utilitarian and contractarian conceptions of individuality because they could neither account for nor envisage the maintenance of the necessary moral density of social relationships. For Durkheim, the modern practice of individuality had still to be socially embedded. The vitality of what Durkheim called 'secondary groups' was crucial to modern social order:

Sociologically, democracy was grounded in the vitality of multiple groups and institutions in society which provided the main foci of the lives of individuals; such strong social groups constituted the intermediate ground of social life — somewhere between 'the individual' and 'the state'.[30]

The Durkheimian tradition of social criticism directs attention to the question of which social formations are to function as 'secondary groups'. Catherine Berndt was pointing to the Aboriginal individual's network of kin, and social scientists who were her contemporaries were beginning to write in positive terms of 'ethnic groups'.[31] It is in keeping with Durkheim's sociological liberalism that 'secondary groups' may include formations and associations held together by common senses of ethnic identity.

Concerned for the moral constitution of the social order, the Durkheimian tradition has conducted an often uneasy dialogue with the strand of liberalism that I am here calling 'juridical' in order to draw attention to its preoccupation with the individual's formal, political and legal autonomy from the claims of others. The historic preoccupation of juridical liberalism has been a robust and often admirable concern to unfetter individuals from pernicious social bonds, and to imagine individuals and to act towards them in terms of their abstract universal equivalence with one another from the point of view of an impartial and inclusive state. The liberal tradition can be understood as an unceasing intercourse and tension between juridical and sociological sub-traditions.

AP Elkin was one of our foremost Durkheimian liberals. Elkin's experience of Australia during the Great Depression made him one of those 1930s liberals who condemned Western liberalism's egoistic individualism, its impoverished conception of the communal life in which individuals were — to their benefit — embedded. To Elkin, rounded and psychologically integrated persons could flourish only in culturally integrated societies. In some essays published in the 1930s and 1940s, Elkin extolled the functional integration of Aboriginal society as exemplary of what egoistic European liberalism was not; Aborigines traditionally enjoyed a condition of community that complex European societies must strive to match lest they sink further into anomic egoism. In Elkin's view, the culture that Aborigines had shared, and in some places still shared, was a source of individual psychological strength for its members.[32]

As an early advocate of 'assimilation', Elkin had advised against thinking of Aborigines as an ensemble of individuals, each to be liberated from their crumbling Aboriginality by the state. In his 1944 book *Citizenship for the Aborigines*, he listed and expounded the principles that he hoped would guide policies for Aboriginal citizenship; one of them was that 'Group — or community — life is of fundamental importance to persons of Aboriginal descent'. Government settlements and missions should therefore preserve

> Aboriginal group life ... with its social and ceremonial aspects, thus aiding the development and integration of the individual personality. The Aborigines, like the whites, need in all normal cases, to belong to a community, and not be mere hangers on and survivals.

By contrast, Hasluck subscribed to notions of the social whole and of the individual that drew on the juridical language of liberalism. In Hasluck's writing, the individual is the bearer of certain democratic rights and allegiances *vis-à vis* the state. His or her entitlements and responsibilities were not contingent on such secondary group affiliations or on such criteria as religion, class or race. In this commitment, Hasluck was a resolute opponent of white Australian racism in the name of national unity. A nation's wholeness depended not only on the majority accepting the members of such minorities as Aborigines, indifferent to their 'Aboriginal' attributes; at the same time, the individuals from those minorities would relinquish their loyalties to any sub-groups of the nation. Under the impact of these two developments, Aboriginal racial identity would lose significance in both public policy and individual consciousness. So it was vital to Hasluck that social policy must hold fast to the essential equality of individuals: their cultural or racial attributes were of little or no account.

In the formulations of 'assimilation' that he advocated in the 1950s and defended to the end of his life, Hasluck's vision of the ultimate homogeneity of Aborigines with non-Aborigines was striking in its abstraction. As he reiterated in 1988:

> The policy of assimilation means that all Aborigines and part-Aborigines will attain the same manner of living as other Australians and live as members of a single Australian community enjoying the same rights and privileges, accepting the same responsibilities, observing the same customs and influenced by the same beliefs, hopes and loyalties as other Australians. Any special

measures taken for Aborigines and part-Aborigines are regarded as temporary measures, not based on race, but intended to meet their need for special care and assistance to protect them from any ill effects of sudden change and to assist them to make the transition from one stage to another in such a way as will be favourable to their social, economic and political advancement.[33]

Simply by repeating the word 'same', Hasluck's formulation avoided specifying the cultural attributes that were to be discouraged or promoted by 'assimilation'. His conception of 'assimilation' was predicated on a primarily juridical conception of nationhood as a condition of formal equality of citizenship. The emotional and cultural textures of human relatedness were conceived by him negatively — that is, in terms of their tendency to compromise his high-minded vision of a social whole of formally equal individuals.

Whereas Elkin could not think about 'assimilation' without considering the dangerous dynamics of Aboriginal cultural disintegration, Hasluck minimised his doubts about the vicissitudes of cultural change by dwelling on the abstractly conceived outcome. He was uneasy about the challenge that any residual cultural difference seemed to offer to a sense of Australia's unity. Keeping 'culture' at bay, Hasluck presumed an emergent individualism with jural, but not cultural, predicates; he imagined 'assimilation' in terms of its end — nationhood unified by the state's gradual dissolution of Aborigines' sense of communal or ethnic identity.

I wonder whether Hasluck was surprised by Elkin's 1959 critique. Perhaps their different philosophies of assimilation had been obscured by their common hostility to many of the government practices inherited from the past: the negative practices of 'protection' and segregation. Elkin and Hasluck had also converged in their views on a particular policy issue that bore on the ties between an individual and his or her 'group life'. In 1951, Elkin criticised the policy of the Commonwealth Director of Social Security not to extend pension benefits to Aborigines living on reserves serviced by government or government-subsidised institutions. The director's eligibility rule insisted that only those Aborigines who were exempt from such official control and care merited pensions. Equitable as this might sound, it had an unfortunate consequence: Aboriginal people had to choose either to get social security or to live with their relations on reserves and missions. Either they were financially induced to desert those with whom they had the closest ties, or they were deprived of cash social security payments as a penalty for remaining with loved ones. Such exemption/eligibility rules were 'inconsiderate', Elkin protested: 'the Aborigines must move up in groups'.[34] Hasluck reportedly agreed with Elkin's criticism of the Department of Social Security's eligibility rule. Perhaps such moments of accord helped to make their divergence of opinions in 1959 as dismaying to Hasluck as Tigger Wise says it was to Elkin.

In 1988, Hasluck recalled that when he began to assemble the ideas that guided him as Minister for Territories in the Menzies government, his outlook was 'still influenced by the evangelism of mid and late Victorian and Edwardian England which placed emphasis on the individual ... The individual made the choice and made the effort and as a result was changed.' He reflected self-critically that 'we did not see clearly the ways in which the individual is bound by membership of a family or a group'.[35]

After Hasluck's time as minister, as I outlined in Chapter 1, government policy towards Indigenous Australians became more receptive to the benefits (for individuals) of being in a group and more receptive to the idea of beneficial political agency of Aboriginal groups — whether 'descent groups' (in land rights legislation) or 'associations' (in service delivery). Anthropology was not the only discipline that contributed to this shift in thinking. One of the foremost critics of Hasluck's legacy, CD Rowley, drew explicitly on social psychology when he advocated a major change in the modalities of government:

> The aim of 'assimilation' has been to winkle out the deviant individual from the group, to persuade him to cut the ties which bind him and his family to it, and to set him up as a householder in the street of the country town. But policies which aim to change social habit by educating individuals, while ignoring the social context which has made him what he is, can have only limited success. A program involving social change must deal with the social group.[36]

CHAPTER 3

Strehlow Damns Coombs

When Australian governments began to consider Aboriginal 'group life' seriously as a source of political capacities, what was the contribution of ethnographic knowledge? By focusing on two students of Aboriginal culture who interacted uncomfortably in the early 1970s — TGH Strehlow and HC Coombs — I hope to illuminate further the intellectual transition from 'assimilation' to 'self-determination'.

Strehlow disappoints Coombs

After graduating from Adelaide University in December 1931, TGH Strehlow spent two years travelling across Central Australia collecting information about Aboriginal songs, myths, ritual and language. He had grown up in the region, the son of Lutheran missionaries Carl and Frieda Strehlow. In 1934 he was back at Adelaide University, as Assistant Lecturer in English Literature. There he wrote three long papers from his fieldwork, later published as *Aranda traditions*.[1] In 1935 he returned to the Centre, and in October 1936 he became a patrol officer in the Northern Territory's Native Affairs Branch, the first person to hold that position. In 1938 he built a house at Jay Creek, a day's camel ride west of Alice Springs. He was soon successful in persuading his superiors to let him open a ration depot there, on a recently gazetted 'Aboriginal reserve'. He worked for the administration in the southern portion of the Territory until May 1942, having risen to the position of Deputy Director of Native Affairs by July 1939. Strehlow served in the army from 1942 to 1946, including a posting as an instructor at Duntroon from January 1945. His civilian academic career resumed with his appointment as Fellow in Australian Linguistics and Lecturer in English Literature at the University of Adelaide in 1946.

Apart from a two-year overseas research fellowship (1949–51), awarded by the fledgling Australian National University, he remained an academic of the University of Adelaide until his retirement in 1973. His association with that university continued until his death in October 1978.

As a 'public intellectual', Strehlow sought to persuade Australians to take more notice of the needs of Aborigines, whom he considered to have been ill-treated. He had recommended Indigenous 'land rights' as early as 1937, thirty-four years before 'land rights' became the policy of a major Australian political party (the Australian Labor Party). It is therefore strange that when 'land rights' were implemented in the Northern Territory (by the *Aboriginal Land Rights (Cth) Act 1976*), Strehlow was among the statute's most outspoken critics. In letters to the Prime Minister and the Minister for Aboriginal Affairs, he both condemned the legislation and vilified the intellectuals who had conceived it, even though his own writings had contributed to the creation of a climate in which 'land rights' were possible. I will try to discern an underlying logic in Strehlow's thinking by contrasting him with another advocate of Indigenous interests, Dr HC Coombs.

When Coombs first actively became involved in advocating the interests of Aboriginal people, as chair of the new policy advisory body the Council for Aboriginal Affairs (CAA), he was 61 years old and about to retire. Trained as an economist, he had been a public servant since 1935. From 1949 to 1968, he was Governor of the Reserve Bank. His only involvement in 'Aboriginal affairs' before November 1967 was in the sphere of arts patronage. As chair of the Australian Elizabethan Theatre Trust from 1954 to 1967, he had helped bring to Southern audiences Indigenous dancers from North Australian communities. If he was not well read in ethnographic studies when he began work with the CAA in November 1967, he soon made it his business to learn. With advice from his Council colleague WEH Stanner, Coombs absorbed the literature — mostly about 'traditional' communities of the North and Centre. He visited such communities — especially the remote missions, settlements and cattle stations of the Northern Territory. Within four years of becoming chair of the CAA, his writings were being received with respect by those interested in Indigenous Australians.

The Holt government had set up the CAA in November 1967 to recommend new Aboriginal Affairs policies in the wake of the 1967 referendum giving the Commonwealth concurrent powers with the

States on Aboriginal Affairs. Coombs and his colleagues were critical of many aspects of the Northern Territory Administration. They valued Strehlow's pamphlets, published in the late 1950s and early 1960s, criticising assimilation policy. Jeremy Long, of the Office of Aboriginal Affairs (OAA), the CAA's administrative arm, had solicited material from Strehlow. The OAA's general program of public information included reprinting WEH Stanner's Boyer Lectures *After the Dreaming*, and a paper by CD Rowley, the director of the 'Aborigines Project' of the Social Science Research Council of Australia. Long asked Strehlow about reprinting *The sustaining ideals of Australian Aboriginal societies* and *Nomads in no-man's land*.[2] Strehlow's critiques were seen to be early contributions to rethinking the policies of the Hasluck era. In December 1973, Coombs wrote to Strehlow, asking him to comment on some of his own papers.

Coombs might have expected Strehlow to sympathise with his attempts to apply ethnographic knowledge to the reform of public policy. However, Strehlow's response was damning. His letter to Coombs began positively, blasting the 'super-racist' policies of the Commonwealth government, against which Coombs and the CAA had themselves been struggling. Strehlow then noted that, under the new Labor government (elected in December 1972), the Commonwealth was seeking to undo this 'destruction of aboriginal authority, culture, and social structure' by a policy of community self-determination. Strehlow had no confidence in this change of policy. He described it as the government selecting pliable Aborigines as the new leaders: 'Only aboriginal leaders who have won prestige and authority in their own groups through their own traditional knowledge can hope to become aboriginal leaders in any meaningful sense.' Limply praising Coombs' papers for their 'useful information', Strehlow endorsed them to the extent that he found in their 'general sentiments ... echoes of statements made by myself and published many years ago'. However, Strehlow doubted that the CAA and the Whitlam government could do any better than Hasluck: 'Canberra never really changes. To the Canberra mind, the men and women whom it controls are — or are expected to be — passive and pliable administrative material rather than human beings.' The Aboriginal people whom Coombs had visited and consulted in Central Australia and Arnhem Land 'are heading for the same future of disillusionment and despair that has already overtaken other Australian groups'. If anything, Whitlam's reformism had only strengthened the hand of 'distant official advisers and bureaucrats' who were not qualified for the tasks they were now undertaking. Clearly Coombs was included in this swipe. One by one, Strehlow dismissed Coombs, Dexter and Stanner, the three members of the CAA. His letter concluded with contemptuous references to 'the large tribe of lesser "experts" and "advisers"', whose 'over-paid efforts', he predicted, would be ineffectual: 'it is time for ruthless changes everywhere, particularly at the top'.[3]

Strehlow's singularity

These words effectively brought Strehlow to a political dead-end. The most likely sources of policy reform at that time were the CAA, its allies within the new Aboriginal Affairs bureaucracies and in the academic world, and the Woodward Royal Commission on Aboriginal Land Rights. Yet Strehlow now despised them all. In March 1974, he even repudiated those who had earlier published his pamphlets critical of government policies.[4] Strehlow's letter to Coombs both endorsed the arguments with which Coombs was reshaping Commonwealth policy — arguments about the need for land rights and the possibility of Indigenous self-determination — and denounced Coombs and his colleagues as power-crazed mountebanks. Strehlow called for policy change, but refused to devote even a sentence to encouraging the available agents and impulses of change. As an intervention in the process of policy reform, his letter to Coombs was fundamentally incoherent. Its only clear theme was Strehlow's continuing alienation from the processes of devising and implementing government policy. Strehlow's criticisms of the implementation of assimilation policy had helped to pave the way for a better policy, yet Strehlow could find no common cause with the new policy's principal advocates. Why?

Strehlow understood himself to have been singularly gifted by Aborigines, but these were gifts he could not share. His letter in July 1971 to WC Wentworth, the minister assisting Prime Minister John Gorton in Aboriginal Affairs matters, made this clear. Strehlow recalled his first research trip as an initiation through hardship:

> During my first year I spent most of the time in travelling about on camels, both through the so-called 'settled' parts (i.e. the unfenced station holdings, which were often so vast that white men could get lost on them and perish for want of food and water when getting off the bush tracks) and through what could at that time still be classified as genuine 'tribal' lands. Here progress depended completely on friendly local group leaders; for I was,

> of course, roaming over the countryside not as a white explorer but as a researcher interested only in ascertaining and recording the linguistic areas, the totemic geography, and the indigenous traditions of the original inhabitants. Under such conditions travelling was always difficult and sometimes dangerous. In those years of wanderings I had to accustom myself to enduring the pangs of hunger, the sharp bite of frosts on nights spent under the stars, days of intolerable heat spent under a blazing sun, days of drenching rain while walking through the sodden bush, and, not infrequently, hours of sleepless panic at night when I could hear my heart hammering in the perfect stillness of a landscape seemingly devoid of all living creatures, wondering whether I should return alive ... I had to survive as best I could, depending on my own knowledge of the country and on the loyalty and bushcraft of my own companions ... I was not interested in the acquisition of a higher degree, but only in recording a unique culture which I believed to be distinguished by an unrivalled richness in some of those very areas in which our European culture was so lamentably weak and deficient. All this meant wrestling also with completely unfamiliar 'dialects', so that I could understand my companions in their own languages, and set down their explanations in their own words.[5]

His stoicism was rewarded:

> Gradually, the dark men, who had watched me critically at first, took me into their complete confidence, and I was shown rich series of secret totemic acts by several Aranda local groups — an honour never extended to white observers by the Aranda before or after the 1896 Imanda festival staged at Alice Springs for the benefit of Spencer and Gillen; and that festival had been enacted purely out of gratitude to Gillen because he had been the man who had ended the police terror of the 1880s in Central Australia.[6]

Strehlow's account — of submission of body and self to the physical and mental stresses of a learning process, of an ordeal embraced for the sake of learning itself, of fealty rewarded by the old men's recognition of his worth — sets out his understanding of his earned entitlement to receive the revealed knowledge of the elders. He added that his standing as a fit receiver of the law was enhanced a few years later when he defended Indigenous interests as a patrol officer (1936–42) in a hostile settler culture.

His narration of his life to Wentworth in 1971 conveys his sense of himself as a special scholar, not only because of the length and intimacy of his field experience, but also because he believed himself to be the repository of the most elevated knowledge of a civilisation hounded to extinction. His knowledge was not only erudition but also a trust. His affinities with his subject were moral, the outcome of a unique disciplining of his whole being as a young man in 1932–34, not just of sustained study in an academic discipline.

Yet Strehlow saw himself marginalised as he watched the academic field of 'Aboriginal studies' grow under the patronage of the Commonwealth government's Australian National University (ANU) founded in 1946 and the Australian Institute of Aboriginal Studies (AIAS) founded in 1961. In a serialised paper published many years later,[7] he argued that the AIAS had strayed from its mission, which he took to be

> the *preservation* of the most comprehensive records of *traditional aboriginal culture* in all its multitudinous aspects so that their richness, interdependence, and intrinsic value could be understood and appreciated by posterity, and — most significantly — set down in a form in which the possibility that this culture might contribute to the enrichment of our 'white' Australian way of life could be recognized by at least the more thoughtful citizens of this country.[8]

According to Strehlow, the perversion of the AIAS had begun with its Interim Council in November 1961. He resented the prominence of Deputy Chairman and Executive Officer WEH Stanner, with whom he had quarrelled in the 1950s over the ANU's claims to some of Strehlow's ethnographic films and recordings. Strehlow saw no good reason for the inclusion in the Interim Council of RM Crawford (Professor of History, University of Melbourne), AD Trendall (Classicist and Master of the ANU's University House), JT Burke (Professor of Fine Arts, University of Melbourne), FJ Fenner (Professor of Microbiology, ANU) or — worst of all from Strehlow's point of view — GH Lawton (Professor of Geography, University of Adelaide). He found the exclusion of Ronald Berndt (Professor of Anthropology, University of Western Australia) and WR Geddes (Professor of Anthropology, University of Sydney) inexcusable. Subsequently, after others' protests, Geddes and Berndt were added to the Interim Council, and WEH Stanner resigned as executive officer in

August 1962 in order to take a year's study leave overseas. Strehlow himself never served on subsequent councils, though he claimed to have been a nominee of the Governor-General, vetoed by the government, in 1968. The advice of 'outsiders' such as himself was not welcome in the AIAS, 'even if they had given a lifetime to aboriginal research'.[9] 'Collection' soon gave way to 'a policy of quickly publishable returns':

> The Institute encouraged short field trips by persons eager to gain easy fame through obtaining material for short papers and theses papers testing new hypotheses and theories advanced by overseas anthropologists, papers leading to higher degrees for new graduates, and theses or articles written to further the personal careers of academics already enjoying the security of established University positions.[10]

Strehlow asserted that the goodwill of Indigenous informants benefited researchers, but not the informants themselves: 'At times the reader will not gain any impression that the researchers were conscious of their common humanity with their studied "subjects".'[11] The researchers made themselves 'at home on the aboriginal settlements and missions', and rarely ventured into 'the old tribal territory'.[12] They remained ignorant of both country and language. Researchers were 'incapable of understanding even ordinary conversations conducted by aboriginal speakers among themselves'.[13]

Strehlow insisted that these researchers should have been financed by universities, not by the Institute. Their esoteric concerns were all too typical of an academic world that had now forsaken 'ordinary educated readers' and displaced Indigenous views. 'It is their [i.e. Indigenous] explanations and their accounts that should be set down for posterity in the greatest detail, and so far as possible in their own words.'[14] The Institute should support

> those few dedicated persons who are willing to spend at least several years in their chosen areas in order to investigate and record all aspects of language, culture, and social structure which their 'informants' are willing to divulge to them … For it is the quality of the 'informants' (and the dedication of the researchers) that will in the end determine the whole worthwhileness of the final results. My own best 'informants' have always been men whom

I respected deeply and admired without reservation for their intelligence and integrity. In their own cultural world these men would have merited a rating as high as that of the best University professors I have known ... It was they who taught me what they thought I should know, see, and hear. I always thought of myself as their pupil, not as their smart examiner.[15]

The autobiographical resonances of Strehlow's critique are unmistakable. If the Institute were to live up to its original purpose, it would champion people who had lived as Strehlow had lived, including Strehlow himself. Such researchers structured their life's project around two faiths to which the typical academic had now ceased to hold. One was belief in the intelligence of the non-academic public — a public with an awakened interest in Indigenous civilisation; the other was a continuing fidelity to the august old men who taught the researcher what they thought he needed, and deserved, to know.

The disputed custody of ethnographic knowledge

Strehlow's distrust of the AIAS as a facility for the Law's custodians should be understood not only in the biographical context that I have sketched so far but also in the context of changing policies for the statutory management of Indigenous knowledge.

In 1964 and 1965, a Select Committee of the Northern Territory Legislative Council reviewed the *Native and Historical Objects and Areas Preservation Ordinance*. Until consulted by that committee, Strehlow said, he had been unaware of the existence of the Ordinance. Strehlow's submission to the committee was nonetheless of such interest that it appeared as an appendix to the committee's report.[16]

Strehlow began with a long autobiographical statement intended to establish his dedication as a witness and recorder of Indigenous Law and his high standing in the eyes of Indigenous custodians — the 'private owners' of the sacred objects. He was obliged to observe secrecy 'while any of the men to whom promises of secrecy have been given remain alive'.[17] The Ordinance was defective, he suggested, in acknowledging neither that 'all sacred sites were once regarded as being owned by all members born into the appropriate local totemic clan', nor that 'the exact locations of sacred caves could not be divulged to any outsiders on pain of death'.[18] If religious rights were to be respected, surely the Ordinance should make it a condition of researchers' access that they be 'invited in the traditional manner by the appropriate totemic clansmen'.[19] Instead, the Ordinance would impose on traditional owners the same penalty as any other person for concealing material or sites from an 'authorized officer or a member of the Police Force'.[20] He recommended that no person 'be permitted to receive sacred objects except from their lawful aboriginal owners, and in the presence and with the approval of the remaining members of the appropriate local totemic clan'.[21] The Ordinance should be redrafted in the light of consultations with Indigenous people, and 'local rules sympathetically ascertained and respected'.[22]

The Select Committee acknowledged Strehlow's importance as a custodian:

> The results of Mr Strehlow's research are held by the University of Adelaide; much of it held in confidence not to be disclosed until the death of the last of those Aboriginals by whom it was entrusted to him. In the absence of a Territory museum or university to which such things could be entrusted [the] Committee believes that we should be grateful to the University of Adelaide.[23]

Such recognition emboldened Strehlow to advise the AIAS about who should be funded to research Aboriginal knowledge in Central Australia. In March 1971, he complained to the chairman of the AIAS about a funded researcher's interest in objects stored near Finke Siding. Strehlow had long known of this cache, and he objected to its proposed relocation to Ernabella and Amata by some Pitjantjatjara men, disputing their right to take such action:

> From my own considerable knowledge of the Lower Southern Aranda traditions of this area, I can assert with confidence that I know infinitely more about the local myths, songs, and rites, and their relationship to the Finke *tjurunga*, than any Pitjantjatjara man who has ever come into the Finke area since the 1930s.[24]

Strehlow conjectured that the South Australian Museum or the Adelaide University Conservatorium was implicated in this 'impudent theft'. Writing of this issue to Ronald Berndt, he doubted that the predatory ways of 'Canberra' officials and researchers could be restrained.[25]

Strehlow's apprehension was at odds with trends in the State and Commonwealth governments' thinking about the protection of

Indigenous heritage. By the early 1970s, the legislative vacuum was being filled by statutes that provided for the registration of sites and objects. In Strehlow's opinion, registration would breach a site's only effective protection — secrecy. As he had commented in his 1969 review of DJ Mulvaney's *The prehistory of Australia*, 'the safety of the ceremonial sites still in present-day aboriginal use depends solely upon the ignorance of white Australian depredators of their very existence'.[26] His strategy for securing sites, objects and knowledge thus conceded no place to the bureaucracies that were then being charged with the management of Indigenous knowledge.

The AIAS was becoming deeply involved in site and object registration. In its 1968–69 *Annual Report*, the AIAS had pointed to a gap 'in our knowledge of Aboriginal culture ... the recording of mythology, an important aspect of which is the mapping of all waterholes, hills, rocks and other places, sacred and otherwise, named in them'.[27] At the Institute's 1972 General Meeting, a 'national seminar on Aboriginal Antiquities in Australia' prompted the Minister of Environment, Aborigines and the Arts, Peter Howson, to set up a national program to record 'sites of significance to the Aboriginal people'. The AIAS was given the task of coordinating the implementation of this program, and between 1972 and 1974 its annual grant from the Australian government tripled to $1.5 million. Much of the extra money was to be allocated by the AIAS's new 'Sites of Significance Committee' (formed in May 1973) to fund the State and Territory authorities that administered Aboriginal site- and relic-protection laws so that they could register sites and store material.

Strehlow was appalled by the intentions revealed and approved at the 1972 seminar. A resolution moved by Dr WDL Ride (Director, Western Australia Museum) and seconded by Mr WC Dix (Registrar of Sacred Sites, Western Australia Museum) said that

> this seminar recognizes that aboriginal sites are an important [and] non-renewable part of the capital equipment of the Australian tourist industry, and asks the Minister to give consideration to appointing a committee to advise on the exploitation of aboriginal monuments, antiquities and sites for tourism and the best means of providing adequate protection for such sites.[28]

The formation of the AIAS 'Sites of Significance Committee' prompted Strehlow to resign from the Institute and to write an article for *The*

Australian saying that the AIAS was now controlled by the despoilers of Indigenous heritage. He would no longer share his knowledge, he told ANU anthropologist Derek Freeman: 'It is better for aboriginal culture to die than to be prostituted in this shameful way.'[29]

Insofar as Coombs developed strategies for Aboriginal heritage protection, they were implicit in his support for land rights, as Woodward was then developing that concept, and in his promotion of the Aboriginal-controlled Aboriginal Arts Board. However, Coombs was sufficiently troubled by the possible consequences of the state becoming so involved in the registration, protection and encouragement of the Indigenous heritage that in 1974 he suggested privately that the AIAS be placed under the control of a 'Society for Aboriginal Civilisation' (SAC). The members of SAC should be 'nominees of Aboriginal communities chosen for their standing in ceremonial and related matters in their own communities.' SAC would have four functions: to foster, promote and develop all aspects of Aboriginal civilisation; to conduct research into the archaeology, history, culture and social life of Aboriginal Australians; to promote and develop (in collaboration with the Australia Council) the contemporary expression of Aboriginal civilisation through the arts; and to collaborate with the Museum authorities in the development of the Gallery of Aboriginal Man. Academics could be members of SAC. Initially, 'the academic membership might be the existing members of the Institute', for the Institute was to be incorporated into SAC. The further admission of academic members would be subject to confirmation of the Council of SAC. SAC would also recommend the appointment of a majority of the members of the Aboriginal Arts Board and recommend the Aboriginal members of whatever board or council eventually governed the Gallery of Aboriginal Man.[30]

Both Strehlow and Coombs were sensitive to the possibility that in mobilising ethnographic knowledge to inform government practice, the custody of Indigenous knowledge — including its objects and its sites — might shift from senior Indigenous persons into the hands of academics and government officials. We might call this the 'governmentalisation' of Indigenous custom — its reworking as an aid to a supposedly more enlightened post-colonial rule, or a further step in its colonisation. Yet the two men responded in very different ways to this ambiguity within the project of enlightened governance. Strehlow chose the path of charisma. Rehearsing his biography like an African chieftain's lineage, he asserted his personal right to this knowledge, as an alternative and antidote to its imminent absorption into the 'iron cage' of rational bureaucracy. Coombs made no such personal claim; rather, he sought to design a better bureaucracy, mobilising Aboriginal customary authority in a new institutional form. The difference between these two political projects — Coombs' hopeful investment in the continuity of Indigenous authority and Strehlow's tendency to obituarise and to substitute himself for an eclipsed authority — can be illuminated further by comparing their views on the problem of generational succession.

Strehlow and Coombs on generational succession

Strehlow held evidently contradictory views about the trajectory of Indigenous society: was it fragile or resilient, decaying or adapting? In his pamphlets *Dark and white Australians* (1958) and *Nomads in no-man's land* (1961), there are passages about youthful insubordination that exemplify this tension in his views.

In *Dark and white Australians*, he attempts to evoke the outlook of the young generation of Central Australian Aboriginal people as he had met them in the last few years:

> Their reasons [for absenting themselves from ceremonies] would run along these lines: 'We are finished with all that. You old people always used to go on walkabouts in order to visit sacred sites. You always tired yourselves out with ceremonies. You were always worrying about your sacred objects in caves and storehouses. But you got little out of it, and you only had kangaroos and emus and grass seeds to eat for your trouble. That's why we want to be like the white people. The white man gets his native "boys" to do the work for him, while he sits in the camp and does the cooking. He never worries about religion; yet he always has plenty of meat, plenty of bread, plenty of tea and sugar and tobacco, and all other good things. He has plenty of clothes and blankets, and a house to live in. He can get a native woman whenever he likes, and he can go to the hotel and get drunk whenever he likes. That's what we want to do too.'[31]

Strehlow granted the logic of this imputed view, but he saw it as the unfortunate logic of materialism and gratification, rather than the nobler logic of spirituality and sacrifice. However, when Strehlow referred a few pages later to 'the cruelties and tyrannies of a semifossilized society', he also implied some sympathy for insubordinate youth.³² Colonial conquest had breached the citadel of tradition. By satisfying wants without compelling sacrifice and subordination to elders, the colonising powers had effectively addressed the insurgent energies of youth: 'Food, clothing, freedom from hunger and want, the breaking of age-old shackles, and above all natural curiosity and the spirit of youthful adventure.'³³ The 'tragedy' was that many of these adventurers were like moths immolated on the flame that drew them. Strehlow's concession to the logic of youthful rebellion was framed within his tragic vision of the history of Indigenous Australians.

A sense of tragic decline poorly equipped him as a reforming critic of contemporary practices of assimilation. When it came to making recommendations about what might now be done, Strehlow explored how elders' authority might be modified so that it could continue:

> The Australian initiation ceremonies were, as we have seen, the foundation of all those things that made up the old aboriginal culture. Upon them rested knowledge and love for the old traditions, pride in the aboriginal heritage, obedience to tribal authority, respect for the norms of social behaviour, and a feeling of security in times of drought, periods of sickness, and the declining years of old age.³⁴

Therefore, 'the responsible authorities should ease off their attacks on these rites and cease undermining the last traces of aboriginal authority.'³⁵ Indigenous people 'should ... be permitted to keep up their initiation rites for the time being, and to punish the persons who reveal the tribal secrets, though no longer to the extent of inflicting capital punishment on the offenders'.³⁶

Strehlow implied that he was available to advise on this strategic attenuation of elders' authority. He was confident that 'some of the undue rigours of the initiation ceremonies can be made to disappear with persuasion given to the tribal elders — many unnecessary rigours have, in fact, already disappeared even without white persuasion'.³⁷ That he saw himself (and the elders) as able to distinguish 'unnecessary' from essential ceremonial rigours implies his continuing sense of himself as an agent of the Law — albeit a reflective agent: he was attuned, but not in thrall, to the old, severe Law. His counsel to government in the 1960s was still in sympathy with the old men to whom he been novice in the 1930s.

Their descendants, the surviving carriers of the Law, from whom he had continued to widen his knowledge in his 1950s fieldwork, should be treated as relevant social authorities, he suggested, not just as mouthpieces for an arcane and ancient Law. Aboriginal authority was to be adapted to the circumstances of the present, not presumed to be in terminal decline nor subverted by official action.

Yet Strehlow's affirmations of the relevance of Indigenous Law to government were qualified by the phrase 'for the time being'. When *Nomads in no-man's land* was approvingly reviewed in the Adelaide *Advertiser,* Strehlow was taken to be pleading 'for a better understanding by Australians of Aboriginal life and lore, especially in schools, and ... that the traditions, social discipline and understanding of these people *before being detribalised* are worth our respect'.[38] The need to distinguish the still 'tribal' from the already 'detribalised' was one of the orthodoxies of any discussion of Indigenous interests in the period 1930–60, and so that distinction was sympathetically read into Strehlow's booklet by the newspaper's reviewer. Yet no ethnographic criterion, no sociological marker of qualitative transition, had ever been established to substantiate the oft-used category 'detribalised'. As well, it was an unstable evaluative category, because the difference between saying that the 'detribalised' had lost culture and that they had adapted was a distinction between perspectives. Strehlow was capable of seeing Aboriginal cultural change, on different occasions and in different publications and passages, as loss and degeneration and as an adaptation securing continuity of authority. By the early 1970s, the gloomier of these emphases was the more prominent in his work.

Coombs was inclined to be optimistic about the possible directions of cultural change, to place the emphasis on adaptation and continuity. In one of its first policy papers for the McMahon government's Ministerial Committee, in July 1971, the CAA called for a 'shift in emphasis' from programs 'narrowing the social gaps which handicap Aborigines' to programs that enabled them to 'find ways to organise themselves for effective social action':

> We believe that wherever the desire to act corporately emerges it should be encouraged and helped with the means to achievement. On Moa Island, in the Pilbara, on the Roper River, at Yirrkala, for example, are Aboriginal communities seeking the right to self-determination and which have shown some capacity to work

together for common purposes. Often when corporate action has been successful the element of traditional continuity has been important. To regard such continuity as always working against adaptation is mistaken. Often the breach of this continuity has led to demoralisation and disintegration.[39]

In the path of the CAA's hopes in adaptation stood an ethnographic orthodoxy that Coombs could hardly ignore. As far he knew, Strehlow may have qualified but he was not known to have repudiated a view he had first put forward in 1934 (when he was twenty-six years old) that Aboriginal culture was so burdened with old men's authority that it left no scope for young men's initiative: Aborigines were 'not so much a primitive as a decadent race'.[40]

On 5 April 1971, Coombs set down his disbelief in what was, in effect, Strehlow's extant political obituary of Aborigines as a people. In a speech to the Anthropological Society of Western Australia, he suggested that Strehlow's prognosis overlooked how much Aboriginal people valued one another's unique individuality and capacity for self-expression. Traditions were not fixed; they were open to change and adaptation — by strong personalities, under new circumstances. Coombs thus likened Aboriginal tradition to British and Australian 'common law'. If Aboriginal traditions were adaptable, it followed that Aboriginal people were quite capable of addressing one of the weaknesses of their political tradition: their 'lack of any machinery for decision-making', through which they could formulate a 'community view' to present to missionaries and bureaucrats. In Coombs' opinion, attempts to establish 'councils' on missions and settlements had demonstrated that such bodies were not consistent with Aboriginal political traditions. Coombs' 1971 address therefore set out reform's difficult task. He insisted that Aboriginal political traditions were legitimately different from those of most Australians. He dissented from Strehlow's view that innovation was beyond the bearers of those traditions, and he suggested that such innovation could not be evaded. Coombs thus presented himself as both an advocate of change in Aboriginal ways, and as a defender of their right to remain different in their traditions. For him, the point of change was to enable Aboriginal people to determine their own future.

Coombs supported this more optimistic account of the adaptive potential of Aboriginal political culture when he noted that individuals were emerging from some communities who were knowledgeable about both Aboriginal and non-Aboriginal ways. He also knew of Aboriginal efforts to review the contemporary relevance of customs, such as the meeting on Goulburn Island that he had witnessed in September 1969; there Arnhem Land elders had discussed changes in customs of marriage. The meeting had featured inter-generational dialogue: younger speakers advocating change had checked with older people, he had noticed, to make sure that they were not stepping beyond what the older people thought would be proper. Coombs also told his audience that Aboriginal people were able to form temporary associations and alliances, without hierarchy and formality, in order to get certain projects done. And when Aboriginal people adopted complementary roles in their ceremonial life — with the 'owners' of ceremonies accepting instruction from that ceremony's 'managers' — they were demonstrating a traditional capacity to share authority and to delegate. Ceremonies were themselves evidence that Aboriginal culture was innovative: Coombs had witnessed some that incorporated and commented upon recent events. He concluded that

> we do not need to despair of the capacity of Aboriginal society to adapt its techniques of decision to contemporary problems. They will no doubt take time to learn, and will make many mistakes, but I do not believe that a society which has survived some 20 to 30 thousand years in widely varying climatic and environmental conditions can really be incapable of adaptation.[41]

Those involved in helping Aboriginal people to form councils and associations should respect Aboriginal customs of assembly and decision-making, said Coombs. Community representatives would stand on more solid ground if more time were allowed for a consensus to emerge from discussions in families and camps. Such representatives would not necessarily be chosen by election, but by Aboriginal processes that non-Aborigines did not have to understand.

Coombs warned in the conclusion to his talk that it was not possible for Aboriginal people to avoid experimenting with their own culture. There was no evading 'a long period of education and of trial and error', in which fidelity to tradition would be matched by commitment to innovation. If Aboriginal people were not to 'continue in a state of economic and social dependence', they would be 'forced by circumstances to face issues, to make mistakes, to resolve their internal problems, to confront our society'. And all others would have to 'learn to respect the Indigenous authority within each community facing that challenge'.[42]

In his 1971 address, Coombs laid out the reform agendas of two cultures. Colonial authority would have to make room for Aborigines' different ways of making collective decisions, and Aboriginal people would have to draw on their customary political capacities in new ways, to acquire by trial and error the political techniques to make and to abide by collective decisions.

CHAPTER 4

'The Whole Aboriginal Problem in Microcosm': The South Australian Land Rights Debate of 1966

In 1966, an Australian legislature grappled for the first time with the problem of how to give legal form to a rights-bearing Aboriginal collective — that is, to recognise Aborigines as a 'people' and to afford them institutions of collective deliberation and action. However, to deal with South Australian Aborigines as a 'people' required the State government to postulate what they had in common. An intellectual device for doing so was at hand: the evident heterogeneity of Aborigines was assumed to be diminishing over time. Thus, explaining South Australia's *Aboriginal Lands Trust Act* — Australia's pioneer 'land rights' law — the Minister for Aboriginal Affairs, Don Dunstan, acknowledged the diversity within Aboriginal South Australia: 'We have the whole Aboriginal problem in microcosm; we have people living in semi-nomadic tribal conditions, and people completely assimilated into the community. We have every stage of social change in between.'[1]

It was common sense, at that time, to consider diversity among Aborigines in historical terms as exhibiting a predictable developmental sequence: the people in the north-west of the State were in an early stage of a process, and those in the cities and towns had advanced to a later stage. The implication of this understanding was that, in time, the people living on South Australia's remote North-West Reserve would become like the Aboriginal people in the towns and cities. Dunstan believed that even the most nomadic and least changed Aborigines were changing in a certain direction:

> Even the tribal areas will come to want material things; there is significant change in their motification [sic] and desires. Previously

> they were not interested in material things, but now at Ernabella, in the North-West Reserve at Musgrave Park, and at Yalata, there is pressure for settled housing and motor cars. They are all very interested in getting better incomes. There will be a very real pressure to get the advantages from the development of mining. They will want to make some arrangement.²

Although no one could tell how long it would take for people in 'the tribal areas' to acquire the same aspirations and way of life as those in the cities, their change would come. The trajectory of the people of the North-West Reserve was clear in direction but opaque in timing. This combination of certainty and uncertainty has been, and continues to be, an important feature of Australian ways of seeing remote Indigenous people. Dunstan's deployment of this historical model allowed him to think of the Aboriginal people of his State as, ultimately, one people.

An incomplete State

It was more than an accident of history that the people of the North-West Reserve had scarcely commenced this transition: well-intentioned South Australians had been striving since the 1930s to reduce the intensity of colonial impact in that region and to slow the pace of its peoples' transformation. The North-West Reserve was not only physically remote from the regions of non-Aboriginal settlement and investment in South Australia; it was emotionally and intellectually beyond the experience of nearly all South Australians. However, the Reserve was part of the State of South Australia, and somehow it had to be encompassed within that State's laws and policies. In 1966, it required an effort of imagination and some statutory ingenuity in order to evoke and pass laws for and about the people of the North-West Reserve. As the parliamentary draftsman WA Wyles admitted:

> I know little about Aboriginal affairs or the North-West Reserve. In fact, I had to check whether my description of the area was correct or not, but the director [of the Department of Aboriginal Affairs] has informed me that it is correct. However, I hardly know where it is.³

At least one South Australian MP, the Member for Burra Mr PH Quirke, spoke as if he had had first-hand experience of the remote north-west, for he evoked it affectionately as a wilderness to be protected:

> This is the last remaining area that is almost, though not entirely, in the same condition as when we found it. It is the last link in this State with the early conditions that must have appeared magnificent when white people first saw them. In this reserve there are still trees that bear right down to the ground, as they did all over the country originally, before they were trimmed by stock and destroyed by rabbits ... [The government] should now consider maintaining that area in its present condition in the interest of not only the Aborigines but also South Australia. Those natives within a few generations will become sophisticated. Their progeny will be educated and they will not want to be nomadic. We want the area not destroyed but preserved forever in its present state; we do not want the cutting feet of sheep on it or the tearing capacity of great stock, which wrench the top cover off the land.[4]

In the year that these words were spoken, the South Australian government understood there to be only 300 Aborigines (on average, for they were nomadic) on the North-West Reserve — less that 4 per cent of the 7760 Aborigines in the State — yet the North-West Reserve comprised 91 per cent of all land set aside as 'Aboriginal reserve'.[5] The government offered little service to these people. It had opened a welfare office on Musgrave Park station in 1961, with two staff — one of whom was on fortnightly circuit (900 miles, or almost 1500 kilometres) through the reserve. At the time of Dunstan's land rights legislation, the Department of Aboriginal Affairs was looking forward to opening a small reserve east of Musgrave Park at Indulkana, on a 12 square mile (over 23 square kilometres) portion purchased from Granite Downs pastoral lease. Indulkana was understood to be 'an important Aboriginal totemic and ceremonial ground', and thus seen as attractive to Aborigines.[6]

The North-West Reserve — an area of 56721 square kilometres — had been declared in 1921. Apart from brief mentions in the Chief Protector's *Annual Reports* for 1924 and 1933, the region had received little government attention,[7] although the residents had been of occasional scientific interest in the interwar period. Humanitarian initiatives had begun in 1937, when the Presbyterian Church opened Ernabella mission, just outside the reserve (marginally extended in 1938) on its eastern edge; the mission was intended to be a buffer between the reserve and the colonised world beyond. When Ronald and Catherine Berndt visited outback South Australia in the late 1940s to gather data for their *From Black to White in*

South Australia, they found a government practice of treating the North-West Reserve as if it were outside the State's operational responsibility. From the nearest police station, at Oodnadatta, ventured a regular patrol; among its duties were

> to drive Bush natives westward from the patrol areas, back to the Great Central Reserve beyond Ernabella. This is said to be for the benefit of the natives themselves, so that they may enjoy tribal life without outside interference, and also to protect the settlers from annoyance and possible attack ... The [Aboriginal] trackers sometimes carry out this part of their work alone; they move about on camels among the stations, keeping in touch with parties of wandering aborigines and pushing them back towards the Reserve.[8]

These encroaching and repelled Aborigines were usually unclothed, and they were experienced by outlying settlers as a low-level menace: bothering and harming livestock, and interfering — sometimes violently — with working natives on cattle and sheep stations.[9] The Berndts had done fieldwork among desert Aborigines in the western parts of South Australia ten years earlier. They now surmised:

> At present, the attractions of the mission station and of the pastoral districts are partially outweighed by the aborigines' broad preference for their own way of life, and by the traditional rituals and ceremonies which they hold from time to time at various sites within their tribal areas. For most of them the mission is still a temporary convenience and holiday resort, rather than a permanent economic necessity.[10]

The buffers — Ernabella Mission, backed up by police patrols — had worked. At mid-century, the acculturation of these people had scarcely begun.

However, by 1966 — less than a generation after Ronald and Catherine Berndt made these observations — the South Australian government was seeking a way to deal with the Aborigines of the North-West Reserve as putative title holders, as subjects within a polity that respected their claims to justice. How could this be done?

The Dunstan government's policies towards the Aborigines of the North-West Reserve constituted a small part of a larger statewide design.

South Australia's Labor government wished to turn the management and ownership of all of the State's Aboriginal reserves over to Aborigines themselves, with some residual supervision by the government. The legislated owning body would be a statewide 'Aboriginal Land Trust'. Not all Aboriginal reserves in South Australia were inhabited, but on the inhabited reserves recent legislation (*Aboriginal Affairs Act 1962*) had provided for the formation of Reserve Councils. Uninhabited reserves would be vested in the Trust, by the new Act. Whether inhabited reserves would come under the Trust was a decision for each Reserve Council to make, subject to the oversight of the Minister for Lands or the Minister for Irrigation. The Trust would consist of a chairman appointed by the Governor and at least two other government appointees. The Trust's other members were to be people of Aboriginal descent recommended by the Aboriginal Reserve Councils, who had agreed to transfer their land to the Trust. The Trust would sell, lease, mortgage or otherwise deal in the land that it owned, and it could 'develop' that land, as long as the Minister saw benefit to Aborigines from such development. The government hoped that eventually revenue from the land — notably, mineral royalties — would make it unnecessary to allocate money from the State budget to 'Aboriginal affairs'.

The debate over the bill — in Parliament and in a Select Committee — showed that the distinction between inhabited and uninhabited reserves was not as straightforward as this description of the statute would indicate. The North-West Reserve was inhabited, to be sure, but it was not possible to imagine its Aboriginal inhabitants in the same terms as one imagined the inhabitants of any of the other reserves. Those discussing the Act acknowledged that there was not yet a North-West Reserve Council that could decide whether or not to transfer the reserve to the Trust. The Act provided that if the North-West Reserve were placed under the Trust, it would not be allowed to 'sell, lease or in any way alienate' (section 16.6) any part of the reserve unless it was to persons of Aboriginal blood. Nor could North-West Reserve land be 'encumbered' without a resolution of both houses of parliament.

This chapter will describe themes in the parliamentary debates and the Select Committee dialogues that envisaged the incorporation of the North-West Reserve in the South Australian land tenure system. Paying particular attention to the evocation of the North-West Reserve, I will argue that these discussions vividly displayed — for the first time in

Australia — some of the problems that confront settler-colonial liberalism once it decides that it is time to recognise a category of citizens whose historically preceding association with the land has come to be seen as constituting them as a people with a morally significant grievance.

Some problems of liberal reason surfaced in Australia's public account of its dealings with Aborigines when 'reserves' changed from being the Crown's benign provision to being the estate of the Aboriginal people. The first time Australian legislators had to deal with this conceptual shift was in 1966, in South Australia. As a political achievement, land rights have been relatively easy because the recognition of Aboriginal entitlement has not required any government to challenge any non-Indigenous property rights: a large proportion of the land that has been conceded to Aborigines had been 'reserves'. However, while the political path from Crown 'reserve' to Indigenous 'estate' has been relatively smooth, the conceptual transition has been more textured, subtle and difficult — and Australia is still finding its way through. To convert those reserves to Aboriginal land, the South Australian government had to deal not with private land-owners but rather with itself, with its own policy heritage. In the 1960s, the rationale of reserves became unclear and increasingly contested.

The 'reserve' under 'assimilation' policy

'Reserves' originated as protective devices, intended as sanctuaries from colonising pressure and, in the post-World War II era, tempering the pressure to assimilate to modern Australia. However, it was the zeal and the idealism of 'assimilation' that every Aboriginal person was, at least in principle, to be included in its benefits. Under 'assimilation', the concept of reserves as indefinite sanctuaries could not survive: even the most remote reserve residents were expected, eventually, to be subject to assimilation. In one scenario, assimilation would lead to the dissolution of all reserves as Aborigines moved out and into urban living. The revocation of reserves seemed an obvious corollary of the assimilation of their residents. However, the application of this logic in Victoria, in the late 1950s and early 1960s, had aroused criticism when the residents of Lake Tyers Reserve — marked for closure in February 1963 by the Victorian government — had objected that they considered Lake Tyers their inalienable home. In New South Wales, there were parallel clashes between Aboriginal reserve residents' senses of entitlement and government views about what was in these residents' long-term interests. South Australian officials and some politicians learned from these controversies that the revocation of reserves (whether actual or anticipated) was experienced by Aborigines as a betrayal; their hurt response was a debilitating contraction from programs of assimilation. As Don Dunstan explained, the granting of land rights was intended to address a significant Aboriginal emotion:

> It is known that Aboriginal people are bitter; it is not surprising that they are, for they have been deprived of the rights which, on the founding of the province [that is, the Colony of South Australia, in 1836] it was stated publicly they would have ...[11]

Whereas, under older policy and existing legislation, individual Aborigines could buy or be granted tenure over land, Dunstan's radical proposal was to convert reserves to Aboriginal *communal* title. To do so was to announce limits to assimilation, to honour what was now perceived to be the Aboriginal residents' continuing difference. Ten years after Dunstan's legislation, the Commonwealth's *Northern Territory Land Rights Act* postulated 'the Traditional Owner' as a figure who was different from other Australian property-owners: the bearer of an ancient law, and not a political, legal or economic subject in ways that other Australians are political, legal and economic subjects. In 1966, when the South Australian parliament legislated communal Aboriginal ownership of the State's reserves (in the Aboriginal Land Trust) and when it differentiated the North-West Reserve from the other inhabited reserves, it was writing Australia's first difficult legislative essay in the recognition of Aborigines as political and legal subjects with different kinds of rights and capacities. Unlike those who drafted the Commonwealth's Bill, legislating in the wake of Justice Blackburn's 1971 judgment and Justice Woodward's 1973 and 1974 reports, the South Australians in 1966 could not look to any signal judicial recognition of ethnographically attested 'Aboriginal law'. In the parliamentary debates in the House of Assembly (July to September 1966), and in the sessions of the Select Committee of the Legislative Council on the Aboriginal Lands Trust Bill (September to November 1966), we find that the terms in which Dunstan and his colleagues and officials evoked South Australian Aborigines as land-owners were not those that anthropology was soon to provide to judges. The South Australian discourse did not evoke Aborigines ethnographically — as bearers of an ancient law — but historically and governmentally — as a people alienated by ill-treatment or with a potential to become alienated from helpful authority as they acculturated.

I will highlight four themes in the discourse of officials and politicians:
1. Aborigines are wronged and alienated *historical subjects*.
2. Aborigines are putative *political subjects* whose further formation as political subjects requires supervision.
3. Aborigines are putative *economic subjects* who are likely to mobilise old and new skills in agriculture, craft and small-scale mining.
4. Aborigines of South Australia are a *people*, communal in their customs of property, with limited aspirations as individuals.

Disaffected subjects of colonial history

Don Dunstan, Minister for Aboriginal Affairs and the Bill's foremost apologist, led his Second Reading Speech on 13 July 1966 by narrating South Australian history, highlighting the dispossession of Aborigines. He said that the government's primary purpose was to address the South Australian Aborigines' bitterness. Not only reserve dwellers but all South Australian Aborigines would get satisfaction from the legislation, Dunstan argued: as all of the State's Aborigines had been wronged, so all would share in the sense of restitution. Addressing the Select Committee, Dunstan introduced the phrase 'chip on the shoulder':

> The most regular and most bitter cry from Aboriginal groups has been, 'the white people have taken our lands, and what is left to us they can take away anyway.' They have seen the removal of their native lands by proclamation in other States, and they have been demanding that they be given protection in this area. The terms of Convention 107 of the ILO reflect the demands of indigenous people. It was felt by the officers of the department that it was very important to do everything we could to remove the chip on the Aborigines' shoulders and to give them protection in the lands which are at present reserved for them so that they can say 'They are ours, as a people. This is not something that the government can simply, by the stroke of the Minister's pen, take away from us.'[12]

Dunstan's Acting Director of Aboriginal affairs, DL Busbridge, also used this expression. He explained that even if Aborigines did not 'personally use' the land they would own through the Trust, they would still benefit from the legislation, as they would not 'retain this chip on their shoulders by believing that further lands are going to be taken from them'. Land did not have to be significant economically, he continued, if it were significant emotionally: 'Certain areas would not create a farm, but it is known that some Aborigines have been buried in the area. I think it does a lot for their morale if such areas are declared Aboriginal reserves so that the Aborigines can, if they wish, visit these places.' As he explained: 'We are trying to live down a strong mistrust [sic] of the government.'[13] However, Busbridge went on to explain that the people of the North-West Reserve felt differently; they did not yet share the negative frame of mind that so worried the government:

> There is no resentment on the North-West Reserve, because they still consider they have their lands, but, as they attain more education and hear more of the present discussions outside their own area, these people will suddenly realize that they do not own their lands. I think it is very important that they do in fact own their lands before they start getting this mistrust.[14]

Pastoral Inspector Mr FJ Vickery agreed that 'this chip on the shoulder applies only to the sophisticates of the settled areas. The chap in the far North-West Reserve has no chip on his shoulder and is quite happy.'[15] Asked if a 'chip on the shoulder' could develop in the North-West Reserve with education, Vickery replied:

> Yes. It is the result of brain-washing by welfare organizations, missionaries, advancement leagues and do-gooders. They exort [sic] the Aborigines to demand what they say are their just rights and tell them that their land has been taken from them. This attitude does them no good at all.[16]

Another pastoral inspector, Mr BF Evans, said that Aborigines acquired the 'chip' by mixing with white men. In the outback regions, he thought, the chip was not yet evident: 'Around Oodnadatta and north and west of there (the area in which I worked) most of the natives were quite happy with their lot.'[17]

The evidence shows rival views about the effects of acculturation. The two pastoral inspectors thought that the Bill — as one of many actions by which people were coming into political consciousness — was at risk of arousing a sense of grievance among the previously contented people of the North-West Reserve. Vickery predicted that they would not understand the Bill and did not desire to change their 'semi-tribalised' life.[18] The government's view, in contrast, was that it could not avoid eventually addressing the least contacted people and so should address them in ways that would pre-empt the dreaded 'chip on the shoulder'.

Aborigines learning politics

The South Australian land rights policy was not only about land title; it also solicited — cautiously, ambivalently — Aborigines' political participation. Dunstan and his government colleagues faced a problem: how plausible was it to suppose that all South Australian reserve inhabitants could form and run councils, to fill the political roles that the Bill provided for them? Here it is relevant to mention South Australia's electoral administration. In South Australia, the franchise was open to all adults, Aborigines included. However, in the administration of the electoral roll the government had not included Aborigines, whom it judged as lacking the cultural capacity to be voters. This informal exemption of certain Aborigines from the electoral roll had been recognised as appropriate in 1961 by a Select Committee of the Commonwealth House of Representatives. Considering the enfranchisement of Aborigines in elections for the national parliament, this committee had recommended that all adults of Aboriginal descent, without exception, be eligible for enrolment, but that their enrolment be optional. This departure from the Australian norm of compulsory voting was necessary, the Committee argued, because in some regions Aboriginal people were 'primitive, illiterate, nomadic, periodically nomadic, or associated only loosely and periodically with missions, or with government agencies for native welfare'.[19] The committee's example was the Aboriginal residents of the North-West Reserve. These were the people that Dunstan's Bill, five years later, would suppose to be political subjects choosing whether or not to place the North-West Reserve under the care of the new Trust.

The proposition was difficult to defend. The deputy leader of the opposition Mr GG Pearson doubted the capacity of even Yalata Reserve Aborigines to vote on whether their lands should be under the Trust: 'Intelligent as they may be in self-preservation, intelligent as they may be in understanding the signs of Nature, I doubt very much whether they are sufficiently educated to understand what is meant when they are asked whether or not they want the Yalata mission, for example to be transferred to the Aboriginal Lands Trust.' He added that 'the farther north we go the more acute this problem becomes'.[20] As another opposition MP,

Mr H Shannon, put it: 'We cannot ask the people concerned, because they are nomadic, difficult to find, and shy.'[21]

Dunstan's discomfort on this point is evident. While insisting that a reserve council could be established in what he called 'the tribal reserve areas' (there was one on Yalata already, he pointed out, formed under the terms of the previous government's *Aboriginal Affairs Act 1962*), Dunstan conceded that on the North-West Reserve, 'it will be some time before an effective reserve council organization ... can be set up'; he remained optimistic that 'it will be possible *in due course* to get an effective expression of opinion from the people on the North-West Reserve'.[22] Later in the same speech, he predicted that 'the likelihood of [the North-West Reserve] coming under the trust in the immediately near future is remote.'[23]

Dunstan explicitly repudiated the 'paternalism' of the European community's past approaches to South Australia's Aboriginal people. He described the effect of such paternalism as 'pauperising'.[24] However, his remarks imply that the government continued to have responsibility for people who had not yet become the responsible subjects of their own political and economic development. In his evocation, the residents of the tribal reserves were vulnerable, not yet fully ready to take care of themselves. I do not dispute his judgment — I merely point out how difficult it is to bear responsibility for others without being 'paternal'.

Dunstan admitted that his Bill was based partly on apprehensions about Aborigines' use of political powers. Citing the unsatisfactory performance of some already existing formal organisations on reserves, he admitted that he had accepted — with reluctance — the advice of the Director of Aboriginal Affairs that the Act should empower the minister to invigilate each council's procedures for choosing their representative on the Trust, to ensure that he or she was 'representative of the majority of the people there' and not the product of 'some clique arrangement'.[25] 'I am reluctant to have oversight of Aborigines' dealings by a Minister,' he told the Select Committee. 'However, at this stage in the creation of the Trust it is quite clearly necessary, but I hope that the day will come when it will not be necessary to have the Minister's consent ...'[26]

For Dunstan, the problem was not only the lack of readiness of the people of the North-West Reserve for participation in councils and in the Trust — the political competence of all South Australia's Aborigines was in question. Speaking to the Select Committee, the chair of the Aboriginal Affairs Board, Professor AA Abbie, said while his Board considered 'the principle of the Act was a good one, we could not, in the foreseeable future, find Aborigines who would be able to cope with it'.[27] Later in his presentation, it became clear that Abbie was thinking about the 'chip on the shoulder':

> I am not saying Aborigines cannot be educated to it. At the moment it is very much a matter of them against us, and I think they have to undergo much more education before they can become sufficiently detached to deal with the problems that will come before the Trust in a reasonable way.[28]

He illustrated his observation with two communities that he described as the 'best educated and most sophisticated' reserves:

> At Point Pearce and Point McLeay a hard core group which has no desire to do much for themselves exists. They are the most vocal of the we-against-them school. Unless their thinking changes they will remain a close-knit unity that is going to get as much out of the Government as it can and give as little as possible in return.[29]

Again, we see a fear that the acculturation of South Australia's Aborigines, while necessary, risked cultivating Aborigines' alienation from the purposes of government.

The opposition's Mr Shannon and Mr Pearson seized upon the ambivalence implicit in Dunstan's Bill: how much would the Act and its regulations actually 'trust' the Aborigines whom they said they were empowering?[30] Dunstan's response clearly expressed the paradox of the prescriptive construction of Aborigines as political subjects: 'The Government has no intention of denying to Aboriginal people the right of having members on the trust board or of overseeing the nominations that they make to get the people they want on the trust board.'[31] Yet 'overseeing the nominations' was exactly what Dunstan had said the government would do. While the intention of his procedures was 'to give effective say in their own affairs to the Aboriginal people', a minister would supervise.[32]

Aborigines as economic developers

During the Assembly's debate, former Premier Sir Thomas Playford moved an amendment to deal with the evident lack of a collective Aboriginal political subject on the North-West Reserve. He wanted to ensure that only a vote by both houses of parliament could transfer the

North-West Reserve into the Aboriginal Land Trust. His intention was to protect 'one of the few rights preserved for Aborigines' who hunted on this reserve, though he did not use the phrase 'land rights'.[33] Playford's amendment powerfully appealed to some South Australians' pride in the natural and cultural heritage values of the State's north-west. In rejecting this amendment, Dunstan also presented himself as the champion of those values. How could Playford be a protector of the reserve when his government (preceding the Labor government in which Dunstan served) had secretly — specifically, without consulting the Aboriginal Affairs Board — granted mineral exploration licences over it? If the North-West Reserve residents placed their land under the Trust, Dunstan argued, such predatory actions would not be repeated. For Dunstan, the Aboriginal Land Trust was to become an Aboriginal agent of economic development.

This was an ambitious and novel projection, as the economic aspirations of Aborigines were subject to an overall suspicion that was expressed in the discourse of experts as their 'intelligent parasitism'. Speaking to the Select Committee, Abbie pointed to the Point Pearce reserve residents as examples of this syndrome, and the idea was there — albeit more self-critically — in Dunstan's point that previous policies had 'pauperised' South Australian Aborigines.[34] A farmer who addressed the Select Committee, AS Wearing, said of Point Pearce: 'I think that these people so live in a maze of misconception and lack of understanding of the present commercial world that it would take many years even with assistance for them to take an active part in the conduct of the affairs of the Trust.'[35] Wearing later referred to Aborigines' 'lack of confidence in themselves' and their 'many jealousies and intrigues' as obstacles to economic development.[36]

It was widely assumed in the House of Assembly debate that economic development of the reserves in the longer settled parts of the State would be agricultural. Some members asked whether reserve dwellers would turn out to be good farmers and, if so, how many families could be supported on the available land. Dunstan denied that he wished to set Aborigines up as farmers: 'That is your own construction. You are going into cloud cuckoo land. We have specifically denied that we have any such intention.'[37] However, his colleague Mr L Hughes implied some economic development ambitions for Aborigines on reserves when he said that: 'By instituting an Aboriginal lands trust, the present Minister is attempting to make the Aboriginal more self-supporting.'[38] Dunstan acknowledged that it would be the government's difficult task to stimulate 'a viable economy to provide employment', so that the children of these reserves would enjoy 'equality of opportunity'.[39]

Dunstan wanted South Australian Aborigines on reserves to face some harsh facts:

> On numbers of the reserves now we are running uneconomic employment in training programmes. Eventually, the councils on the reserves will face the fact, and they have been told this: we are not going to continue uneconomic employment on reserves, and that the training programme should reach the stage where they are either are in gainful employment on the reserve or in employment off the reserve. They may go off the reserve, making the reserve their base. They must turn to economic employment in due course ...[40]

Busbridge spoke along the same lines. Referring to the Point Pearce residents, he predicted:

> [I]f they take over the management of the reserves themselves and are faced with a few economic facts I think then that even though Government assistance may be necessary in a decreasing sum for several years, that sum, on the one hand, would be taking effect more readily than the present grant of Aboriginal wages, and would be forcing people themselves to make the decision.[41]

The North-West Reserve was already subject to mineral exploration, and Dunstan wished to vest ownership of minerals in the Trust, arguing that 'in every comparable country the indigenous people have been holding mineral rights and it has been shown time and again that the holding of these rights has been able to provide, in many instances, a viable economy for reserve areas ...'[42] One opposition MP said that he could not imagine Aborigines becoming mining entrepreneurs who would search for 'rare and valuable substances' such as petroleum and helium.[43]

Dunstan's hopes for the North-West Reserve were not limited to mining: he envisaged a 'craft industry in clothing, pottery, jewellery-making, wool scouring, cloth weaving and so on. We believe that, with the giving of these new techniques to the Aborigines, the extraordinary fund of their artistic inspiration will be immediately released.'[44] As well — and perhaps in implicit qualification of everything else to which I have pointed — Dunstan acknowledged the natural heritage value of the

North-West Reserve. He explained that his government's intention was to maintain the reserve 'inviolate', and that 'whatever development takes place it must fit in with the maintenance of the natural surroundings and the background of tribal culture that the people desire to maintain'.[45] The Select Committee asked Abbie whether the North-West Reserve could be developed as a station property. 'It could be,' he replied. 'It would be no better or worse than any other station property in that district. It would lead a fairly precarious existence.' Reminding the Committee of the region's very low rainfall, he warned:

> It would be a tragedy to convert it into a cattle station. At the moment it is a valuable reserve of fauna and flora, probably one of the last remaining in the State of any size. If it were converted into a cattle station, it would produce only second grade beef, and would be competing with people trying to earn their living.[46]

The South Australian Aborigines as a people

Dunstan sought to include the North-West Reserve people in his reformed policy, even though he conceded that they were different from Aboriginal people in the rest of South Australia in many important respects. He thus sought to recognise all of South Australia's Aborigines as a people with common entitlements. Three considerations made this inclusive project reasonable. One was that the heterogeneity of the State's Aborigines was diminishing as the remote nomads became acculturated; it was difficult to say how quickly this was happening, but Aboriginal policy must assume some future, and this was the most plausible future to assume. A second reason for an all-embracing policy was that South Australia was a single jurisdiction: its sovereignty as a State of the Commonwealth was territorially exhaustive. To continue to act as if the North-West were somehow beyond South Australia effectively betrayed this fundamental legal principle. The third and most problematic reason for including the North-West people was that South Australia's Aborigines could be conceived as falling within a common historical narrative. As explained by Dunstan, this was the story of the failure of the colony to honour its foundational duty to Aborigines, resulting in their debilitating 'chip on the shoulder' and estrangement from the beneficial programs of government. If some South Australian Aborigines did not yet have the 'chip' through being remote from colonial pressure, they were nonetheless destined to get it, and governments had best pre-empt it by addressing the common grievance: land insecurity. Dunstan attributed to the State's Aborigines the sentiment that the lands 'are ours, as a people'.[47]

The supposition that the jurisdictional boundary of South Australia determined the boundaries of the Aboriginal 'people' of South Australia was a fiction of debatable necessity. As the two pastoral inspectors pointed out, from the point of view of its Aboriginal residents, the North-West Reserve was part of a larger cultural bloc that spilled over into Western Australia and the Northern Territory. The government would find this out, they predicted, as soon as financial rewards began to issue from the economic development of the reserve. Mr Evans predicted that nothing would stop the people from the adjoining reserves in Western Australian and the Northern Territory from 'migrating in masses to the reserve',[48] and Mr Vickery warned that 'chaps from other States' would claim part of any North West Reserve 'bonanza'.[49]

The idea that the Aboriginal people of South Australia made up a collective interlocutor of government nonetheless persisted in the land rights debate. Busbridge, when responding to a question about whether the formation of the Trust would encourage Aborigines to see themselves as 'detached' rather than 'closer to us', demonstrated the terms in which that figure could be evoked: he linked blood, collective memory and people-hood:

> While there is any fair proportion of Aboriginal blood in the people there will always be a unity in a recognition of their past lands. Although the people may be integrated in the community and living in acceptable standards and economically employed, there will always be this recognition of their indigenous past, as well as a value in Point Pearce and Point McLeay remaining even if in years to come they are only somewhere to go at weekends to see where their forebears lived.[50]

He acknowledged that there were different ways by which South Australian Aborigines could feel an association with the land:

> In the south there are Aboriginal people living on reserves that are nowhere near the land of their forefathers, and they have a strong resentment at the fact that the land was taken from the Aborigines. They are often people who have very little to do with the land themselves, and they would not be capable of developing it.[51]

But in the southern reserves, some people had been relocated generations ago, and so 'regard the present land as their land'.[52]

Dunstan also attached some significance to 'blood' as the basis of peoplehood. When Playford tried to make the parliament the only authority that could alienate portions of the North-West Reserve, Dunstan proposed to keep that power in the hands of the Trust, but to bind the Trust to grant leases only to people of Aboriginal descent.

When Dunstan hoped that his chief institutional innovation — a statewide Land Trust — would be that people's political vehicle, it was easy to point to the likely difficulties. Pastoral Inspector Vickery predicted that even if the North-West Reserve formed its own council, it would work 'only in relation to that reserve. I believe that a representative from, say, the North-West reserve on and Aboriginal Lands Trust would be a fish out of water amongst the more sophisticated members of the trust who would come from the southern reserves.'[53] Busbridge saw this difficulty, but expressed it more hopefully: 'Many Aborigines would have very little knowledge of or would see any direct bearing with the central Trust, but I believe they would have considerable faith in their own councils as an interim step to that Trust.'[54]

To the extent that Dunstan and Busbridge saw South Australian Aborigines as a 'people' with a shared memory of dispossession and shared instruments of restitution (communal title, a statewide Trust), they were wary of the incipient 'individualism' of Aborigines about which opposition MPs continued to speak hopefully. The government's study of Indian land tenure in North America had taught that individualisation of land tenure had led to loss of the native land base, as it was so tempting for individuals to sell. The Australian Labor Party's admiration of Israel also contributed to Dunstan's respect for the 'communal'. He had sent a public servant to Israel in search of social models that tempered individualism with communalism; Aborigines on the Gerard Council, he told the Select Committee, wanted to know more about Israel's 'Moshav Communities': 'These are cooperative communities where the people sometimes individually work the land and sometimes together. The marketing and buying are done cooperatively.'[55] Busbridge acknowledged that 'some Aborigines look at what opportunity might arise to them to gain individual land from the Trust' but, as he explained: 'I personally certainly have not encouraged that thought.' Later he added that 'there is much danger in the individual distribution of Aboriginal lands' and this 'would need to be looked at carefully'.[56]

However, Dunstan was not dogmatically hostile to the growth of individualistic tendencies among the South Australian Aboriginal people. In explaining how he would limit the Trust to granting leases in the north-west to persons of Aboriginal descent, Dunstan evoked with approval what he saw as the emerging desire of the North-West Reserve Aborigines for modern houses:

> [Some] are seeking settled housing, and some people purchase houses themselves out of their Savings bank money. We have several prototypes of settled houses for people moving there. Those people wish to put these houses up close to Musgrave Park station. We have to give them some security of tenure with the settled houses they put up, and even giving them a licence with an interest to use a little plot of earth around them is in itself some alienation from the authority, because it takes away the authority's exclusive rights, whoever is holding them (at the moment it is I), to use that little bit of land. It is an alienation in form.[57]

Conclusion

Compared with other ways of thinking about Aboriginal people-hood that were about to emerge in Australia, the discourse of the Dunstan government about Aborigines was comparatively free of evocations of their traditional custom and law. Dunstan's approach to them was not so much that they were a people rich in their own distinctive political and legal heritage, but that they were a people understandably aggrieved and alienated by colonial dispossession. The South Australian debate (whatever the merits of the legislation) has something to tell us about the variety of terms in which Indigenous Australians may be evoked as a people.

CHAPTER 5

The Politics of Enumerating the Stolen Generations

That Indigenous Australians suffered from the separation of children from their natural parents by state and church authorities has now been acknowledged in statements of apology from Premiers, Chief Ministers, the Prime Minister, the Leader of the Opposition and some church officials. Their apologies since 1997 have validated an Indigenous grievance, and it is often said — without contradiction — that their words contributed to 'healing' the aggrieved. With the Stolen Generations now relatively securely included in the national story, it is open to Indigenous Australians to characterise their own lives or the history of their family as being blighted by having been among the Stolen Generations.[1]

In 2010, I heard a Warlpiri man, Martin Johnson, explicitly include himself as a member of the Stolen Generations when he told a story about the Northern Territory Welfare Branch shifting his family and scores of other Warlpiri from one government settlement to another. His family's memory is of removal from ancestral country without consent. His declaration of himself as one of the 'Stolen Generations' attached that particular Warlpiri story to an already familiar and widely accepted narrative of state coercion. As well as arousing sympathy, his self-inclusion raised a question that was both political and methodological: Should there be criteria for 'membership' of the Stolen Generations, as if it were a quantifiable empirical category? Or is it best to see 'Stolen Generations' as an 'ethical category' — a morally and politically resonant term that is outside the analytical vocabulary of the historian, but various usages of which may be objects of historical inquiry? To put these questions in another way, does 'the Stolen Generations' name a strictly bounded sub-set of the Aboriginal and Torres Strait Islander 'population', or is it better understood as an item in our vocabulary for thinking of Aborigines and Torres Strait Islanders as 'peoples'?

There have been at least two reasons to refer to the Stolen Generations as if they were an empirically specifiable sub-set of a 'population'. First, when the Howard government and its intellectual allies responded coolly and even scornfully to the moral fervour of the *Bringing them home* report, partisans of the report countered with quantitative arguments: counting or estimating the Stolen Generations really mattered.[2] Second, those considering reparations for the individuals and families who are 'members' of the Stolen Generations have had to consider the empirical inadequacies of the term 'Stolen Generations'. In *Healing: a legacy of generations*, the Senate Legal and Constitutional Affairs Committee found it 'not entirely clear … who was to be included in the target group of various recommendations relating to reparation, and to compensation'.[3] The Committee took submissions in 1999 and 2000 in order to assess the Commonwealth government's response to the recommendations made by *Bringing them home*. Noting that the Human Rights and Equal Opportunity Commission (HREOC) inquiry had allowed a broad use of the word 'separated', the Committee went on to say:

> Although *Bringing Them Home* made statements about no family having been unaffected by the removal process, this … was not seen by the Committee as meaning that the funding would be distributed to every indigenous person on the basis they were either a separated person, descended from them or had been affected by the removal of others. While there was broad agreement from witnesses that, overall, much of the indigenous population suffered from similar problems and had been locked into low socio-economic status, the 'separated' population was seen by many to be somewhat more limited. Evidence to this Committee suggested that the 'stolen generation' group was quite distinct within a broader group of 'separated' people.[4]

After quoting complaints from some Aborigines that the distinct entitlements of the Stolen Generations had been obscured in public debate, the Committee concluded that the *Bringing them home* report itself had not consistently treated them as a discrete constituency of grievance. Some of the *Bringing them home* recommendations were intended to:

address specific and apparently identifiable groups and individuals, and [were] not directed to the indigenous community generally, regardless of the arguments over the extent of 'stolen generations' and the percentage and numbers of those removed. However, some of the recommendations are not sufficiently precise, and others do appear to be generic in effect.[5]

The HREOC inquiry had been ambivalent about the possibility and necessity of delimiting the Stolen Generations as a distinct portion of the Indigenous population. Martin Johnson's inclusion of himself and his family as wronged by a process of removal points to the likely continuing popularity of an inclusive usage of 'Stolen Generations' that blurs the boundary with the wider Indigenous population. Many people could feel themselves to have been addressed by Kevin Rudd and Brendan Nelson when they offered the Australian parliament's apology on 13 February 2008. The term 'Stolen Generations' is becoming metonymic: what happened to certain people signifies what happened to many more. The Stolen Generations have become an allegory of colonisation itself, evoking many different experiences of colonising authority.

However, there remains an expectation — shared by those who sympathise with the Stolen Generations and those who are more sceptical of the story — that the history of the Stolen Generations needs to be anchored firmly in population data, including the possibility of knowing how many were 'Stolen'.

It is therefore frustrating that Australian governments have not kept good records of their administration of Aboriginal people — as WEH Stanner once remarked, 'the very absence of more precise information is itself the best evidence of past indifference'.[6] Peter Read, the longest serving historian of the Stolen Generations, has confirmed this critical assessment of official records.[7] Government neglect of record-keeping may sometimes have combined with popular resistance to it, as Alec Kruger — a Stolen Generations litigant in 1997 — has speculated. In 1989, upon his retirement, Kruger had discovered that 'getting a birth certificate [to prove his age when seeking a pension] wasn't the easiest thing in the world':

> The Northern Territory Department of Births, Deaths and Marriages couldn't even find me, except as someone who had married Nita and fathered a lot of kids. They couldn't even identify

my mother and it seemed that my birth hadn't been recorded anywhere. In December 1924, with Christmas and the wet season settled in, my father must have skipped over notifying them about me. Perhaps by the mid-twenties it was a lot trickier, legally, for him to be fathering children with my mother. Perhaps they would have been out to steal us anyway. No hospital records registered my entry into the world. I was born at Donkey Camp before there was even a nursing station at Katherine. No school records were available. Everything was a bit of a guess really.[8]

The Northern Territory Administration's paper trail of Kruger's custody as a child at Kahlin Institution, Pine Creek and the Bungalow was incomplete. Notwithstanding Kruger's vivid memories of being an inmate of each of those places, 'I even started to have doubts myself'.[9]

Hobbled by such an unhelpful archive, the *Bringing them home* report concludes that: 'It is not possible to state with any precision how many children were forcibly removed, even if that enquiry is confined to those removed officially. Many records have not survived. Others fail to record the children's Aboriginality.'[10] As the report notes, it is of limited use to survey those who now identify as Aborigines and Torres Strait Islanders, to ask them whether they or their parents were ever removed, because that method would leave out 'those people whose Aboriginality is now unknown even to themselves' because of their own or their forebears' removal.[11] Nonetheless, the report concludes 'with confidence' that 'between one in three and one in ten Indigenous children were forcibly removed from their families and communities in the period from approximately 1910 until 1970 ... Most families have been affected, in one or more generations, by the forcible removal of one or more children.'[12]

The report's estimate was soon discovered to be based, at least in part, on misreading available studies. For example, HREOC misreported Max Kamien's research in Bourke. The report said that one-third of 320 adults told Kamien of having been separated from their families in childhood for five or more years. In fact, what Kamien had found was that 34 per cent of adults recalled experiencing the absence of one parent for more than five years between the ages of five and fourteen, and only 5 per cent of males and 7 per cent of females had experienced the absence of both parents. Kamien did not say what had caused these separations of children from parents; indeed, he gave no basis for inferring that all separations had resulted from governments removing children.[13]

In finding weaknesses in the report's quantification, critics have sometimes been understood as threatening the moral appeal of its recommendations. In 2000, the Australian government's submission to the Senate Legal and Constitutional Affairs Committee argued that the report's own statistics of removal did not justify the term 'Stolen Generation', as probably only one in ten Indigenous children was removed (and not necessarily 'forcibly', the Commonwealth added). The Commonwealth's submission derived its 10 per cent from two main sources. The first was the ABS National Aboriginal and Torres Strait Islander Survey 1994 (NATSIS) — a random sample of 5000 Indigenous households (17,500 individuals). NATSIS had asked: 'Were you taken away from your natural family by a mission, the government or welfare?' and 'During the time you were taken away, who brought you up?' Of those asked, 10.2 per cent responded that they had been taken. The second source was Peter Read's 1981 estimate of 5625 taken in New South Wales between 1883 and 1969. Although the Commonwealth admitted that it had no reliable figure for the total number of Aboriginal people of New South Wales in that period, it asserted that Read's figure was not more than 11 per cent of the total. The Commonwealth ignored Read's own recent critique of his 1981 estimate as being too low.

The Commonwealth's submission did not accept as indicative of Australia-wide rates of removal the findings of local studies by authors such as Kamien (Bourke) and Jane McKendrick (a Victorian GP). Finally, the Commonwealth drew on its own records of the Northern Territory Administration to produce a figure of 6–7 per cent for that Territory.[14] In summary:

> The available evidence, including that cited by HREOC as its source and authority, clearly suggests that [one-tenth to one-third] is an inflated estimate which has led to the assumption of vast numbers having been affected and whole generations of trauma across the entire indigenous community. In its fundamentals there is no research to support the enormous weight of the conclusions that have been drawn. At most it might be inferred that up to 10 per cent of children were separated for a variety of reasons, both protective and otherwise, some forcibly and some not. This does not constitute a 'generation' of 'stolen' children. The phrase 'stolen generation' is rhetorical.[15]

We should note that the Commonwealth did not estimate an absolute number of children removed (by any definition of 'removed'). In preferring to make its estimate in the language of proportions — one in ten — the Commonwealth's point was to discredit the very term 'stolen generation'. That this provoked outrage (e.g. see *The Koori Mail*, 19 April 2000) confirms how important both 'Stolen' and 'Generations' had become. Colin Tatz showed how one could accept the Commonwealth's proportion without conceding rhetorical defeat: 'If [Aboriginal Affairs Minister John Herron would] rather talk about the *decimation* of the Aboriginal population, I'm happy to talk to him on that basis.'[16]

In 2000, Robert Manne considered the criticisms that had been made of the *Bringing them home* report. Like the Commonwealth, he did not think that a plausible national figure could be derived by generalising from the handful of local studies cited by the report. And, like the Commonwealth, he judged the 1994 NATSIS survey to be the best available source. Thus he agreed that around 10 per cent of Indigenous Australians living in 1994 had, at some time, been taken from their family to be brought up by others. Unlike the Commonwealth, however, he insisted on presenting a plausible absolute number. He was not persuaded by Peter Read's suggestion that a total of 50,000 children had been taken in Australia. This estimate entailed figures for Queensland and the Northern Territory that he found implausible.[17] Using NATSIS data, Manne estimated that the national total for the years 1910–70 was between 20,000 and 25,000 children removed from their parents — 'a far from trifling sum'.[18] Acknowledging that 'removal' encompassed a great variety of processes and circumstances, he asserted that nearly all removed children had been people of mixed descent.

Since 2000, there have been two more attempts to quantify the Stolen Generations: Mark Copland's Griffith University thesis about Queensland, submitted in 2005, and the third volume of Keith Windschuttle's *The fabrication of Australian history*.

Queensland

To 'relocate' or 'remove' Aborigines from one place in order to gather them under official supervision in another place had been the central mechanism in Queensland's approach to controlling Aborigines after 1897. In their accounts of such 'removals', neither Thom Blake nor Raymond Evans drew attention to a possible consequence of such removals: the separation of children from parents.[19] In Thom Blake's analysis, 'the removals program fulfilled a variety of objectives: removing the old and unemployable from station and fringe camps; controlling behaviour in fringe camps, on settlements and labour relations; as means of extending prison sentences and punishment over and beyond the legal system'.[20] The theme of Ray Evans' paper was the policy's distinction between Aborigines who were useful to colonists and those who were useless and/or threatening in some way: the latter were targeted for removal.[21]

In the wake of the *Bringing them home* report, the policy of 'removal' acquired new interest for historians as the context for the Queensland chapter of 'the Stolen Generations'. Collaboration between Griffith University and the Queensland government created a 'Removals Database', using State government records from 1859 to the 1980s. Mark Copland devoted his PhD thesis to analysing this database, including his attempt to quantify the forced removal of children from their parents. Copland uses the word 'removed', not 'stolen'. He defines 'removal' as 'the forcible removal of an Aboriginal person to a church or state-run institution'.[22] Importantly, his definition highlights *where* children and adults were removed to, not from *whom* they were removed. I am not sure how much it matters that Copland defines 'removals' as those movements that were 'forcible'. As it turns out, Copland never adduces data on whether a removal was effected through force; rather, he tends to assume that if Aboriginal people were subject to a law that empowered the state to 'remove' them, then all removals can be treated as 'forcible'. In his thesis, the phrase 'forcible removal' is effectively a tautology.

It is commonly understood that the term 'Stolen Generations' refers to the removal — not necessarily without parental consent — of children to an authority other than their natural parents. As Copland points out, in Queensland many of the removed children were accompanied by their parents. Indeed, one of the more common reasons given in Queensland records for removing a child was so that the child could continue to be with his or her parents in an institution.[23] That is, Queensland child removals occurred in the context of the massive institutionalisation of kin-based groups. If this is so, how can the Queensland Removals Database tell us anything about the Stolen Generations? This raises the important issue of how we should interpret the dynamics of the institutions to which people were removed: were children and parents who lived in the same institution separated or together?

One of the differences between Copland and Windschuttle is that they give conflicting answers to this question.[24] This difference emerges in Windschuttle's book when he discusses Copland's finding that there were 660 'documented removals of Aboriginal children where they were not accompanied by their parents'.[25] Windschuttle disputes this figure, preferring the Queensland government's number of 249 (as reported by Anna Haebich from an unpublished government submission to HREOC).[26] Windschuttle says that Copland's 660 is based on too long a date range and includes children whose removal resulted in their living in the same institution as their parents.[27] Certainly, Copland does count as 'separated' from their parents all children living in dormitories — whether or not they were admitted to the same institution as their parents. Dormitories effected the separation of more children than those who were 'orphans, incorrigibles and neglected', he writes.[28] He is suspicious of official judgments that children were otherwise 'neglected' by their natural parents, and he emphasises the material deprivation experienced by children in dormitories. He cites dormitory girl Ruth Hegarty's memoir of estrangement from her mother, even though both lived within Cherbourg.[29] Without disputing that institutional life was materially austere, Windschuttle argues that when whole families were removed to Queensland institutions, the child's ensuing relationship with parents can better be understood as attenuated than separated: 'most dormitories for children on government stations and missions in northern Australia were not fully segregated from the parents' quarters. The children slept and ate apart but saw their parents most days.'[30] How far can attenuation go before we can call it 'separation'? And to what interactions does the phrase 'saw their parents' refer? It seems to me that both Copland and Windschuttle offer tendentious summary accounts of a complex and varied set of circumstances.

Accepting for the moment that the process of removal studied by Copland was larger than (but included) the forced separation of children from their mothers and fathers, how does Copland quantify 'removal'? There are two units to be counted: 'removals' and 'removees'. In the Removals Database, each person who was removed at least once is represented by a 'Personal Card' recording certain attributes of that person. The database includes another series — 'Removal Cards' — that record certain features of each act of removal: 'Where it was possible to identify that the same person was being removed more than once, a number of removal cards were attached to the same personal card.'[31] Copland reports the number of removals as

12,576.[32] Although Copland's primary unit of analysis is the 'removal', not the individual removed, it is more relevant to our topic — enumerating the Stolen Generations — to focus on his account of the numbers of 'removees'. The total of 'children removed' would have equalled the total of 'removals of children' only if each child had been removed only once. As Copland explains, some people — including some children — were subject to more than one act of removal.[33] Copland uses the term 'removee' to distinguish a removed individual from an act of 'removal' and so will I.

Thus we can ask: how many persons were removed in these 12,576 episodes of removal? That is, how many personal cards were in the database (some of them with more than one removal card attached)? Copland gives or implies three different answers to this question. Without drawing attention to it, Copland implies in Figure 2.3 that the number of removees was 11,723.[34] However, when discussing the sex of those removed he implies a different total: 11,190 — or 5797 males, 4377 females and 1016 whose sex was not clear from the available records.[35] Later, he reports that his database consists of 11,570 'personal records'.[36] That is, depending on which figure we use for the number of removees, the quantity of 'removees' is between 0.89 and 0.92 times the number of 'removals'. Roughly, for every ten removals there were nine removees.

How many of these removees were children? Copland found that the State records often omitted information about the age of persons removed — for 7657 out of 11,723 removees, age was unknown.[37] He thus had to estimate the proportion of removees who were children. Of those 3616 removees whose ages were known, 3077 — or 85 per cent — were aged between birth and 18 years. Were we to assume that 85 per cent of removees of unknown age were aged under 18, then between 9900 and 10,000 of the removees would have been aged under 18. However, this figure would imply that very few of the removees (roughly, only between 1500 and 1700) were adults. This would be a surprising result, given what historians such as Blake and Evans have written: removal was largely targeted at those Aborigines judged recalcitrant and/or useless — an account that implies a relatively high proportion of adult removees. And as Copland himself acknowledges, removal dealt with kin-based groups of removees. Copland seems to think (or judges it prudent to assume) that the authorities recorded age more diligently when the removee was a young person, so that the removees whose ages were recorded as under eighteen years (3077 removees) would constitute a large proportion of all child removees.[38]

Thus Copland comes up with a figure of 3077 or more children removed between 1897 and 1972 when he uses his Removals Database. However, Copland argues that there must have been more than 3077; as a source for quantifying the Stolen Generations in Queensland, the Removals Database is insufficient in that it does not necessarily include all children removed to dormitories, mainstream children's institutions and employment.[39] In attending to these three additional components of 'children removed', Copland found gaps in the official record: officials did not quantify their work every year. In years for which he could find no records, Copland found it necessary to estimate children removed to dormitories (some of whom may have been already included in the Removals Data base), 'mainstream children's institutions' and 'employment'.[40] He projected numbers for those years for which he lacked data on the basis of previous and subsequent years. He also needed to make an estimate to overcome the lack of data about boys' employment: he simply assumed that for every girl employed there was also a boy. To allow for the possibility that a child taken into an institution was subsequently taken out of it, he used other State administrative data to estimate that this happened to half his removees.

Putting all this together gave him a figure of 8827 'separated children' for the years 1897–1971.[41] However, there was one more step for Copland to take, for the 8827 'does not take into account children adopted or fostered by non-Aboriginal parents'.[42] To estimate how many children were fostered or adopted, Copland turns to the 1994 NATSIS finding that about three out of every ten removed children (31.7 per cent) were adopted or fostered by non-Aboriginal parents. The addition of this component (that is, treating the 8827 removed to institutions as 68.3 per cent of the true total of children removed) brought Copland's estimate to '13,076 children separated from their natural families in Queensland between 1897 and 1971'.[43] Copland estimated that from 1900 to 1970, 81,000 Aboriginal children were born in Queensland; to these he added an already present child population of 8250 and subtracted an estimated total of children who died in infancy in the years 1900–70. The result was a total of 77,100 children who *could* have been removed in the period 1897–1972. His 13,076 thus makes up about one in six of the estimated number of Queensland Aboriginal children who survived infancy.

Two discretionary judgments tend to enlarge this proportion. One is that Copland defines childhood as up to eighteen years of age (high from the perspective of the early twentieth century); the other is that Copland includes removal to employment (almost three out every 10 of those removed), not only removal to institutions and foster homes. Derived by such steps of reasoning and definition, Copland's proportion — one in every six (or 16 per cent) — is higher than the national proportion of 10 per cent on which the Commonwealth and Manne converged.

In considering Copland's figure, we should keep in mind two features of Copland's definition of 'removal'. One is that it focuses on what children were removed *to*, not on what they were removed *from*: he cannot assume that every one of these removed children was 'separated from their parents', though it is plausible that many of them were.[44] By definition, 'removed' children were 'separated from their parents' if they were adopted or fostered. If they were removed to a 'mainstream children's institution' then it would also seem that many, if not all, were separated from their parents — at least for some time, if not for ever. It is likely that removal to employment also involved separation from parents, though for how long is not clear from Copland's data. However, to add these three 'likely' categories of removal to the 3077 or more child removees on the Removals Database is to pile plausible conjecture upon plausible conjecture. Recall that the Removals Database encompasses the relocation of whole families — kin-related persons — to institutions: child removees on the Database were not necessarily separated from their parents unless we agree with Copland's conjecture that these institutions' attenuation of parent–child relationships always amounted to 'separation'.

The other point to keep in mind is that Copland includes the word 'forcible' in his definition of removal. How can we be sure that every child removee in the Removals Database and every child added as a removee to a dormitory, to a mainstream children's institution, to employment or to adoption or fostering by a non-Aboriginal family was separated as a result of state or church coercion of unwilling parents or other kin? We cannot know this from the data available to Copland and cited by him. As I pointed out above, Copland writes as if there were no removals or separations that were not 'forcible', and that did not result in 'separation' from parents for some time, if not forever.

In summary, while Windschuttle is being too parsimonious in accepting only the Queensland government's 249, Copland's figure of 13,076 is an estimate that includes confident judgments about the following issues: (1) that the attenuation of parent–child relations that dormitories effected is best seen as 'separation'; (2) that there is no need to distinguish between separations for finite periods (such as those occasioned by employment) and those that lasted until death; and (3) that a removal subject to State authority is 'forcible' — no matter what the disposition of the parents. Unlike Copland, Windschuttle does not include children removed to employment, and nor does he include as 'removed' the thousands of children (in Copland's estimate) fostered or adopted. Finally, if a child lived in the same institution as his or her parents, Windschuttle doubts that they were separated, as he thinks that dormitories usually did not sever the parent–child relationship.

New South Wales: Windschuttle vs Read

Peter Read has acknowledged the difficulty of estimating a number for the Stolen Generations in New South Wales.[45] In his pioneering *The stolen generations*, he included a table titled 'Estimates of Aboriginal children removed, 1883–1969' for New South Wales, in which he qualified almost every category of removal as 'approximate figures due to lack of records'. Only two sub-totals did not require this warning — for Kinchela and Cootamundra Homes 1939–69 and for Aborigines Protection Board placements 1916–38 — but it is difficult to follow Read's calculation for the former, as he appears to multiply 31 by 25 to get 825, an excess of 50. Read wrote that while his total of 5625 removed children was no more than an educated guess, the figure warranted the inference that the removal of children had affected all the Aboriginal families of New South Wales. Later, he declared his 1981 estimate to be 'an underestimation':

> A surer figure can be estimated on the approximately 84,000 files held by the NSW Welfare Service of all children in care in the period 1921, when the records began, to 1985. If 15 per cent of the children represented in these files were Aboriginal (which is probably an underestimation) the number of New South Wales children would therefore be close to 10,000. This figure is the number of removed children, not their descendants. *The total number of New South Wales individuals deprived of an Aboriginal identity ... would be much higher than this.*[46]

Mark Copland has commented that while Peter Read has never made clear the steps that have led him to his quantifications, the estimates for New South Wales are 'reasonable' and 'not necessarily outrageous'.[47] Richard Broome implies a similar assessment when he cites Read's national estimates without querying them.[48] Keith Windschuttle, in contrast, will not accept intuitive plausibility as a substitute for method. But what is Windschuttle's method?

To focus his critique of Read, Windschuttle quotes his 1981 statement that highlights a particular New South Wales record series covering the first 800 children removed under the 1915 Amendment to the *Aborigines Protection Act 1909*. These files (comprising 1220 pages) are a very large sample, Windschuttle argues, of the removals that took place between 1915 and 1940, so their analysis allows testing of Read's characterisation of the Stolen Generations.[49] Windschuttle comes to the following conclusions about these 800 cases:

- Not all separations were permanent: 54 per cent of cases, between 1907 and 1932, returned either to their immediate family or to their community of origin.[50]
- Only 10.6 per cent of children removed between 1907 and 1932 were aged less than five years. Two out of three were adolescents (aged thirteen to nineteen).[51]
- Females constituted 71 per cent of removed children (a point on which he and Read agree, though they offer different explanations).[52]
- Some 43 per cent of removed children/youth were placed in jobs (and not taken to institutions).[53]
- A high proportion of children were either orphans or from single-parent families — that is, they were not able to depend on a male breadwinner and did not have a relative who could substitute for such a figure.[54]
- 'Being Aboriginal' was rarely stated as a reason for removing a child: the common reasons given for those aged between birth and twelve years were 'neglect', 'orphan', 'lacking parental care/control' and 'request of State Children's Relief Board', while for those aged thirteen to eighteen, they were apprenticeship, training and education.[55]

Using such data, Windschuttle challenges the argument that child removal in New South Wales was motivated largely by a wish to eliminate Aborigines as a distinct people. His counter-argument — made plausible by his figures and quotations from government documents — is that there were many genuine welfare cases and that the State was responding as best it could, with humanitarian motivation (though not necessarily with beneficial effect). I hope that historians who know the New South Wales archives consider Windschuttle's challenge to be worthy of a reply that is no less grounded in such evidence.

Windschuttle also comments critically on Read's estimate that 5625 children were removed in New South Wales between 1883 and 1969. He considers each component of that estimate, arguing that Read has misunderstood evidence and counted some children twice. Only a scholar who has worked on the New South Wales files will be able to evaluate Windschuttle's and Read's use of them confidently. Until we see an informed rebuttal of Windschuttle, then I suggest that we cease citing Read's estimates for New South Wales and use Windschuttle's estimate for New South Wales: 2600 'in care'. Given Windschuttle's tendency to methodological and emotional parsimony, I suggest that we treat his figure as a minimum.

Peter Read and the birthright population

In quantifying the Stolen Generations, it has been relevant to estimate the size of the total Indigenous population for two reasons. One is that we cannot calculate a rate of removal without having a base population as a denominator. Thus Copland went to some trouble to estimate how many Aboriginal children there were in Queensland who could have been removed. In addition, as my citations of Manne and the Commonwealth show, the 1994 NATSIS survey is an important source on both the size and the 'rate' of removal. The survey data represent a sample of the known Indigenous population. Drawing a representative sample requires that we know the size and composition of the base population — but what if we don't?

Peter Read has argued that this is the case. He has been concerned not only with the numbers of Aboriginal children removed *from parents*, but also with the number of Aborigines 'stolen' *from the Aboriginal people*. Read wishes to use his statistics on child removals as a basis for estimating how many people — now deprived of Aboriginal identity — do not identify as 'Aboriginal' in the Census. In *The lost children*, he and Coral Edwards estimate that 'there may be one hundred thousand people of Aboriginal descent who do not know their families or communities'.[56] Adding those identity-deprived people back into the Indigenous population is Read's exercise in counter-factual demography. The Howard government was addressing Read's counter-factual when, after quoting the NATSIS 1994 result, it declined to add an estimate of those people who were now ignorant of their 'Aboriginal background' and so were excluded from samples drawn from the self-identified Indigenous population. As that government explained, such people 'would not put themselves within the class of people seeking access to government services for reasons of removal from their families and would not claim compensation'.[57]

Read's approach invites us to rethink the question: From whom were the 'Stolen Generations' stolen? He is not content with the obvious answer: the child's natural parents. That answer is prompted by a scene that no viewer of *Rabbit-proof fence* is likely to forget: the police confronting and overwhelming a helpless Aboriginal mother as they snatch her child and force her into a car. This moment of official kidnap has become emblematic of the Stolen Generation process, warranting shame and outrage. However, as the case of Lowitja O'Donoghue illustrates, some children were removed with parents' consent, and the points of grievance now relate to the conditions under which parents/mothers were making this painful decision, as well as how the removed child subsequently was treated.

If it was not necessarily from 'parent(s)' that a child was 'stolen', is the term 'stolen' too tendentious? As I understand Read, he could well agree that *not all* the children removed were 'stolen' from unconsenting parents/families, but he nonetheless would insist that every removed child was 'stolen' from the Aboriginal people. That is, the socialisation of the removed children into a non-Aboriginal identity — and not merely the removal itself — is what gives effect to this theft. Many of those who were removed and brought up in non-Aboriginal homes and institutions did not learn that they were of Aboriginal descent, nor did they learn to value that descent as the basis of their identity. Their non-Aboriginal upbringing induced them to 'deny their own birth-right' to be Aboriginal.[58] Thus, no matter how they were removed, their progeny were lost to the Aboriginal population. That loss is part of what Read means by 'stolen'. His estimate of 100,000 refers to those who did not (in 1989) 'identify as Aborigines but *who were entitled to do so because their parent or grandparent had been removed*'.[59]

'Entitled' and 'birth-right' are words to ponder. Read's idea that a 'people' can have members stolen from it is dependent on the assumption that there is a 'people' defined by descent: to align one's identity with one's descent is to claim one's 'birth-right'. Read is here emphasising 'descent' as a criterion of Aboriginal people-hood. In contemporary Australia, the idea 'Aboriginal' assigns some importance to descent — but perhaps not as much as Read commends. Descent has been joined by 'identity' as a criterion for counting who belongs to the Indigenous peoples of Australia.

As retired Commonwealth public servant Barrie Dexter has recently reminded us, the Gorton government in 1968 adopted self-classification as the government's way of demarcating the Aboriginal population:

> 'An Aboriginal or Islander is a person of Aboriginal or Islander descent *who identifies as an Aboriginal or Islander and is so accepted by the community with which he or she is associated*'. There were, in other words, three tests: descent (with no question of relative proportions of mixed ancestry, as in the past); identity; and acceptance.[60]

The italicised words are important: since the late 1960s, descent has been recognised by governments as a necessary but not sufficient criterion of Aboriginality. There must also be a subjective element, some self- and community recognition. In the counting of the Aboriginal population, it is only self-recognition as Aboriginal that is important. Up to and including the 1966 Census, Aborigines were classified, and were asked to classify themselves, according to degree of Aboriginal descent. Since the 1971 Census, the Aboriginal population has been constituted, statistically, by a request for self-identification that makes no reference to 'descent', 'cast' or 'blood'. The revised Census practice has continued to be an invitation to 'ethnic' self-classification. The Census does not ask a 'factual' question about 'racial origin' or descent, and it does not ask the 'community' to verify a person's claim to be 'Aboriginal'; the Census enumeration privileges the subjective identity of the respondent. The principle behind this invitation is that each individual (or the responsible person caring for that individual, such as a parent) knows best what his or her 'ethnicity' or 'heritage' is, and neither community verification of identity nor officials' grading of a person's descent is significant.

As a co-founder and activist within Link-Up, Read doubts that some people's self-knowledge is adequate to their 'real self': government policies have obscured the 'real self' of many people of Aboriginal descent.[61] The state's respect for each respondent's self-classification now means that a person might really be of Aboriginal descent — in ways real to Peter Read, that is — but not tick Aboriginal and/or Torres Strait Islander boxes in the Census and so not be enumerated as a member of the Aboriginal or Torres Strait Islander populations. In Peter Read's counter-factual demography, the emphasis of the Census on subjective identity effectively works to narrow the definition of the Aboriginal population. His view implies scepticism about Mick Dodson's hailing of self-classification in the Census as the exercise of a 'right', a welcome instance of 'self-determination'.[62] A favourable assessment of the change in the Census from 'race' and 'descent' to self-classification is that it admits people of any degree of descent to the 'Aboriginal population', if they so desire.[63] In contrast, it is implicit in Read's approach that the Australian government's 1968–71 revision of the Census criterion of 'Aboriginal' — from objective descent to subjective identity — consummated a significant attack on Aboriginal people-hood. Influenced by their own and their family's history, people of Aboriginal descent might choose not to identify. For the state to permit such a choice after years of intervening in Aboriginal identity-formation was to further what Read calls 'a concerted effort by the state to terminate and further prevent Aboriginal self-identification' and 'a violent and premeditated attack not only on Aboriginal family structure but on the very basis of Aboriginality itself'.[64] Read is thus critical of our current notion of the Aboriginal population, insofar as 'Aboriginal population' is constituted by many individual acts of identification that have been affected by the state's coercive practices; he presents us with a counter-factual population consisting of those who would be entitled by descent to be the 'Aboriginal people'.

Read sees the Stolen Generations and their descendants as including those who have been induced by their own or their ancestors' experience of removal not to exercise their birth-right — that is, not to align their identity with their Aboriginal descent as they are entitled to do. As I understand Read's argument, to deny one's birth-right and/or to be denied one's entitlement to be Aboriginal is to be a person lost not only to the Aboriginal population, but also to the Aboriginal people. That such individuals might, with help, be reinstated to the Aboriginal people — accorded their birth entitlement — is an important theme of *A rape of the soul so profound*, a book written 'from the point of view of the Aboriginal race as a whole'.[65]

Read's counter-factual demography gives the concepts 'race' and 'descent' more analytic weight than any Australian scholar I can think of.[66] If his is a racial conception of 'Aboriginal', it nonetheless eschews the ideas from nineteenth century racial science that one's intellectual capacities and behavioural patterns are determined by the race into which one is born, and that the Aboriginal racial inheritance is inferior. If there is a notion of inherency in Read's concept of the birth-right Aboriginal population, it is a thoroughly political one: those of Aboriginal descent inherit an entitlement to belong to the Aboriginal people. For Read, the point of quantifying the Stolen Generations is that we need to know how many have been denied that entitlement, and the point of scholarship and government policy is now to restore the entitlement to be Aboriginal by linking people up to the kin from whom they have been severed.

Conclusion: The Stolen Generations as a bounded constituency

Confronting any effort to quantify the Stolen Generations is the fact that government records are patchy and unreliable. However, even had the records been better maintained, problems would remain. My comparison of three scholars — Copland, Read and Windschuttle — illustrates some issues of interpretation that are difficult to resolve. The terms 'stolen', 'removed' and 'separated' have not been stabilised into a descriptively precise vocabulary for delimiting the topic under study. The quantification of the Stolen Generations will always be determined by the interpretive decisions made by scholars about such issues as the Indigenous experience of employment and dormitories, the meaning of neglect and the determination of parental consent. One's judgments about these issues cannot be politically innocent: they will be embedded in our wider underlying views of the aims, practices and effects of the British colonisation of Aboriginal people.

Moreover, whatever estimate of absolute numbers a scholar may plausibly propose, it will not be possible to express that number as a proportion of the Aboriginal population. Neither the definition nor the administrative application of a key term — 'Aboriginal' — has been constant through history (it remains a problem even now, in some State governments' death-registration practices). Not only have there been variations, across governments and through time, in the official definition of 'Aboriginal', but people themselves cannot be assumed to be consistent over time in their self-identification, for reasons that Peter Read discusses. To express the Stolen Generations as a proportion of the 'Indigenous population' will never be an exact exercise because, even if we could come up with a number of those 'Stolen', the population denominator will be an over-determined artefact of politics, administration and popular culture. Finally, let us not forget that the *Bringing them home* report itself is undecided (though not in a reflective way) about whether to present the Stolen Generations as a discrete division within the Australian population that scholars can identify and quantify, or whether they were the entire Indigenous population, viewed from the standpoint of their collective suffering as subjects of colonial power. We know enough, however, to be sure that the state's interference in Indigenous family life was so widespread, persistent and negative in its effects as to warrant Prime Minister Rudd's and Opposition Leader Nelson's apologies in February 2008 to all Indigenous Australians.

Part III

CRITICAL REFLECTIONS ON POLITICAL CAPACITY

CHAPTER 6

The Changing Cultural Constitution of the Indigenous Sector

> They are the critical ingredient in Aboriginal people's material security, an expression of Aboriginal political identity and an appropriate modernisation strategy with the evolution of an Aboriginal civil society.[1]

Thus Patrick Sullivan writes on 'the Indigenous sector'. I agree with him that the Indigenous sector is of fundamental importance in contemporary Indigenous affairs, and in this chapter I review some of the anthropological and public policy writings that help us understand it.

The Indigenous sector consists of thousands of organisations: statutory authorities mandated to act for Indigenous title-holders; incorporated 'councils' performing the functions of local governments in remote parts of the continent; employers and job-placement agencies (formerly known as Community Development Employment Projects (CDEP) schemes); as well as health services, legal services, housing associations, mining royalty-distribution bodies, schools, childcare agencies and sporting clubs. The rise of the Indigenous sector is the most important product of the national Indigenous policy era known as 'self-determination' (though there were Indigenous organisations well before it began).

As Sullivan argues, the 'Indigenous sector' has features in common with the 'not-for-profit sector'. However, he points to what makes the Indigenous sector different:

> Mainstream not-for-profit sector organisations are not normally run by the people whose needs they propose to meet. Aboriginal

not-for-profit sector organisations, on the other hand, are usually directed by a board elected from the client group, and much of the staff is also recruited from this group. Second, mainstream not-for-profit sector organisations do not usually aim to meet the needs of entire polities comprised of both genders, all age groups and the full range of potential competencies, and with pre-colonial norms of governance that are, to a greater or lesser extent, still intact. It could be argued that these norms are often maladapted or dysfunctional, but they still produce self-organising communities.[2]

The 'pre-colonial norms of governance' are among those realities that governments began to recognise sympathetically in the 1970s, encouraged by anthropologists, pivotal court judgments and Indigenous actors themselves. I will argue in this chapter that the survival and flourishing of the Indigenous sector raises the following questions: What are these norms? And how distinctive need they be? First I will describe some features of the Indigenous sector.

We do not know how many organisations make up the sector. In 2003, David Martin estimated 'perhaps more than 6000'.[3] Diane Smith wrote in 2002 of 'a tidal wave of organisational incorporation … in Indigenous communities … there is a legally incorporated body [i.e. Indigenous] for approximately every 100 Indigenous people in the country'.[4] In 2008, she estimated 5000.[5] It is not possible to get an Australian total of incorporated Indigenous bodies because not all governments administer their laws of incorporation in such a way as to distinguish companies that are 'Indigenous' from those that are not. We have reliable data about that unknown proportion of the Indigenous sector that is incorporated under the Commonwealth legislation. I will review some figures from the Office of the Registrar of Aboriginal Corporations later in this chapter.

What does the Indigenous sector do? Four distinguishable functions or goals come to mind, and it is possible for an Indigenous organisation to have more than one of them.

- *Representation.* There is a range of senses in which an Indigenous organisation may be representative. The fact that it receives or manages resources on behalf of its clientele requires routines of reporting that 'represent'; the body may also hold elections for its leaders; it may collect client data; it may brief counsel. Some devote much of their

resources to advocacy — writing submissions and discussing the needs of their members and clients with politicians and government officials.
- *Title-holding.* Some Indigenous organisations have been created primarily or exclusively because Australian laws of real property assume that there is a legal entity that holds title, and because Australian policy has strongly favoured the principle that for Indigenous property (land and sea rights), that entity is communal.
- *Service delivery.* Since the 1970s, governments have judged that some public services to Indigenous Australians are best administered through a publicly funded Indigenous organisation that does not operate for profit.
- *Profit-making.* Sometimes Indigenous people form corporations that are designed to sell a good or service for profit. Governments have encouraged them with grants and soft loans, but there is some concern that these ventures have so far failed at a high rate.

Though the profit-making ambition of Indigenous Australians is a phenomenon worthy of study, the focus of this chapter is on the other three functions or goals of the organisations of the Indigenous sector — the governmental functions of representation, territorial possession and public administration. In a paper advocating what she calls 'jurisdictional devolution', Diane Smith writes that 'the challenge will be to create a "space" for new kinds of Indigenous authority within zones of jurisdiction already occupied by federal, State and local governments'.[6] I see four kinds of authority:
- *Over physical resources.* Land rights legislation, including land-purchase programs, have resulted in the transfer of considerable physical resources (land and sea rights, capital) to Indigenous control. These resources may or may not have income-generating potential, and their controllers may or may not wish to exploit such potential. As well, according to some Indigenous knowledge systems there are powers embodied in certain physical features of land and sea, and it is the responsibility of Indigenous people to 'manage' those inherent powers, even if legal title is not vested in the proper Indigenous custodian.
- *Over employees.* It has been the primary function of some Indigenous organisations — such as CDEP schemes — to create and administer a publicly funded workforce. However, beyond CDEP it is difficult to imagine an organisation of the Indigenous sector that is *not* also an employer. Under Australian industrial laws, to be an employer is to

have certain defined powers and responsibilities. The employees of the organisations of the Indigenous sector are both Indigenous and non-Indigenous.

- *Over 'voice'.* All Australian governments recognise, in some way and to some degree, that there is an Indigenous constituency with which they must remain in touch. Organisations of the Indigenous sector have the power to be the tangible 'voice' of that constituency. There is no guarantee that governments will take any notice of this voice, but this does not make it any less compelling for Indigenous people to struggle to exercise control over it. To be an official or office-bearer in an Indigenous organisation is to possess to some degree the power of Indigenous 'voice'.
- *Over access to entitlements (some of which may be 'citizenship entitlements').* When Australian governments devolve some service delivery to Indigenous organisations, they confer a certain power on those organisations: the power to classify clientele according to some notion of need or desert specified in public policy. Is this person Indigenous? Does this person have the need that this program is designed to meet? Does the urgency of this person's need exceed that of another? These are among the decisions that are routinely (and most of the time without controversy) made by many Indigenous organisations — about housing, employment, schooling, clinical services, legal representation and other matters. It is a very considerable power that we are likely to take for granted because its exercise is so susceptible to routine.

Cultural difference and the Indigenous sector

Advocates of 'self-determination' demand that public policy respect 'cultural difference'. If empowering Indigenous Australians means conceding much to their customs of governance, then for law and public administration to impose norms and procedures on Indigenous organisations is, in this conception, to compromise 'self-determination' by extending indefinitely the frankly tutelary program of 'assimilation'. After surveying legislation governing Indigenous incorporation, Reilly and colleagues offer a version of this tug-of-war between imposed and immanent approaches to Indigenous corporate governance: 'the internal governance, auditing and administration requirements in legislation establishing Indigenous governance bodies and mechanisms are burdensome, and take valuable time and resources away from the core representative functions and responsibilities of Indigenous organisations'.[7] The authors complain that the corporate structure provided within the *Aboriginal Councils and Associations Act* seeks to establish organisations to fit Aboriginal people into a non-Aboriginal bureaucracy and governance practice, and so offer 'very little scope for the exploration of self-governance, except as an unintended by-product'.[8] As a result, in the regulation of bodies incorporated under the Commonwealth Act, 'the high level of prescription in the rule ... gives rise to the need for special assistance. The assistance is not based on the strength or particularity of Aboriginal culture, but on its frailty.'[9] These Jumbunna authors were writing in the spirit of the 199th recommendation of the Royal Commission into Aboriginal Deaths in Custody: that governments refrain from prescribing the internal structures of Indigenous organisations.

There is no doubt that the Indigenous sector works within a tutelary regime, and this is made explicit for those Indigenous bodies that have incorporated under Commonwealth legislation. When the Howard government passed the *Aborigines and Torres Strait Islander (Corporation) Act 2006* to replace the *Aboriginal Councils and Associations Act 1976*, the intention — based on the recommendations of a 2002 review — was to assist and to induce Indigenous Australians' embrace of the norms and procedures of 'good governance'. As Table 6.1 shows, the Office of the Regulator of Indigenous Corporations (ORIC), has continued to be willing to deregister corporations — whether for non-compliance or inactivity.

The regulatory impact of the two successive Acts seems to fall into two periods. In the first 20 years of the Act's operation, 2999 corporations were registered and there seems to have been little if any review of their performance by the registering authority; since June 1998, there has been more scrutiny, resulting in more deregistrations (2591) than registrations (1878). In this second period, the high volume of deregistrations until the commencement of the amended *Aboriginal and Torres Strait Islander (Corporations) Act* in 2006 may well reflect problems in the older incorporation statute, not necessarily impropriety in the Indigenous sector. Those who reviewed the *Aboriginal Councils and Associations* Act in 2001–02 concluded that the Act did not give the Office of the Registrar of Aboriginal Corporations (ORAC) many options, other than deregistration, in order to 'help' a corporation that was experiencing difficulty in complying with reporting requirements. The review recommended amendment of the Act

Table 6.1: Corporations registered and deregistered under the *Aboriginal Councils and Associations Act* and the *Aboriginal and Torres Strait Islander (Corporations) Act*, 1978-2011 (annual figures at 30 June for financial years 1986-87 to 2010-11)

Year	New	Deregistered	Net total
1978-86	456		456
1986-87	98		554
1987-88	109		663
1988-89	180		843
1989-90	181		1024
1990-91	220		1244
1991-92	230		1474
1992-93	298		1772
1993-94	304		2076
1994-95	313		2389
1995-96	265		2654
1996-97	162		2816
1997-98	183		2999
1998-99	128	274	2853
1999-2000	183	333	2703
2000-01	171	165	2709
2001-02	187	113	2783
2002-03	183	105	2861
2003-04	134	282	2713
2004-05	120	248	2585
2005-06	102	158	2529
2006-07	111	88	2552
2007-08	84	31	2605
2008-09	125	7	2723
2009-10	163	676	2210
2010-11	187	111	2286

Source: ORAC and ORIC, Annual Reports.

so as to shift the registrar's work from a 'traditional enforcement-based approach' to a 'facilitative approach'.[10] In particular, the review envisaged:

> Assistance to members and directors of corporations in developing the skills necessary to participate effectively in corporate processes and to satisfy the requirements of regulatory compliance. This may require education and training. Assistance to corporations facing corporate governance difficulties and insolvency. Context-sensitive enforcement of certain statutory obligations and easy access to incorporation. Regulatory intervention to protect members of the corporation from abuses.[11]

The reviewers were not committed to an alternative set of 'Indigenous cultural' norms of corporate action that might be enabled by a less prescriptive approach: 'The notion of "culturally appropriate" incorporation has ... proved to be problematic.'[12] In justifying treating Indigenous corporations differently, the reviewers suggested that 'special regulatory assistance' would be 'a temporary measure of "positive discrimination" *based on race* which will enable Indigenous people to enjoy, on an equal basis with other Australians, the same legal facilities (and attendant socio-economic benefits) that incorporation can confer'.[13]

In its self-presentation (in annual reports, other publications, and the conduct of its staff and delivery of its programs), the Office of the Registrar of Indigenous Corporations (ORIC) has worked hard since this review to make itself a helpful and encouraging body. Nonetheless, as the volume of deregistrations since 2006–07 shows, the registrar continues to use this potentially punitive instrument. The tables and graphs in ORIC Reports do not include annual numbers of deregistrations; I have inferred the quantity of deregistrations from these data. ORIC evokes its Indigenous constituency in terms of its learning needs: terms of distinction such as 'race', 'culture' and 'people' are absent from ORIC's discourse. While insisting on, and imparting, certain standards of corporate governance, ORIC has distanced itself from the rhetoric of commentators such as Helen Hughes (see Chapter 7). ORIC's carefully developed persona upholds the premise that Indigenous Australians are honestly engaged in their organisations for the public good, and are handicapped by specific and remediable deficits in the skills of governance. ORIC is teaching, and Indigenous Australians are willingly learning, how to govern.

A study of corporate delinquents commissioned by ORIC made the following points about some organisations' failure:

> There are three common symptoms of failure found in cases of corporate failure — failure to produce financial accounts, not holding annual general meetings and poor record keeping of members' records. Each of these common symptoms of failure can be improved by providing corporate governance support services. Corporate insolvency, in both the literature and this paper, is most often linked with poor management of the corporation by directors and staff. The largest cases of corporate failure involving people's intentions and behaviours relate to disputes within and between corporations. There are only five cases (5 per cent) involving fraud and just one case (1 per cent) involving a bankrupt director.

> The research findings suggest that early external intervention in Indigenous corporations exhibiting poor corporate governance and management issues or potential insolvency is important and effective. The findings also suggest that Indigenous corporations need support and capacity development in managing the corporation's affairs and not only in the governing of corporations. It is important that both directors and staff acquire skills and competencies in business management to perform their duties and fulfil their responsibilities in this area. The research findings are consistent with mainstream research on corporate governance and business failure ... Over 40 per cent of Indigenous corporations that had experienced corporate failure were returned to members after external administration. This increased to 70 per cent when liquidation only cases were excluded.[14]

Such a diagnosis of 'failure' does not make the Indigenous sector sound different from non-Indigenous corporations, and it points to the obvious solution: training.

Research by anthropologists has begun to illuminate this new (but not unprecedented) mode of engagement between Indigenous Australians and the state.[15] Emphasising the historical dynamism of indigenous culture, recent anthropological theories of culture have facilitated the empirical observation of Indigenous adaptation. Alan Howard, commenting on cultural change across Oceania, notes that the political mobilisation of Pacific peoples does not merely *draw on* cultural identities and on customary ways of thinking and enacting social relatedness; it also *reconstructs* these identities and ways:

> The fact that much of the discourse concerning cultural identity takes place within political arenas raises questions about its relevance for social reconstruction and social transformation. Can political discourse and action effectively generate commitment to cultural identities, particularly newly formed ones? To what extent do political definitions of cultural identity carry over into other areas of social life? What are the organisational effects of redefining 'tradition' for political purposes? Obviously Oceanic societies are not the first to face these dilemmas. They are part and parcel of nation building everywhere, especially where indigenous social, linguistic, religious, and cultural divisions are pronounced.[16]

Ronald Niezen has written that under the stimulus of their mobilisation within nation-states and through the multilateral discourse of human rights, Indigenous peoples are re-forming their social relations. The Indigenous peoples' movement:

> seeks to protect the values and institutions of individual-absorbing societies within a global movement that affirms individual rights and liberties. Once the basis of membership in indigenous communities or organizations shifts from ascribed to chosen identities, the controls and constraints that define indigenous or 'segmentary' societies, and that give them permanence and power, are dispensed with.[17]

In the recent research commentary by Australian anthropologists, this anti-essentialist conception of culture works by locating Aboriginal organisations in what some of them call an 'inter-cultural' space (or field) in which it is difficult to label norms and practices as either 'Indigenous' (Aboriginal) or non-Indigenous. This review leads me to argue in the remainder of this chapter that the threat to self-determination comes not from the contamination of Indigenous governance traditions by alien governance traditions but via changes in the structures and norms of Australian government itself.

Indigenous, learning to be corporate

One vignette of the tutelary state is Christina Lange's account of the response to ORIC of a community living on an Aboriginal pastoral lease, Windidda. In 2006, ORIC told Ngangganawili Community Incorporated (the community's corporate face) that it was not complying with its legal obligations and was at risk of deregistration: 'Receipt of the notice challenged the community's assumption that a lack of interest from the regulatory body equated to the satisfactory fulfilment of corporate responsibilities.'[18] Lange worked with the Windidda residents to help them come to terms with what it meant to be not just a 'community' but also a 'corporation', and to work out how to 'disengage' the implications of one from those of the other.[19] Making that distinction was contrary to the Windidda folk's habits of thought: as a 'community', they were content with their informal processes for holding money collectively, but as a 'corporation' those same funds had to be accounted for in prescribed ways.

'Close attendance to governance' became essential to the community's survival.[20] It would be difficult to read Lange's story as a *complaint* that these Aborigines had to learn to be 'corporate' as well as 'communal': as she tells it, they were well able to make the changes required. The process added to their repertoire of political subjectivities; it did not displace something authentic with something alien.

When Zohl de Ishtar and her Balgo colleagues report the collective deliberation processes of the women of Balgo, acting as the Kapululangu Aboriginal Women's Law and Culture Centre, they give the impression that the women do things in their own 'Walawalarra' way:

> In bringing Indigenous law together with the *Corporations (Aboriginal and Torres Strait Islander) Act 2006* (Cth), it has been decided that only women Elders can be Chairwomen, while middle generation women may be Vice Chairs. This is in deference to the Elders' Lawful authority, their relationship with Country, and their knowledge of the *Tjukurrpa* (Cosmology). It also respects that Kapululangu was established by Balgo Elders, and reaffirms their central position within their organisation. Middle-generation women are, however, equal members and also bring vital skills and knowledge to the Board. While these younger women defer to their Elders in all matters pertaining to law, and often in other matters as well, they are respected for their own knowledge — particularly in matters pertaining to the *Kartiya* world.[21]

The obligations of the Act can also be met by devices such as 'Two Companions':

> In any [Board] task there are always at least two women acting together and sharing responsibility. There are, for example, two Chairs and two Vice Chairs. This duality ensures that all of the Elders have a chance to be Chairs of the organisation. While one chair is more skilled in the *Kartiya* governance processes and can sign her name, for example, the other may still be recognised for her deep knowledge of the Law.[22]

The women refer to the 'Australian rules' — their statutory obligations and the governance norms in which they are occasionally coached in workshops. The authors acknowledge that some Elders have found it difficult to participate in and make sense of ORIC's training.[23] But to be reminded of these differences between worlds does not in itself threaten the Aboriginal domain. 'Kapululangu women have successfully included Settler ways into their operation without forfeiting their right to determine their own self-governance.'[24]

Frances Morphy has provided a more cautionary account, based partly on a 'governance' training workshop for Yolngu that she attended. The language of this workshop was (of course) English, and it included terms basic to 'governance' training — such as 'fairness' and 'honesty'. Morphy (a student of Yolngu-matha since the 1970s) pointed out that there are no obvious equivalents for these terms in Yolngu-matha. She comments: 'Attempts at "capacity-building" that assume a set of universal principles underlying all human actions, whatever their surface form, are doomed to failure.'[25] However, she acknowledges that once the teachers became aware that their cherished governance concepts were not 'universal', they might still (and most likely would) decide to propagate these terms among Yolngu as new, helpful and necessary concepts. In Morphy's view, it is an open (and, in her paper, unaddressed) question 'whether people should be *persuaded* that concepts such as "fairness" *ought to be* universal'.[26] Later in her paper, she concedes that 'perhaps it is checks and balances that are the universal principles for good governance'.[27] If so, then Yolngu practise them already. As she explains: 'leaders [whose status is based on male primogeniture, not on democratic election] who lead by consensus are constrained by the need to reproduce consensus. Disaffected constituents can "vote with their feet", withdraw their support, and align themselves with another leader.'[28] She urges trainers in governance to acknowledge and build upon the governmental capacities that are already in Yolngu custom. She concludes her paper by arguing that both trainers and trained should acknowledge that while translation of the key English terms of good governance is not possible, an 'explication' of their operational significance is imperative. In her view, the bicultural individuals who are skilled at such explication tend to be Yolngu; their historical circumstances have necessitated their cultivation of skills in cultural brokerage, while most white Australians can get away with being monocultural. Such skilled explicators should not be the recipients of governance training; they should be among its deliverers. She concludes:

> When they are in a position to understand more accurately what western governance terms mean, Indigenous people might go one of two ways. They might agree to be positioned, or to work towards being positioned as 'well-governing Indigenous persons',

but then again they might use the information systematically to articulate alternative models of good governance.[29]

Diane Smith's research among Indigenous leaders in the region of Western Arnhem Land reinforces the impression we get from the above accounts: of Aboriginal learners with bicultural aptitude. Her examples include a chairperson consulting his committee and making up rules so that '*Bininj* etiquette' was respected in the use of members' names; this adaptive chairperson also explicitly suspended avoidance etiquette within meetings — again after seeking his colleagues' support — to enable committee members to participate fully. She draws attention to the useful 'cognitive tool of compartmentalisation', so that different rules are understood to apply in different, bounded and specifiable contexts, such as meetings.[30] Biculturally adept leaders such as this chairperson thus construct 'buffers' between custom and the demands of 'good governance'. Smith generalises that 'good governance' processes are likely to be adopted by Indigenous Australians if those innovations meet four demands:

> First, they give priority to people's pre-existing cultural knowledge, norms, systems of authority, and experiences. Second, they have been designed collectively and in a practical governance context. Third, they can be put to immediate practical use; and fourth, they can continue to be adapted to suit changing governance needs.[31]

The supposition that all this guiding, teaching, adaptation and (sometimes) deregistration inhibits or betrays the 'self-determination' of those Indigenous Australians who maintain continuity with 'pre-colonial norms' is difficult to sustain when we see such examples. While it remains reasonable and useful to pose the question of whether incorporation puts custom and culture at risk, it is a mistake to equate that question with the issue of whether incorporation serves or betrays Indigenous self-determination. It is possible that self-determination is a project that stimulates Indigenous willingness to change ways of thinking about the distribution of authority among Indigenous people.

The ambivalence with which Kathryn Thorburn closes her 2008 study of the Kurungal organisation should teach us something. On the one hand, she invites more sustained conversation about 'governance' within the organisation, and between the organisation and consultants and regulators; on the other, she warns that such help may change the role of Kurungal, making it less a cultural and political mediator and thus 'no longer characterisable as "Indigenous" in any meaningful way'.[32] Why should that matter? If it does, then whose notion of 'Indigenous' matters in this situation? Jon Altman's conclusion about Bawaninga Aboriginal Corporation (BAC) is that it has been effective because non-Indigenous managers have served for long periods and have been allowed much discretion by an elected executive whose members serve short terms: 'Long-term managerialism has probably inhibited Aboriginal executive decision-making,' he admits, and BAC has not been successful 'in genuinely representing and empowering its Aboriginal membership'.[33] An observer such as Thorburn might say that BAC has not been very 'Indigenous'; however, Altman hails BAC as 'a progressive organisation advocating for appropriate forms of development for its membership'.[34] Altman's criterion of success is implicit: BAC's longevity and its ability to limit trouble from governments, from members, from white professional employees. The corporation includes informal mechanisms that allow ongoing accommodation of diverse authorities and interests. As Altman suggests in his conclusion, trouble may come: BAC is vulnerable to government policy changes about the goals and obligations of CDEP. To the extent that the 'success' of BAC has been determined extrinsically (that is, by a relatively permissive CDEP policy), then the question of this (or any) organisation's 'Indigenous' character is of less importance.

Reading recent anthropological studies of Aboriginal organisations has taught me not to presume that self-determination is rooted in Indigenous organisations' fidelity to Indigenous custom, and that (thus) self-determination is vitiated by state-taught norms and procedures. That way of thinking would require someone to formulate authoritatively what Indigenous custom and culture *are* in the context of Indigenous organisations, but does such authority — scientific? political? — exist?

Among recent anthropological researchers on Australian Indigenous organisations, there are pleas for recognition of intact Indigenous approaches to politics. For example, at Port Keats (Wadeye), Bill Ivory summarises what he has found to be the characteristics of local Indigenous leadership. However, his account does not encourage confidence that it is an adaptive political mode, for many of Wadeye's younger folk, he writes, see their leaders as being impotent to engage the state. Ivory's solution appears to be to document that there is an Indigenous system of leadership, in the hope that the state will engage sympathetically with it and thus give that approach to politics legitimacy in the eyes of sceptical youth.[35] Ivory's stance — hoping/obliging the state to recognise as adequate an existing mode of Indigenous authority — seems to me to be atypical of recent studies of Indigenous self-determination in Australia. It has been more common *not* to postulate an 'Indigenous' governance norm, conceding the necessity for customs to adapt. 'Indigeneity' becomes a quality that actors invoke strategically as they urge this or that adaptation.[36]

As soon as anthropologists began to consider the historical dynamics of the 'cultures' they study, it became impossible to pose the question of fidelity to custom and more interesting to observe the creative manipulation of the multiple norms with which Indigenous persons must deal. Francesca Merlan's ethnography of the Jawoyn illustrates this. Merlan invokes Taussig's concept of 'mimesis' to describe how self-determination policy proceeds by two steps. First, the state elicits 'from indigenous people what are taken to exist as their own modes of organisation and … recast(s) the management of Aboriginal affairs in what are seen to be indigenous terms'. (She gives the example of the salience of 'tribe' in governmental thinking.) Second, these powerful 'representations of Aboriginality … come to affect who and what Aborigines consider themselves to be'.[37] How much do Aboriginal people actually change in the course of this second mimetic step? The term 'mimesis', as I understand it, offers no secure ground on which to distinguish Indigenous adaptations that are opportunistic and thus make only a shallow claim on actors' understandings and loyalties, and adaptations that substantively reconstruct Indigenous social being. Is Indigenous mimesis a superficial or a profound refashioning of selves? Merlan shows the Jawoyn to be changing, generation by generation, in their conception of themselves as entitled land-holders. She does not present these generational differences as the attrition of tradition.[38]

Working with the Rembarrnga, Cowlishaw did not invoke the concept 'mimesis'. However, her ethnography of the interface between the public agencies and the Indigenous clients of self-determination also demonstrates the difficulty of judging the depth of Aborigines' efforts to be the fitting subjects of that policy. She was manifestly undecided about the terms in which it would continue to be accurate to characterise Rembarrnga people as 'different' from non-Aborigines. On the one hand, she writes that 'robust "racial" difference is being inexorably squeezed out while a malleable, tractable kind of "cultural" difference is encouraged'.[39] On the other, she seems to distance herself from the celebratory description of 'robust' difference when she refers to it as an 'orthodoxy' cherished by 'anthropologists and cultural studies scholars' who are unlikely to appreciate that 'Aborigines' attempts to embrace modernity' constitute a 'dialectical process'.[40]

In 1997, David Martin wrote insightfully that Indigenous organisations would soon face tougher tests of their fitness to receive public funds: 'The hitherto largely unexamined claims that "community control" of service provision will necessarily lead to improved outcomes, whether for Aboriginal communities or mainstream ones, are likely to receive much closer scrutiny against the new criteria being developed within bureaucracies.'[41] Martin and his CAEPR colleagues accepted the challenge to think more critically about the ways in which the Indigenous sector might be enabled or disabled by being, in part, an expression of Indigenous culture. For example, Diane Smith refers, in positive terms, to 'universally accepted guiding principles of good governance (such as equity, fairness, flexibility, transparency, accountability, efficiency and effectiveness)'.[42]

The issue of whether such notions of good government (universal or European-Australian) are an imposition on Indigenous Australians was a theme of James Fingleton's review of the ACA in 1996. Fingleton urged that Aboriginal corporations be enabled by the Act to pursue both internal and external accountability. By internal accountability he meant that 'the incorporation has been culturally appropriate, such that the group has legal mechanisms in place which it has approved, understands and can be expected to observe in a reliable way'.[43] When he invoked 'cultural appropriateness', however, Fingleton did not have in mind a regulatory model of 'Aboriginal culture'; rather, he wished to give each incorporated body more latitude to define its *modus operandi*. For example, the Act should not prohibit Indigenous organisations from accepting non-Indigenous people as members — that was an issue for each organisation to decide. And in some regions, Indigenous norms might not favour annual elections: why not allow a variety of pathways to office? Finally, why did a member of an Indigenous organisation have to be a 'natural person'? Might not some Indigenous organisations wish to include as members other Indigenous organisations? Fingleton's way of accommodating cultural difference was to highlight the need for local choice and to make as few suppositions about 'Indigenous culture' as he could. The 2002 review by Corrs/Westgarth echoed this approach, and these recommendations became part of the Howard government's reforming Act in 2006.

If it is not possible to generalise about how 'Aboriginal culture' is 'different' from and resistant to the state's solicitous templates of Indigenous collective action, then what does 'culturally appropriate' mean? The thrust of recent work by Sullivan and Martin has been to warn against recognising/formulating a 'customary' or 'traditional' Aboriginal or Islander way of conducting collective action.[44] It is not possible to identify the *cultural* ground from which to mount a cultural critique of government policy as *culturally* coercive. Nonetheless, the impulse to consider culture to be at risk has been strong among that generation of Australian anthropologists who, in the context of land and native title claims, have been obliged to emphasise the continuity of Indigenous custom. For David Martin in 2003, under prevailing schemes of self-determination Aborigines were at risk of recognition that entailed 'juridification': 'the problem of *the underlying social relations being distorted or dominated* by the legally enforceable expression of the same relations'.[45] He hoped that '*as much social and political process as possible* should be left within the realm of informal indigenous social practices, not codified within formal corporate governance structures and processes'.[46] Notwithstanding his wish to preserve 'informal processes' against creeping 'juridification', Martin states that 'there is no such thing as an autonomous arena of indigenous values and practices'; rather, there is a 'contested intercultural field of transforming and transformed practices and values'.[47] This would seem to undercut any Indigenous cultural critique of the effects on Indigenous Australians of their engagement with 'the formal and informal institutions of the dominant Australian society'. However, Martin does not go that far. He prefers to say that it is 'inadequate to leave the construction and evaluation of such judgments *solely to the indigenous people concerned* and to a domain of supposedly uniquely indigenous values'.[48] He adds that 'more effective governance … must draw *not only from the values and practices of indigenous people*, but also from those of the general Australian society'.[49]

It has not been easy for anthropological commentary to abandon fully the idea of an 'Aboriginal' way — for good or ill — of doing politics. In their first paper on these problems of political–cultural development, Martin and Finlayson put forward what they consider to be the 'core cultural themes' of Aborigines' approach to politics: 'the tendency of Aboriginal societies and groups towards "fission" and disaggregation rather than aggregation and corporateness' — a tendency they call 'localism':

> The Aboriginal domain is typically highly factionalised, and characterised by the complex and often cross-cutting allegiances which people have to groupings based on families, clans, ancestral

lands and so forth, as well as to contemporary forms such as Aboriginal organisations. A defining characteristic of this domain lies in its localism, in which the political, economic, and social imperatives lie, pre-eminently in more restricted forms and institutions rather than in broader and more encompassing ones. 'Local' can be either social or geographic or both, and the two are frequently related, for example, through relations based on affiliation to traditional lands. Localism is characterised by such features as a strong emphasis on individual autonomy, and by priority being accorded to values and issues which are grounded in the particular and local, rather than in the general and regional or national.[50]

Localism is a problematic feature of Indigenous peoples' ways of doing political work, to the extent that 'aggregation' and 'corporateness' are, generally speaking, what the available institutions of self-determination demand of Indigenous people.[51] Martin and Finlayson were encouraged in 1996 by the fact that Aboriginal people seemed to be getting better at 'aggregation':

> Organisations such as Land Councils and ATSIC itself are becoming powerful vehicles through which new forms of Aboriginal collective political and economic enterprises are being forged, at regional and national levels. Arguably, they have provided the institutional base from which both a regionally-based leadership and in informal coalition of Aboriginal leaders has emerged in recent years.[52]

For Finlayson, the plight of native title representative bodies in the second half of the 1990s had much to do with the novelty of some of these bodies' practices of 'representation' and 'accountability'. She writes that 'it is the culture of Indigenous community politics, rather than models of managerialism or technical knowledge, which determine[s] Indigenous organisational action and behaviour', and that 'community organisational accountability is very firmly (even too firmly) tailored to Aboriginal cultural conceptions of kin-based obligations and the necessary flow of goods and services'. If there is to be reconciliation of this kind of accountability with that demanded by governments, she suggests, there must be a 'conceptual and cultural shift' in Indigenous political culture 'from exclusive to inclusive, from local to the regional, from the personal and familial to the wider general community'.[53] In these words we can see the metaphorical extension of 'localism' to refer to any strategy of exit, any factional assertion and any elevation of personal interest over impersonal obligation. Cultural constructs such as 'impersonality' were strongly resisted by the governing committee of one NTRB with which Finlayson worked, causing tensions with the organisation's administrative arm, whose officers were well socialised into 'impersonality'.[54]

In studies of the operation of Aboriginal organisations, the management of 'localism' has been a prominent theme. In 2002, Diane Smith saw the management of localism 'in the historical development and funding of the outstation movement in Australia, where the trend has been for smaller outstations to aggregate themselves around a larger "hub" community for the purposes of securing service delivery and administration'.[55] Citing 1999 data, she asked whether 'the 942 Indigenous communities with populations of less than 50 wanted to have their own separate governing structures and administrative processes, separate financial management systems, direct funding allocations, and service delivery responsibilities'. She implied that their answer would be 'no',[56] and proposed that the Indigenous sector be organised into layered jurisdictions — a pattern of hubs and spokes: 'Local community jurisdiction would remain in place, but specific areas of authority and responsibility could be delegated to governance layers of greater collective scope.'[57] To define and secure such higher level units in a political culture with a strong tendency to disaggregation required 'local leaderships who can mobilise constituents to provide mandates, who are widely seen to be representative, and who can give direction to the transfer process'.[58]

Smith tended to see aggregation as the object and fragile outcome of political effort to overcome the default tendencies towards 'localism' that governments had coddled by a relaxed regime of corporate registration and funding. She evoked the myriad entities that had been funded as Indigenous 'selves':

> individuals ... their extended families ... tribal and clan groupings; local communities; regional geographic areas and regional organisations. All these different layers have been developed and funded in Australia, but in a *haphazard and poorly coordinated* manner. As a consequence, *competing representative voices, duplication of services, program ineffectiveness* and arguably, barriers to self-determination have been multiplied on the ground.[59]

Will Sanders questioned this perspective: he worried that the effort of aggregation would and should be tempered by conceding that governance might be achieved by a loose knit network of semi-autonomous agents. In a series of papers delivered in Canberra and Darwin in 2002 and 2003, he renamed 'localism' as 'dispersed governance' — a recurrent feature of Indigenous practice:

> As part of the attempt to move towards policies of Indigenous self-determination and self-management in which upper-tier Australian governments have been engaged over recent years, Indigenous people have been allowed some considerable degree of choice in the organisational structure to be developed for the conduct of Indigenous governance. The pattern which has emerged from this choice tends to be both highly localised and highly dispersed. Indigenous people seem to have preferred to group themselves into organisations of quite small geographic scale, for quite limited organisational purposes. Many little organisations have emerged, with somewhat different, although at times somewhat vaguely stated and inter-related purposes.[60]

His theory was that dispersed governance 'divides the task of community and regional collective decision-making into "do-able" bits and pieces [such as health, housing, land rights advocacy]. And second, it offers opportunities for the representation of a diverse range of interests and points of view.'[61]

In subsequent research on the Anmatjere Community Government Council in Central Australia, Sanders saw a regional political structure that was effective because its local cells — ten wards each with equal representation on the council — were allowed to be strong. He has narrated how he and fellow researcher Sarah Holcombe advised the council to operationalise 'a guarded regional federalism that had considerable respect for the autonomy of its constituent parts' in the face of certain pressures towards centralisation of authority.[62] Similarly, when discussing the motive for Aborigines to be open to the formation of a tier of regional government in the Northern Territory, Diane Smith presented the principle of 'subsidiarity' as a concept in political theory that is relevant to a strong Aboriginal impulse towards the dispersion and localisation of authority:

the Indigenous principle of subsidiarity enables federalised systems of governance that accommodate interdependent layers, including the possibility of both centred and decentred social formations. This constitutes a form of 'networked governance'. It is generated out of the interconnectedness of locally autonomous groups (and categories) of people, and via the negotiated allocation of roles, rights and responsibilities across those parts.[63]

The Aboriginal leaders who promoted this model 'referred to the corpus of *Bininj* [Indigenous] institutions, values, and behaviours as the foundation from which they then consider what might be the best rules and procedures for [their organisation]'.[64] Being true to culture is both motivation and legitimating ideology.

Trends in the form of the state

The culture of the Indigenous organisation — whatever we say about it — may be less important in determining the effectiveness of Indigenous corporations than the wider 'culture of governance'. The phrase is Diane's Smith's. As she explains it:

> [A] culture of governance is based on institutionalised forms of policy, program and grant funding that are supported by the tools of financial compliance and accountability, service delivery outcomes, administrative review, and technical audits. These tools are activated by the ever-changing face of government departments, agencies and committees, which work to defend their relative influence, functional 'territories' and budgetary power. Aligned to departmental territories are vast bureaucratic networks where influential senior officials formulate policy frameworks and devise implementation strategies for government consideration. In doing so, they create their own internal language for the operation of Indigenous affairs.[65]

In the era of Indigenous self-determination, the 'culture of governance' has changed in ways that we can summarise under two headings: the centralisation of accountability and the scaling up of the 'local'. Ian Marsh has recently summarised four changes in public sector accountability processes since 1983:[66]

1. 'Centralised policy control was enhanced by budgetary, organisational and personnel changes that were designed to give the centre the language, technologies and administrative capacity to drive wider changes. As a first step, the control of ministers and key co-ordinating departments was strengthened. Within this framework, the focus has shifted progressively from economic structures and regulatory frameworks to, most recently, the delivery of human services.'[67]
2. The state withdrew from employment-creating interventions into markets. This eventually determined the expectations that were placed on CDEP. Since 2005, there has been increasing pressure for CDEP effectively to be a transition to what have sometimes been called 'real' jobs, severely limiting local discretion over the use of CDEP resources.
3. Public services were contracted out to non-government organisations (NGOs).
4. Where government activity required the attention of multiple agencies and levels of government, the government aspired to coordinate them in a 'whole of government' approach, beginning in 2002.

With the abolition of ATSIC in 2004–05, its programs — most importantly CDEP (employment) and the Community Housing and Infrastructure Program (CHIP) — were redistributed across several government agencies in a process that some called 'mainstreaming'. Indigenous communities had already been dealing with many government agencies; with the loss of ATSIC, they no longer had an agency dedicated to the advocacy of Indigenous needs. It thus became even more important to attempt to coordinate multiple agencies in a 'whole-of-government' approach. According to Marsh, there have been at least nine reviews of the 'whole-of-government' experiments, and their cumulative finding is that 'whole-of-government' will not work without devolution of authority, funding, accountability and coordinated organisation to regional and local levels — a development inhibited by the centralisation of policy control (point 1 above): 'It has not proved possible to reconcile centralised "siloed" organisation and funding with devolved authority and flexible resource management.'[68] That must be due partly to the reasonable case that can be made for centralised accountability. As one Canberra-based public servant told me, 'at regional and local levels staff are unable to see the big picture'.

Patrick Sullivan has similarly reviewed these changes in the form of the Australian state, drawing the conclusion that Indigenous organisations have become more accountable to centrally determined performance criteria and less answerable to locally voiced needs and aspirations. As Sullivan goes on to point out, one of the motives for these changes is a genuine commitment to giving more substantial and effective public support to Indigenous Australians, especially those in remote regions where the state has arguably 'failed'.[69] The commitment to increase public provision has included the Commonwealth's re-engagement of the State governments, and in turn they have been reorganising local government in the Northern Territory, Western Australia and Queensland. In the reform of local government, the scale of municipal units has come under critical scrutiny: can small units of Aboriginal self-determination deliver the infrastructure and services to which Aborigines are entitled? Is it necessary to make remote and rural units of government larger as a means to make them better? The chronic difficulty of recruiting competent professional staff to remote Indigenous organisations is one reason to increase the size of such units.

Here it is relevant to recall a point made by Diane Smith in her study of the approach taken by Western Arnhem Land Aborigines to the formation of regional government in the period 2004–08. Comparing *Bininj* (Aboriginal) and *balanda* (non-Aboriginal, white) notions of a region, she observes that *balanda* tend to emphasise economies of scale and to set clear cadastral boundaries, while *Bininj* take more notice of long-acquired conceptions of a collective self, including ceremonial practices, inter-marriage and land ownership, with boundaries less precise and more mutable.[70] The struggle between these two conceptions of 'region' was about who should be included and excluded in enlarged local government areas. *Bininj* in Western Arnhem Land would have liked to exclude the townships Jabiru and Maningrida;[71] however, for reasons of economy and social philosophy, the Northern Territory government has insisted that shires be not only large but also more culturally mixed.

In the resulting map of local government jurisdictions since 2008, Aboriginal communities in the Northern Territory find themselves in large shires whose size and composition is not of their choosing. Until 2008, 'the majority of residents in rural and remote areas of the [Northern Territory] were under the jurisdictions of 55 community government councils ... many with single settlement jurisdictions ... In 2006–07, their estimated median population was 475.'[72] The populations of some communities with their own councils had been as small as 200, and they had controlled their own CDEP programs. In 2007, changes in CDEP policy prohibited the use of CDEP for delivery of local government services. The stated intention was to convert local government CDEP roles under Commonwealth–State partnerships to salaried positions for the same work. Then, in 2008, came the shire system, and these small units were subsumed into shires whose electoral system does not guarantee representation on council to small communities; council meetings on which a community might be represented are likely to be held further away. After such changes to the economy and polity of rural and remote Aboriginal government in the Northern Territory, it is no surprise that a recent field study found 'sentiments of loss of community control and ownership over local government institutions and resources, and a lack of effective communication and responsiveness from senior Shire management and headquarters staff'.[73]

In Queensland, the state government's 2008 local government restructure exempted fourteen Aboriginal communities from being subsumed within large regional units, while joining five Cape York councils into a new Northern Peninsula Area Regional Council and amalgamating fifteen Torres Strait Island councils into a new Torres Strait Island Regional Council. All of the units issuing from this program of selective amalgamation are small (260 to 2640 residents, according to 2010 population data). Morton Consulting Service's review of their needs points to a continuing problem that is relevant to the theme of this chapter: the many Aboriginal councillors required are recruited from a small and relatively poorly educated pool of available adults. This review argues that 'orthodox governance principles' (such as the distinguishing of political from administrative roles, respect for the rule of law and community engagement) are not yet well understood or practised.[74]

The government of Western Australia has invited voluntary amalgamations of local governments. There are twenty-two shires whose Indigenous population is considered to be a high proportion (between 8 and 84 per cent). In ten of these shires, the proportion is above 40 per cent. In the Kimberley region, where there are 218 Indigenous communities across four shires, the Indigenous proportion of the population ranges from 32 per cent in Broome shire to 84 per cent in Halls Creek shire. Until 2007, CDEP supplied the funding for municipal services in many of these communities, and decisions about CDEP were made locally by Indigenous organisations. Since 2007, when CDEP was reformed, more funds for municipal services have come from Commonwealth and State agencies, imposing more centralised control on how such monies are to be spent. While there is an undoubted commitment from both Commonwealth and State governments to increase public spending in order to overcome historic deficits in infrastructure and basic services, the commitment has entailed rethinking the role of local decision-making. A recent study of the dimensions of local government reform in Western Australia remarked critically of 'self-determination', it 'has been used as an excuse by governments and service providers to provide an inequitable level of service and to tolerate conditions and activities that would not be accepted in any other sector of the community'.[75] This warning echoes Dillon and Westbury's 'failed state' observation that 'the rationale for substantive non-engagement [by governments] has been that self-determination and self-management, by definition, exclude the need for government involvement (apart from the ongoing funding arrangements)'.[76] These words capture very well the association that contemporary policy technicians have begun to make between certain conceptions of social justice — regional and racial equality of entitlement to public goods, sameness of standards in the judgment of these goods' quality — and suspicion of the legacy and motives of past practices of devolving decision-making to small local Indigenous units. Insofar as this critique becomes influential within governments, Aboriginal services from local governments are likely to be both better funded and more severely measured against universal standards of effectiveness.

In each of the three jurisdictions — Western Australia, the Northern Territory and Queensland — that include a large proportion of the small, remote Indigenous communities that make up 'remote and very remote' Australia, the funding and structure of local government have been changed substantially since the demise of ATSIC in 2004–05, and the expectations placed on Indigenous Australians as participants in local structures of government — councils and corporations — have changed. Three ideas have become associated as drivers of this new political environment: that Indigenous Australians have been under-serviced, with disastrous effects on their well-being; that the standards by which reformed government service delivery must be judged can be encoded in statistical measures of socio-economic and health outcomes, designed to measure (dis)parity between Indigenous and Australian populations; and that public provision will be more effective if it is centrally accountable and professionally administered by a combination of national and State agencies with professionally administered Indigenous corporations as junior partners. There is much to be said in favour of each of these ideas, and for some policy intellectuals their virtue as a new social justice paradigm is unquestionable. However, the impact of this paradigm includes intensifying pressures on Indigenous Australians to become adept in corporate governance — whether or not that is at the expense of something called 'custom'. Thus, in the interests of social justice, the stage is set for an intensified program of experimentation, adaptation and learning by remote Indigenous Australians in the arts and ethics of government. As Martin has argued, the different requirements of different domains of collective action — service delivery, advocacy, royalty management — are making themselves apparent, so we should not expect this to be a uniform and predictable sequence of 'acculturation'.[77]

There are Indigenous intellectuals who have prepared for these challenges and welcome them. For example, Mick Dodson and Diane Smith call upon 'Indigenous governing bodies ... to promote a clear separation between the powers and responsibilities of leaders and boards, and the daily management of community businesses and services':

> Preferably, leaders and boards should make the overarching policies, enforce the rules, and provide strategic direction. But leaders and governing boards should not be routinely interfering with the daily implementation of those policies by their managers and staff. Inserting local politics and the interests of powerful leaders into day-to-day business decisions invariably runs economic and other development projects into the ground.[78]

What could justify the relative autonomy of this managerial stratum? The answer can be found in Dodson's and Smith's exposition of the core ingredients and principles of what they see as good governance: the managers' respect for the 'rules of the game', such as those that they could read in publications of the Australian Stock Exchange;[79] their commitment to procedures of appeal and dispute resolution;[80] their ability to explain financial management systems to governing boards;[81] their collection and analysis of data relevant to planning for their communities — 'for example, information about community and regional assets, locally meaningful indicators of current and future population change, data on health, education, training, employment, welfare and income levels, community grant funding and service delivery';[82] their understanding of options in economic development;[83] their ability to manage the tension between 'individual and group autonomy ... (a tendency towards localism, smallness of scale and separatism)' and 'connectedness … (wider territorial and cultural alliances, and a desire for larger scale political and economic action)'.[84] While Martin more recently has emphasised the functional differentiation of Indigenous organisations (and thus of the ethical formations that they require of leaders and functionaries), in 2003 he endorsed Dodson and Smith's generalising promotion of the institutional relative autonomy of managers: 'boards set policy and priorities; management implements them, but without direct and day-to-day interference by board members'.[85]

Martin has also pointed out that to recruit such disinterested and knowledgeable people as managers requires that Indigenous organisations go beyond local people to 'outsiders'. This is not only because there may be too few 'locals' with the necessary training, but also because such 'outside' recruitment is a corrective to 'localism' (in one of its senses):

> Skilled 'outsiders' — whether they be relatively better educated Queensland 'Murris' in Northern Territory organisations or non-indigenous people in Native Title Representative Bodies, health and legal services, and so forth — are necessary along with local indigenous people precisely because they can ensure that there is a diversity of perspectives and values brought to bear on an organisation's operations.[86]

It is important that 'outsiders' can be 'Indigenous'. The historical geography of Australia's colonisation makes that possible: the process of acculturation is older and has changed people more in some regions than in others. As early as the 1930s, William Cooper advocated that Aborigines from the longer-settled, temperate regions be delegated to guide the 'advancement' of the more recently colonised people of the remote North and Centre of the continent. Today, the vehicle of what Cooper called 'uplift' is a sustainable Indigenous organisation (and thus an Indigenous sector) that cultivates a professional-managerial class that will include Indigenous people:

> We suggest that the proper method of dealing with the primitive people would be to send educated and cultured Aborigines to their own uncivilized people. These men, of the same blood, would understand their people and would be able to suggest to the government means whereby the hardships and sufferings of these people could be alleviated or removed.[87]

The language used by Cooper nowadays makes one wince, but his vision that a stratum of leaders must emerge to realise the potential of people-hood is essentially what animates some of the advocates of today's Indigenous sector. The defining ethic of that leading stratum, however, cannot be ascribed to any particular cultural tradition or identity: it is an ethic of 'service'. Mick Dodson and Diane Smith wrote in 2003 that:

> *Like all other communities*, Indigenous communities need systems and processes which prevent those people who exercise legitimate powers from using that power for their own personal gain and from changing the rules to suit their own interests. Self-determination should not mean 'selfish' determination.[88]

These words suggest that the rise of the Indigenous sector entails a regime of ethical development that is more focused and specific than any of the policy regimes ('protection', 'assimilation') that preceded it. It requires the formation of a new class to staff an Indigenous sector that has become embedded in the apparatuses of Australian government over the last four decades.

CHAPTER 7

The Ambivalence of Helen Hughes

In the *Weekend Australian* (18–19 August 2007), Robert Manne urged 'those who want to grasp the philosophic direction of the [Howard] government's policy' on Indigenous Australians to read Helen Hughes' *Lands of shame*. This was good advice. Many of the Howard government's policy innovations (endorsed by the Rudd opposition in August 2007), such as limiting the application of communal land tenure and abolishing many Community Development Employment Projects (CDEP), are consistent with Hughes' ideas.

However, Manne was generous when he said that Hughes argued her proposals 'cogently and persuasively'. A book with such significant inconsistencies and gaps falls short of 'cogency', and its persuasiveness relies heavily on readers sharing the author's suspicion of Indigenous leaders (a feeling that may well be widely shared in the Coalition and Labor Parties but not, I would have thought, by Robert Manne).

To give an immediate example of the book's lack of 'cogency', take one of Hughes' prescriptions for rooting out the corruption that she believes to be widespread among Aboriginal leaders. They are effectively protected, she suggests, by corporate regulation that has been enfeebled by misplaced regard for cultural difference.[1] She complains that the Office of the Registrar of Aboriginal Corporations (ORAC, renamed the Office of the Regulator of Indigenous Corporations, or ORIC) treats Indigenous corporations as children, talking down to them while letting them get away with inadequate reporting of their affairs.[2] To deal with this allegedly indulgent regime, Hughes would amend or repeal the legislation that authorises ORIC. Incorporated Indigenous associations would then have to comply with the reporting requirements of the Australian

Securities and Investments Commission (ASIC).[3] However, in another part of her book she presents incorporation under ASIC as a ploy used by corrupt Aborigines who wish to shield their business affairs from public scrutiny.[4] What would an Attorney-General do if moved to action by Hughes' denunciations? There are other inconsistencies and gaps, but before attending to them it is necessary to understand Hughes' account of the Indigenous Australian situation.

Hughes distinguishes three types of condition in which Indigenous Australians now live. About 160,000 'work in mainstream jobs in cities, towns and country' and 'have mainstream living standards'.[5] Hughes is not concerned with them, other than suspecting that some of them are enjoying at others' expense the advantages conferred by their power and skill. She is much more worried about the well-being of those who live 'on the fringes of towns and in major city ghettos' and those who live in some 1200 tiny settlements in remote Australia that she refers to as 'homelands'. Most of her book is about this third group, the remote homelanders, and she estimates that there are between 90,000 and 120,000 such people.[6]

Hughes' vision for the future of the homeland Aborigines is that they would become a more centralised population by living in a number of 'core centres', where economies of scale would allow essential services and retailing to be provided at a proper standard. There would need to be about 100 such centres, she estimates, but she does not suggest which current townships in remote and very remote Australia should be the beneficiaries of her strategy, other than suggesting the 'rehabilitation' of Wadeye, Maningrida, Mutitjulu and Palm Island 'to decent civic standards'.[7] She later adds Warburton to this list.[8]

Hughes does not see her proposal as an assault on Indigenous culture. After all, she understands that those 160,000 who 'participate fully in the mainstream' remain 'proud of their traditional culture and ties to their ancestral lands'.[9] If homelands people migrate to core centres such as Warburton, she suggests, they can still 'own houses in their own "country" and preserve their culture'.[10]

Hughes' attitude to Indigenous culture is that it is acceptable as long as it is not allowed to excuse governments for Indigenous Australians' continuing socio-economic disadvantage. In critically considering policy-makers' recognition of cultural difference, she condemns what she calls 'exceptionalism' — a philosophy that has flourished in the last thirty years. Though exceptionalism 'was intended to make up for past mistreatment',[11] it has led to such practices as the recognition of customary law, the 'imposition of communal instead of private property rights', the use of languages other than English in teaching, special local government arrangements,[12] curricula that defer or stint basic training in literacy and numeracy,[13] and undue tolerance of Aborigines' unhygienic and degraded living conditions.[14] What she calls the 'Coombs model' or the 'Coombs experiment' has been an instance of 'exceptionalism'.[15] She attributes to Coombs extraordinary executive powers when she writes that 'the Coombs experiment moved Aborigines to remote regions'.[16] In fact, Coombs' admiring account (in 1973) of Aborigines' decentralising movement from settlements and missions to outstations was his response to Indigenous initiatives. In seeking to understand their actions sympathetically, he did not have to move the people about whom he was writing. They were capable of moving themselves, with or without policy intellectuals' approval, partly because a sequence of Coalition and Labor government decisions had declared nomadic Aborigines to be eligible for welfare payments. A reader has to make a conscious effort not to be distracted by Hughes' odd fixation on Coombs as the mastermind of 'exceptionalism'.

Facing all governments that respectfully recognise Indigenous difference and facing all policy intellectuals who invoke that difference when making Indigenous policy proposals is the troubling interplay of two liberal democratic ideals: equality and difference. Hughes shares in the dilemmas of contemporary post-colonial liberalism when she affirms her support for the survival of Indigenous culture while worrying about the perversely discriminatory effects of 'exceptionalism'.[17] The question that Hughes' readers must answer is: What are *her* proposed trade-offs between respecting the right of Indigenous Australians to be different and upholding their right to conditions of life that are not scandalously inferior to those of Australians who live long and more or less healthy lives and whose cultural choices do not condemn them to squalid insecurity? The characteristic tendency of her answer to that question favours the choices made by governments over the choices made by Indigenous Australians.

However, Hughes is no apologist for extant governmental practice. Far from it: she excoriates at least six of Australia's nine governments for not spending enough on Indigenous Australians. In the provision of housing, schooling and health care, governments have been able to get away with not doing enough: 'The Northern Territory, Queensland, Western Australia and South Australia with "homeland", fringe and ghetto Indigenous populations, and New South Wales with the largest fringe and ghetto Indigenous populations, appear to be satisfied with present Aboriginal and Torres Strait Islander living standards.'[18] In their derogation of their duties to support Indigenous living standards, their 'bureaucratic insensibility' has combined with the 'philosophical' error of 'exceptionalism'.[19]

Disdain for accountability is high among the qualities to which Hughes refers in her phrase 'bureaucratic insensibility'. She is scathing not only about public under-spending but also about the weakness of the mechanisms of audit and evaluation that governments arrange for themselves.[20] The Department of Finance has 'driven out concepts of efficiency and effectiveness throughout the Commonwealth bureaucracy'.[21] The ten COAG 'whole-of-government' trials were not real trials in that the agencies responsible did not collect baseline data, other than in a 'limited' study of Wadeye.[22] The new (since 2004) 'Indigenous Coordination Centres' (ICC) are 'process rather than results driven'.[23] Most Commonwealth departments do not publish budget or expenditure data: 'Their voluminous reports are entirely qualitative so that it is impossible to derive any sense of where funding is going or what it has achieved.'[24] She criticises as 'information free' an 'outcome' report on expenditures under the Indigenous Women's Program in 2004–05,[25] and demands that the Productivity Commission disaggregate by region its national 'average' socio-economic indicators. Hughes invites the Commonwealth to learn from AusAID, a government agency whose intellectual rigor derives, she believes, from its association with the World Bank.[26] These complaints and suggestions are reasonable.

However, Hughes' declared respect for rigorous, independent evaluation sits oddly with her tendency to dogmatic judgment. She confidently conjectures that the unevaluated Women's Program is 'unlikely' to have achieved its stated aims, but she does not say what reasoning leads her to that view.[27] She is equally dismissive in her discussion of Shared Responsibility Agreements (SRAs). As she points out, they were not set up in such a way that would enable them to be evaluated carefully. One would expect that defect to induce caution in her own evaluation, but it does not: 'Shared Responsibility Agreements have degenerated into slush funds for politically smart operators and their bureaucratic supporters because they have not been willing to tackle basic deficiencies, notably in education … education and health have not been improved so that people have not been made more work-ready.'[28]

Compare Hughes' swift appraisal of all SRA with the study of them published by the ATSI Social Justice Commissioner Tom Calma in the *Social justice report 2006*: Calma's ambivalent conclusions rest on data that his staff collected, while Hughes' judgment is not encumbered by evidence. Towards the end of 2006, Calma surveyed 108 SRAs, involving 124 communities, that had been signed before 31 December 2005. A total of sixty-seven communities with SRAs replied to his survey. They told Calma that their SRAs were about ten different concerns, the four most frequent of which were 'cultural revitalisation', 'capacity-building', 'sport and recreation' and 'health and nutrition'. Two out of every five of the reported SRAs were suggested by the government (the local Indigenous Coordination Centre), and another two out of five were initiated by the community's own perception of its needs.[29] About half said they were satisfied with the pace of the SRA negotiations (45 per cent), the amount of information provide by the government (53 per cent) and the way the government met its obligations (57 per cent).[30] We could not call these survey results a glowing Indigenous endorsement of SRAs, but nor do Calma's data support Hughes' generalised description of them as 'slush funds for politically smart operators and their bureaucratic supporters'.[31] The conclusion that stands out from Calma's survey is that no generalised conclusion about SRAs is possible. Sometimes empirical evaluation does not lead to clear-cut conclusions about the worth of programs. This is inconvenient for Hughes, for whom no assertion is worth making if it is not made boldly: whether advocating policy evaluation or blithely exhibiting her indifference to it, she seeks to impress the reader with her unequivocal disdain for extant practices.

Confident over-statement is indeed her signature tune. She writes that 'decent education and living standards' represent 'the only known way to reduce levels of alcoholism and drug addiction'.[32] This assertion ignores the extensive literature that seeks to gauge precisely the effectiveness of various forms of therapeutic intervention into drug and alcohol abuse. I would not contradict her insistence on 'decent education and living standards', but no good can come from disregarding therapies when they are shown to be effective. In being insistently dismissive, Hughes is deaf to good news. Thus, when she cites data that indicates program success — such as in the numeracy and literacy achieved recently by Pitjantjatjara children — she does not pause to wonder what the ingredients of success might be.[33] Instead, she calls for an audit of the health of 'all children', and says it is 'high time' that someone evaluated Aboriginal Community Controlled Health Organisations (ACCHOs).[34] Why bother? Hughes knows already what such a study would reveal: 'In the "homelands", Australian taxpayers are asked to pay for a multiplicity of inefficient health providers that waste the scarce medical practitioner and nursing skills. Communal medicine is not working.'[35] It is not 'inadequate funding' that renders ineffective such public services as health, she adds later, but 'inherent structural defects'.[36]

What are the 'structures' to which Hughes refers? In her book, there are two kinds of obstacle to the better government of Indigenous Australians. One is an inappropriate form of land tenure; the other is the interests of bureaucrats and Big Men. In the past, Hughes has pointed to a connection between land tenure and corruption. In an interview with Frank Devine, she portrayed the *Aboriginal Land Rights (Northern Territory) Act* as an avatar of the Soviet Union:

> The theory is that all decisions are communal, because ownership of property is communal. In practice, the 'elders', the members of land councils, the local government organizations, the health organisations make the decisions, and get most of the benefits. It's not stretching too far into ideological analogy to think of them as commissars … *excessive central planning always creates corruption.* The old Soviet Union relied on corruption to keep it moving. It developed a vast black market because it had no other market. But the corruption in our remote Aboriginal communities confers no benefits at all on the majority. Moreover, it is deeply entrenched. The commissars stop at nothing to protect their rackets.[37]

It is difficult to think of a socio-political order more unlike Soviet society under central planning than the Northern Territory homelands. The one feature that the situations have in common is that state activity looms large in economic affairs, circumscribing market activity.

Hughes cannot resist sneering at public servants. She describes one intervention into petrol sniffing in the following way: '"Truckloads of bureaucrats", social workers and police bribes in the shape of sports equipment and even motor bikes were ineffective.'[38] When she deplores the adoption of CDEP schemes by Indigenous communities, she says that 'bureaucrats spread it'.[39] When she praises the potential for mining companies to employ local Indigenous labour, she cannot resist concluding her point with a *non sequitur*: 'Progress will be achieved by the entrepreneurial initiatives of competing mines *rather than by* government and mining industry bureaucrats sitting around tables.'[40] There are 'bureaucrats' everywhere, fouling the Indigenous scene. ACCHO bureaucrats 'often see [information systems] as an attempt to monitor their performance and so resist their introduction and use'.[41] Governments should avoid using 'bureaucrats' to engage the residents of her proposed 100 'core centres' because Indigenous people have learned to resent and distrust them. Instead, the government should mobilise retirees active in such service clubs as Rotary.[42]

Worse than 'bureaucrats', in the Hughes bestiary, are Big Men (she seems, in this book, to have abandoned the term 'commissars'). Big Men need not be men, for they 'may also be grandmothers'.[43] To the extent that 'Big Men' is a metaphor, it refers to the institutionalised beneficiaries of the policies that Hughes would abolish. Hughes introduces the term by citing the Bennelong Society's Peter Howson: 'He showed that a *rentier* class of Indigenous "Big Men" as well as academics, cultural consultants, politicians, public servants, administrators and service providers soaked up the bulk of considerable taxpayer funding devoted to keeping the Coombs model in place.'[44] There is no denying that some people — both Indigenous and non-Indigenous — earn wages, salaries and consultancy fees because the governing of Indigenous Australians creates a demand for their labour. In Hughes' view, all those who do so are under suspicion of being Big Men or their accomplices.

Hughes makes grave allegations against Big Men. One type of organisation in which they thrive, she says, is the Northern Territory Land Councils. She accuses elected and appointed Land Council personnel of securing their power to 'run the Land Councils' by 'kinship relations that include child marriage, polygamy, sorcery and pay-back'.[45] She acknowledges that Land Councils are effective in settling disputes between clans that courts would not be able to resolve, but the sentence in which she makes this concession concludes with the begrudging comment 'so that the councils absorb resources like sponges'.[46] Land Council Big Men, she declares, appropriate royalties from mining on Aboriginal land, rather than distributing them equitably.[47] Land Council Big Men bitterly opposed the Howard government's amendment of the leasing provisions of the *Aboriginal Land Rights (Northern Territory) Act* in 2006.[48] Hughes accounts for their stance by suggesting that the Land Councils have been able to 'channel … rents into a few pockets'.[49] Failing to distinguish their private interests from their public duties, Big Men also derive monopoly profits from the 'communal businesses' that they run on remote Aboriginal lands.⁵⁰ Hughes thus casts Northern Territory Land Council leaders as corrupt, but she offers no evidence for her accusations. She goes further, however: the alleged criminal predations of Big Men have vitiated the politics, as well as misdirected the finances, of the homelands. Local government in remote Australia is under the thumb of Big Men,⁵¹ and the Big Men who run the ACCHOs and their peak body NACCHO are 'well satisfied with the services that they deliver' and with Aborigines' levels of 'health and short expectation of life'.⁵²

The most disturbing feature of these accusations is not that they are unsubstantiated. They do not require substantiation if we concede that it would be surprising if Hughes' accusations of political bullying and financial corruption were always and everywhere untrue. We should assume that among Indigenous Australians — a section of the human race — there are some greedy, unscrupulous and violent people. The occasional exposure of such individuals in the political process and in the courts is a necessary antidote to the wishful thought that Indigenous Australians are virtuous children of Nature.

However, there is more than this salutary reminder of Indigenous imperfections in Hughes' preoccupation with Big Men. To an extent that she probably has not realised, Hughes' 'Big Men' metaphor betrays her contempt for Indigenous Australians' success. The vile things that Big Men do, Hughes insists on telling us, include sending their children to good schools, being politically articulate and organisationally effective, earning an income in the Australian average range, and being role models for those undertaking a mainstream education. This is how Hughes lets slip her loathing of the emergent Indigenous middle class.

Hughes warns that 'all parents — Indigenous and non-Indigenous — who choose to live in remote areas must recognize that if they are not to cripple their children, they have to send them away to board during term time'.⁵³ But when she comes across instances of Indigenous parents doing so, she is outraged, for if you send your kids to boarding school you arouse her suspicion that you are a Big Man who cares only for his/her own children: 'The sons and daughters of "Big Men" frequently [sic] attend mainstream boarding schools so that in the absence of secondary schooling the "homeland" elite is perpetuating itself.'⁵⁴

Hughes is tough on those Indigenous people who benefit from education. Ostensibly, she admires educated Aborigines. She quotes, in apparent agreement, an educationist who complains that children in the homelands are not given the chance to observe the 'benefits of education': they do not see enough 'adults working and earning mainstream incomes so that they can buy a house, a car and travel'.[55] You would think that Hughes would not lose the chance to admire such achievers herself — particularly after reading her insistence that if Aborigines are to be 'effective land care agents' they must become literate and numerate and able to communicate in English.[56] Literacy and numeracy are essential skills for artists as well, if they are to avoid exploitation.[57] And 'illiteracy in corporation managers has to be tackled by intensive adult education'.[58] Few would dispute the benefits that the acquisition of literacy brings to Indigenous Australians — yet Hughes finds a way to do so. Instead of praising Indigenous people who share her faith in literacy, numeracy and articulateness in English, she holds them in suspicion, for these skills are the toolkit of Big Men who lord it over their illiterate, innumerate and inarticulate fellow residents, checked neither by (ineffective) electoral systems nor by the homelands' (poorly attended) meetings.[59]

In her book's most remarkable use of statistical evidence, Hughes shows the reader four graphs of the incidence of low and high incomes among Indigenous households in the Northern Territory, Queensland, South Australia and Western Australia, from the 2001 Census. The curves on these graphs have two peaks: one shows that many families got only the low incomes ($300–399 per week) allowed by welfare payments; the other, secondary peak was around $1000 per week. Hughes labels the latter group of families 'a high income Indigenous elite'. Big Men are the 'homelands' members of this elite, she assures the reader, their bank accounts fattened by 'their appropriation of a high share of public funding through official positions'.[60] There are Big Men in the cities too: she offers the example of the former Aboriginal and Torres Strait Islander Social Justice Commissioner Tom Calma. Among the perquisites of these Indigenous voluptuaries are helicopters in which each Big Man visits his 'several wives' and carries his beer.[61]

There are two Helen Hughes. One, a development economist of neo-liberal persuasion, advocates that Indigenous Australians acquire human capital so that they can participate successfully in the mainstream labour market. The other Hughes despises those who have already done so: she attributes their success to deviousness, luck, greed and bad public policy. She labels their middle-class incomes 'appropriation' by Big Men, and she pities other Indigenous people as the Big Men's victims. Her cynicism about Indigenous communities no doubt resonates among some of Australia's more bilious radio personalities and their public.

One of the tasks of public policy reform, according to this second, ardently populist Hughes, is to dismantle the structures that have given some Indigenous Australians advantages over others. It is this crusade against Big Men that lends moral fervour to her case for strong government intervention into the lives of Indigenous Australians. She urges governments to act for the least politically effective Indigenous Australians against vested Indigenous interests.

Central to her proposals is the policy problem of land tenure. Communal tenure should not be allowed to survive: it gives no security or real sense of ownership;[62] it frustrates economic development; and it undermines pest eradication.[63] Private ownership would instil pride in the family home. If people cling to communal ownership, suggests Hughes, it is because they 'fear change because of its uncertainty and risks'.[64] If they are to taste the advantages of private land ownership, they will have to submit to the Commonwealth's unilateral amendment of land rights legislation: the Commonwealth will stand up to the Land Council Big Men on behalf of those who are intimidated.[65] Governments can also exert pressure to end communal tenure through the provision of public housing. The Commonwealth should fund house repairs in the homelands only for those 'who opt [sic] for 99-year lease house and garden plots', 'with core communities being given priority'.[66]

Not only is she ambivalent (at best) about Indigenous people who prosper from their political skills, their entrepreneurial flair or the sale of their human capital on the labour market, there is another unresolved dilemma in her policy prescription: what to do about the under-investment in remote and very remote community infrastructure. To see her inconsistency about this problem, we need to return to Hughes' three-part account of the situations facing Indigenous Australians. In fact, there are two such accounts in the book, and in the subtle differences between them (not acknowledged by Hughes) we find her policy confusion. Recall that she regards about one-third (160,000) of the Indigenous population as not needing any special help because they are 'in mainstream jobs' and enjoy 'mainstream living standards'. The other two-thirds are problematic: about 250,000 'on the fringes of towns and in major city ghettoes' and between 90,000 and 120,000 in impoverished, job-scarce 'homelands'. Hughes offers two significantly different accounts of the dynamic relationship between these three sectors.

In the first scenario, she sees an already existing tendency for the homelanders to move to where many of the 250,000 live. She refers to the 'the decline of the total homeland' population, and it is implicit that those who leave the homelands arrive on the fringes of towns and in city ghettos (for where else can they go?). She gives no data to evidence this 'flight' from the homelands, and she remarks that we do not know what proportion of homelanders' visits to larger settlements 'become permanent'.[67] Whether or not there is already such movement, one version of Hughes' 'core centre' strategy would encourage this flight from the homelands. Economies in servicing homelanders would arise if they came in from their scattered and very remote habitations to live in the 100 'core' centres that she has in mind (though some would probably move further, into the cities). Depending on where the 100 core centres are (and Hughes names only five examples of core centres), her core centre strategy implies rapid growth, over the next few years, in many Indigenous town populations — adding to the 250,000 people living 'on the fringes of towns and in major city ghettos'.

Note that in this scenario the two more problematic sectors of the population (homelanders and town/urban fringe dwellers) are both characterised by unemployment and low living standards. Where Hughes becomes confusing (and perhaps she is confused herself) is that in her other presentation of these two sectors of the Indigenous population, she emphasises how different they are. Hughes argues that government policy should be based on the 'fundamentally different' situations of the town fringe/city ghetto 250,000 and the homelands 90–120,000.[68] Most of the fringe and ghetto dwellers 'are located in areas of ample employment, mainstream infrastructure, functioning local government, police and law, and literate English speaking populations'.[69] The homelands people, in contrast, are locationally disadvantaged, so the government must address them with different solutions. This appeal for fundamentally differentiated policy implies not that the homelands must be emptied (through migration to towns and cities) but that the homelands somehow will be made more liveable — with more ample government services, investment and employment programs. This scenario is consistent with her advocating that Wadeye, Maningrida, Mutitjulu, Warburton and Palm Island be funded to support 'decent civic standards'.[70]

Is Hughes hoping to empty the homelands or to render them more liveable? It is this question that her book fails to answer. (It is also a hard question for the governments of Australia, Northern Territory, Queensland, South Australia and Western Australia to answer.) How many of the core centres would she build up within the 'homeland' regions if she proposes to continue treating the homelanders as a distinct policy problem? Alternatively, how many of the 'core centres' are to be in the town/city zones into which the 90–120,000 homeland residents are to be encouraged to move? The regional impacts of Hughes' strategy are impossible to project unless she names more of the 100 proposed 'core centres' than the five that she mentions.

Is there political cowardice or political innocence in Hughes' failure to name more than five of her projected 100 core centres? The places not named would have to include towns such as Port Augusta, Kalgoorlie, Wiluna, Newman, Dubbo, Broken Hill, Cloncurry, Cairns, Cooktown, Coen, Mount Isa, Tennant Creek, Katherine, Alice Springs, even Darwin. Hughes does not explicitly deal with the way that her strategy for depopulating the Indigenous homelands — if that is her proposal — necessitates public investment in scores of regional towns in which there are already substantial Indigenous minorities. And even if granted the necessary investment, will these towns welcome the influx of homelanders impoverished and bewildered by governments' calculated neglect?

If Robert Manne was right to present Hughes' book as an influence over the Howard government, then Hughes' crucial vagueness about what she is proposing may also be a vacuum in the social and economic planning of the Australian government (whether Labor or Coalition). *Lands of shame* may be a guide not only to the 'philosophy' but also to the intellectual vacuity of Australia's current political elites. The appealing chords that Helen Hughes has struck in *The Australian*'s op-ed pages — profound ambivalence about the emergent Indigenous middle class, scorn for the homelands as Coombs' 'socialist' experiment — are no substitute for policy realism. Hughes' call for greater public investment in Indigenous Australians is dogged by a simple question that she does not answer: where best to spend that investment?

THINKING HISTORICALLY ABOUT 1967-76

CHAPTER 8

'If We are to Survive as a People ...':
Noel Pearson's Economic History

The representation of Indigenous Australians as a 'population' scarcely enters into the work of Noel Pearson. His is a discourse of people-hood. 'Australia is a country shared by two peoples,' he declared in his 2004 Judith Wright Lecture.[1] He rarely refers to statistical disparity when he writes about the relationship between these two peoples: 'closing the gaps' is not the social justice idea that drives him.[2] Rather, the crucial relationship to get right, he wrote in 2007, is between 'Indigenous governance institutions' and Australia's governments. He asks: 'Is the relationship based on negotiation, and is there mutual accountability in the relationship?'[3] These are questions about the quality of relationships between peoples, not about the size of the socio-economic gaps between populations. In Pearson's thoughts on people-hood, the 'link with ancestral lands and culture' is fundamental, as he made clear in his 2005 Mabo Oration.[4] However, his notion of people-hood is more than 'cultural'. He titled his Wright Lecture 'Peoplehood', and devoted not a single sentence to evoking Indigenous cultural heritage; rather, he declared the 'economic context' to be 'ultimate'.[5]

In this chapter, I will make sense of Pearson's thought by paying attention to his stories, for empathy with the past is fundamental to his politics. However, he has warned: 'Without first having a thorough understanding of the political economy of [the] past, any act of imagination based on contemporary feelings, values and moral convictions will be teleologically silly and misleading.'[6]

What are Pearson's stories? And how does political economy discipline his historical imagination?

The Law story

Pearson read the High Court's 1992 judgment in the *Mabo* case 'rapturously':[7] it 'reinforced my enthusiasm for the capacity of the common law'.[8] The judgment and its successor, the 1996 *Wik* decision, combine to make possible a revised narrative of the arrival of British law in Australia. Pearson understands the new narrative as permitting 'compromise' between British-Australian law and the law of Australia's Indigenous peoples. For him, this compromise is worth defending — but first its demands on both sides must be understood. Explaining the compromise offered by the High Court has been the aim of several essays by Pearson since 1993.

In Pearson's account, the High Court's decisions about 'native title' rest on the following revised story of the common law in Australia. When the British brought their law to Australia, they encountered a law that was already there. In British common law, as formulated by the High Court's two judgments, Indigenous law appears in the recognisable form of 'native title'. By the forceful assertion of their colonial sovereignty, the British were able to extinguish 'native title' over much — but certainly not all — of Australia's land and seas. For Pearson, it is very important that the effect of the Crown's lawful actions of granting title to colonists was not the extinguishing of Aboriginal law, but merely the extinguishing of 'native title': in respect to certain portions of land, the Crown ceased to recognise something that had preceded its existence in Australia. In some actions of the Crown, ceasing to recognise native title was final: on those land portions, native title can never more apply. In other actions of the Crown, the extinguishment was only partial and temporary: in those places, native title may apply. In much of Australia, native title certainly still applies, because no action of the Crown — in respect of certain portions of land — has ever been inconsistent with the common law's recognition of title under Aboriginal law.

In this narrative, which is so fundamental to Pearson's thinking, the laws and customs of the Aboriginal people exist whether or not the Crown recognises them. That there are 'two systems of law running in relation to land' is, in his view, 'a matter of fact' — even if it is not a matter of British-Australian law:[9]

> No matter what the common law might say about the existence of native title in respect of land that is subject to an inconsistent grant, the fact is that Aboriginal law still allocates entitlement to

those traditionally connected with the land. The extinguishment of native title should therefore be understood as extinguishment of recognition of Aboriginal title. The extinguishment of recognition does not result in the extinguishment of Aboriginal title in relation to the land. *It survives as a social reality under Aboriginal law.*[10]

And:

A common law scheme which sees technical legal events as fatal extinguishing events, even where Aboriginal traditional connection with the land is being maintained, would be a perverse law, and inconsistent with the *Mabo* compromise.[11]

These words were written in 1996. In a paper delivered in October 2003 and published in 2009, Pearson reviewed the judgments of the High Court from 1996 to 2003, and found that most of the judges had indeed begun to stray from 'the *Mabo* compromise' as he understands it. I gave the gist of his critique in Chapter 1: that the judges were formulating 'native title' not by reference to the common law but by reference to a section of the *Native Title Act* that directs attention to Aboriginal law and custom that has been attested to be 'traditional'. The resulting tenures have disappointed native title holders. I will not return to that important argument here.

Pearson concedes that, as a matter of fact and not merely a matter of law, Aboriginal law may cease to exist. 'Aboriginal law is also a reality,' he asserts, 'and we are unanimous in our resolve that it continue to be so.'[12] Unfortunately, in some parts of Australia it is too late to save Aboriginal law, while in other parts Aboriginal law is imperilled, due partly to the behaviour of Aboriginal people themselves. He asks 'What strategies can we pursue to make Aboriginal law have consequence for our colonial condition?'[13] His 2000 essay, 'Our right to take responsibility', attempts to answer this question: its opening words are 'If we are to survive as a people …'[14] 'Central to the recovery and empowerment of Aboriginal society will be the restoration of Aboriginal values and Aboriginal relationships, which have their roots in our traditional society.'[15] To continue Aboriginal law as a fact is a struggle that his people are not guaranteed to win. The 'ultimate context' of their endeavour is 'the economic context'.[16] To understand what he means by insisting on 'the economic', we need to know Pearson's stories of Australia's colonisation. There are two levels: the local (what happened in his home region) and the national.

Australian colonial history: 'dispossessed from the real economy'[17]

Pearson once remarked that 'both black and white Australians have struggled for two centuries for that elusive ideal: a moral community in the Antipodes'.[18] While this may seem at first to be surprisingly generous towards the colonists, Pearson's approach to Australian history highlights some sincerely and zealously pursued visions of moral community that have done his people much harm. The good intentions of ill-conceived 'progressive' policy and the moral vanity of the critics of racism are prominent targets of his critique. He is a tricky figure to place within the History Wars.

On the one hand, it is taken by Pearson to be obvious that the Australian colonial process featured 'racism, dispossession and trauma'. His own region — Cape York — suffered:

> Until recently there were old people still living at my community who told of massacres of their people on their land. Testimony to a brutal past is written on the landscape of my homeland: places such as Battle Camp and Police Lagoon and Hell's Gate. Aboriginal stockmen mustering at Cape Melville in the 1950s found the bones of their people littering the landscape.[19]

He regrets that 'there is a strong tradition of denial in Australia'.[20] His comment on the work of Keith Windschuttle — which adopts minimal estimates of frontier bloodshed and views the casualties of colonisation largely as the justifiable incidents of the assertion of law and order — is that it is empirically wrong and that it lacks empathy with Indigenous Australians. In diminishing the public's empathy, such 'denial' histories subvert 'the prospects of successful co-operation between Aboriginal Australians and conservatives'.[21]

On the other hand, Pearson does not align with what he calls the 'stifling orthodoxies' that give comfort to 'progressives'. He offers a periodisation of Australian history in which the late 1960s and early 1970s — one of the peaks of liberal effectiveness — emerge as the moment of most damaging impact. Here it is important to realise that Pearson — like Karl Polanyi in *The great transformation* — stands at the intersection of anthropology and economics: for both thinkers, relationships of exchange are embedded in and imply cultures and moralities — 'every economic relationship is also necessarily a social relationship'.[22] A history of moral community must also be an economic history. Accordingly, the adapting Aboriginal economy must be the central topic of colonial history. In their economic history, we see the changing 'options for Aboriginal people'. Pearson lists four options, implying (I take it) an historical sequence between the first and the final three:

- trying to survive by moving between the traditional economy where possible and working in the white economy (this itinerant existence became increasingly difficult and in time impossible)
- begging for scraps on the fringes of the white economy and being exploited as prostitutes and slaves (and therefore soon dying out)
- being removed from white society and its slave economy to missions and government settlements
- finding a more stable situation in the white economy, usually as exploited labour at the lowest end of the economy (for instance, in the cattle industry or as domestic labourers).[23]

If I understand him correctly, Pearson sees most Aborigines who are alive today as the products of the final two Aboriginal adaptations: being an inmate of a mission or a government settlement, or being in low-paid manual employment. 'Aboriginal society survived where it was isolated from the white economy ... an institutional subsistence economy' [or] 'an informal system of slave labour'.[24] How could this be 'survival'? He remarked in 2004:

> There was probably a time when the pastoral economy in which Aboriginal people were involved in northern Australia was conducive to the maintenance of traditional cultural forms, because it gave stockworkers and their families access to their traditional country and economy.[25]

What redeemed these 'harsh and cruel' economic niches was that they were not 'passive welfare or charity'.[26] The moral constitution of Aboriginal people persisted partly because, in both the pre-contact and post-contact economies, you were not rewarded for doing nothing. When Pearson salutes his 'ancestors', he is not necessarily looking any further back in history than to those who adapted to colonial conditions:

> Resilience and strong values and relationships were not features only of our pre-colonial classical society (which we understandably hearken back to). Our ancestors actually managed to retain these values and relationships despite all of the hardships and assaults

of our colonial history. It is a testament to the achievement of our grandparents that these values and relationships secured our survival. Our grandparents struggled heroically to keep us alive as a people, and to rebuild and defend our families in the teeth of sustained and vicious maltreatment by white Australian society.[27]

If the dignity of self-help (even in materially deprived conditions) is a central value in Pearson's vision of people-hood, then the moment of catastrophe for his people was around 1970, when work became materially unnecessary. He points to four public policy decisions that effected 'revolutionary change' in remote Australia:

> The equal wages decision of 1966, which mandated equal payment for Aboriginal stock-workers, contributed to the large-scale exodus from the long-standing employment and lifestyle Indigenous people had carved out in the pastoral industry of northern Australia (and elsewhere) ... The Commonwealth Government's solution for Aboriginal people displaced from the pastoral industry was to provide access to social security payments ... This provided young men with work-free income. Citizenship brought to Aboriginal people the right to drink.[28]

Shortly after these changes, the inception of Legal Aid services for Aborigines undermined 'elders and other local justice mechanisms'.[29] Whereas in a liberal historical perspective the step-by-step accumulation of citizenship rights is a story of the nation's emancipation of Indigenous Australians from arbitrary colonial power and civil inequality, for Pearson these reforms were hammer blows against Aborigines' hitherto robust adaptations to the colonial economy. Liberalism's triumph was in fact the delayed assault on a neo-traditional order that had survived dispossession. In Pearson's periodisation of the story of how difficult it has become for his people to be a people, the period 1967–76 was the threshold of lethal emancipation.

Since first presenting that revisionist economic history of people-hood in 2000, Pearson has augmented it with a comparison. Using the work of US historian Shelby Steele, he has argued that Australian and American liberals have been on parallel paths in their dealings with Aborigines and with African Americans. Pearson first notes that after the formal end of slavery (in the 1860s), Black Americans faced the issue of how much it was their responsibility to advance themselves, despite institutionalised discrimination against them: should African-Americans predicate their advancement on the reform of racist institutions or was there much that they could do — by embracing education and by working hard — to improve their position within a society that continued to be racially discriminatory? The success of the civil rights campaigns of the 1950s and 1960s seemed to vindicate the view that changes in law and public policy were not only important but possible; the triumph of civil rights seemed to overshadow the rival strategy of African-American accommodation and self-improvement. However, Pearson argues, one of the consequences of effective political mobilisation by African-Americans in the 1950s and 1960s was to alter the 'distribution of responsibility'. Through the social policies of 'the Great Society' and through 'affirmative action', the liberal political establishment of the 1960s and 1970s effectively assumed responsibility for African-American social advancement. 'The devastating effect of this redistribution of responsibility for black advancement to white institutions,' Pearson writes, 'is to perpetually project blacks as weak and incapable of achieving advancement on their own merit.'[30] White and Black America have become locked in moral complementarity that damages each of them: Whites guiltily assume responsibility for more than they should; Blacks discount their own agency as they adopt the posture of permanently aggrieved victim.

Using Shelby Steele's historical thesis, Pearson thus takes aim at what he calls 'post-citizenship' Aboriginal political consciousness, in which 'black rights become white responsibilities'.[31] He points to 'the difference between the responses of Rosa Parks and Vincent Lingiari to the racist victimisation they endured — and the victim politics which the post-civil rights and post-citizenship leadership cultivated'.[32]

The significance of Pearson's comparison of 'black politics' in the United States and Australia is that it allows him to link his revisionist history of liberalism — a liberalism that fails to grasp the real effects of its emancipatory intentions in the public policy reforms of the late 1960s and early 1970s — with a history of the rise of a complementary 'black' sense of victimhood. However, when he adds this Steele-derived history of liberalism to his earlier account of the unintended effects of citizenship on remote Aborigines, a problem arises. Has Pearson not blurred the geographical focus of his history? He seems to me to have shifted his attention, unannounced, from what happened in the late 1960s and early 1970s to the remote Aborigines (displaced from the remote industries and institutions in which they had made a viable adjustment and suddenly admitted into the welfare state) to all Aborigines. In making this generalising step in his argument, Pearson does not pause to consider how distinct the economic and cultural history of those Aborigines in the southern regions of Australia may be. Their modes of adjustment (still under-studied by historians) were more various, more likely to have included movement between cities and their hinterlands, not so dependent on the patronage of state-surrogates such as pastoralists and missionaries, not so rapidly and uniformly disrupted by the demise of rural employment and by the disbanding of institutional authority.

A fracture appears in Pearson's history when he attempts it at the national level, between two arguments. One of these is about the unintended effects of citizenship rights on remote Aborigines whose modes of economic adjustment were coincidentally collapsing because of structural economic change. The other is a more generalised critique of liberalism and its associated mentalities (guilt and victimhood). This second argument may be plausible when applied to some Aboriginal people of the towns and cities who — with open admiration for Martin Luther King and for 'Black Power' — led the 'civil rights' campaigns that pushed 'assimilation' to its limits. However, I doubt that either of these arguments applies to those Aborigines such as the dissenting Ngarrindjeri who, in the mid-1990s, asserted a heritage of 'respectable' sympathy for the aims of assimilation policy.[33] I suggest that there are three 'Aboriginal Australias' that have fared differently since the 1970s. One has asserted its claim to land rights — with some success — and faces the issue now of deciding how land could be a factor in an adaptive economy; it is also under pressure to acquire the human capital needed to participate in the labour market. The other two, having long experienced acculturation and the more intrusive programs of assimilation, have had little or no benefit from land rights and native title legislation; they have controversially articulated identities through heritage struggles and through the promotion of the Stolen Generations identity, and many of them would be as critical of 'victim' identity as Pearson himself.[34] Of course, I am not referring here to three well-defined and discrete categories (let alone 'groups') of people. However, I do discern distinct twentieth-century traditions of adjustment, grievance and identity that have their material base in the differentiated geography and timing of Australian colonial pressures. The differences between these trajectories of Aboriginal response are blurred by Pearson when he simply adds the historical model that he derives from Shelby Steele's work on the

African Americans of the United States to the economic/moral history of remote Aborigines, which he sketched — persuasively — in *Our right to take responsibility*.

It is difficult for any of us to write a 'national' history of Australian colonial authority and Indigenous responses. The problem of regional specificity erupts in Pearson's revisionist explorations for reasons with which any historian can sympathise, but also because, in his case, the ambition of Pearson the historian to be 'national' is reinforced by the ambition of Pearson the policy intellectual to be credible in Canberra about policy issues that are national in scope. To present a generalised model of the Aboriginal psychology of welfare dependency has met an ideological need.

The community history

When first stretching his wings as an historian — his BA (Hons) thesis in history at the University of Sydney — Pearson eschewed histories of Australian colonisation that were national in scope. Pan-Aboriginal narratives of the Aboriginal response to colonisation seemed to him to be too generalised to be interesting; he commended histories that documented local and regional particularities.[35] Writing on the Lutheran mission at Cape Bedford and its successor at Hope Vale, where he had grown up with his family, Pearson was fascinated by the response of his forbears — the parental and grandparental generations — to the Lutherans' paternalistic authority.

After the brutal colonial invasion of the Cooktown–Palmer River region in the last 30 years of the nineteenth century, his surviving people — the Guugu-Yimidhirr (father's side) and Kuku Yalanji (mother's side) — were forced to compromise with the authoritarian refuge offered by the Cape Bedford Lutheran mission (founded in 1886). The most far-reaching thrust of Lutheran supervision was their control of young women, and in particular women's access to marriage. Lutherans shared in the persisting frontier view that the Aborigines of Cape York were suffering from 'cannibalism, infanticide, rampant sexuality, constant revenge killings and the degraded position of women'.[36] Pearson agrees that there was much male violence against women among the Aborigines who had become visible to colonists at the frontier. However, Pearson suggests that the observed violence was itself an effect of frontier conditions: those men were responding to their dispossession and social alienation.[37]

To the extent that it was successful, the missionaries' curbing of male violence included imparting to mission residents a story about what kind of folk they had been and what, with guidance, they had since become: the Lutherans' representation of Aborigines' pre-contact savagery had been 'internalized by many Guugu-Yimithirr people'.[38] With this view of their pre-contact past, it was no wonder that many Guugu-Yimithirr accepted Lutheran authority — in more than a grudging way: it had brought peace and wholesome relations between the sexes to a new community of survivors. Lutheran authority also reconciled the Guugu-Yimithirr to God. To explain the effective and durable paternalism of Lutheran Pastor Schwarz (known to Guugu-Yimithirr as 'Muni', and attributed with supernatural powers), Pearson writes:

> Muni was able to teach a Christianity which commanded the subservience of the people without necessarily alienating them, because this subservience was commanded by god and expressed the biblical values of 'meekness' and 'humility', and the belief that one's rewards lay not in the present but in the after-life.[39]

Muni's authority was transmitted by parents: 'the mission leaders and elders insured that the religious life was to be kept alive, that the young would be brought up with the mission's traditions and values. Informants often refer to the mission leaders as having played the role of teaching them.'[40]

By the time Pearson was growing up, the Guugu-Yimithirr formed by this ethos were old and were finding their young folk resistant to the habits and imperatives of the old mission institutions: the 'Sunday School, Bible Study, Church Services, "Fellowship" groups'.[41] The mood of the young was more than just 'disinterest in Christianity', observed Pearson in 1986: it 'reflects a wider social change and possibly disillusionment with traditions or an inability to make those traditions relevant to the changed times'.[42] Pearson was atypical of his cohort in one way: encouraged by trends in the writing of academic history, he made it his business to empathise with the older people from whom those in his generation were becoming estranged.

In his lectures and articles since the mid-1990s, when Pearson occasionally offers readers glimpses of this originating culture and its demise he demonstrates his empathy with two different eras of Aboriginal experience. In 2000, he wrote that to grow up materially poor in Hope Vale was nonetheless to experience the human riches of a true community.[43] In 1987, writing with Merv Gibson, he evoked the erstwhile morality of that community as Aboriginal and Christian, spurning alcohol and gambling.[44] In 1997, he recalled arriving in Brisbane to attend a Lutheran secondary school, very much the product of a confessional community; there he discovered — through his admiration of the Ella brothers (Rugby Union stars of the 1970s and 1980s) — that he was also a Queenslander and an Australian.[45] In his 1993 Boyer Lecture, Pearson recalled his generation's growing disquiet about the Hope Vale ethos of submission to church and state authority and of resigned acceptance of White racism.[46] By the early 1980s, his generation had come to a painful and indignant realisation that while 'paternalism within the family might be a natural, affectionate relationship ... when it involved adults of different races it was undeniably racist'.[47] The authority of the church could hardly survive this growing critical awareness. Thus Pearson recalled in 2007 that:

> I served on the Hope Vale Aboriginal Community Council when the last vestiges of the Lutheran Church's administrative involvement in the affairs of our people were removed in the late 1980s. We cut these last ties with a relishing sense of historic reckoning. The awful truth is that we threw the baby out with the bathwater: the role of the church in the secular and spiritual life of our community was conflated; both the church and our people should have found a way to move beyond the paternalism of the past without destroying the moral and cultural order which had been such a strong quality of our community.[48]

So that is now Pearson's policy question, one grounded in his sustained effort of local and trans-generational historical imagination: What is to replace 'paternalism' as the authority on which 'community' — for a time — rested? For Hope Vale people, the question has attained existential urgency. Pearson's 2006 piece in *The Weekend Australian*, 'Hope Vale lost',[49] portrayed the town where he grew up in 'community' as a place where childhood was now ruined by neglectful, predatory, substance-abusing adults.

The left-right story

If that is a locally generated question, does it have to be answered in a statewide or nationwide way? In Pearson's analysis it does, because what governments have done and must do is important, and governments conceive their actions through large, generalising philosophies, understandings and programs. The fourth of the stories that Pearson tells is about the conservative, liberal and social democratic assumptions underpinning Australian social policy debates. In two addresses that honoured politicians from the Australian Labor Party — the Ben Chifley Memorial Lecture in 2000 and the John Button Oration in 2010 — Pearson promoted a class analysis of Australian history in order to make sense of the clash of values and philosophies in the discussion of social policy.

In the Chifley Lecture, he advocated that Labor rethink its commitment to the welfare state. He proceeded by an historical narrative. The welfare state was the framework of 'class cooperation' and 'compromise', lasting from just after Federation until the 1980s.[50] While the welfare state has been mildly redistributive of wealth, it has also been 'reciprocal', in that its benefits have been funded from taxation: 'the principle is that you receive approximately what you contribute'.[51] However, as capitalism has made more and more use of labour that is not organised to present collective demands, the organised 'lower classes' have lost much of their bargaining power, and those who do well from contemporary capitalism — and here Pearson refers to the highly skilled knowledge workers — have less reason to defend the welfare state. 'Lower-class Australians' now face uncertainty.

Pearson then differentiated the relationship of 'my mob' to the welfare state. In contrast with other lower-class Australians for whom the welfare state has been enabling and civilising, access to the welfare state by 'my people in Cape York' has been damaging: the result has been passive welfare. Welfare has become the basis of contemporary Aboriginal livelihood, rather than a safety net beneath Indigenous peoples' occasional transitions in 'the real economy': 'two generations of life in the safety net have produced a social disaster'.[52]

That the welfare state is now politically vulnerable, and that 'my mob' has been damaged by accessing the welfare state, are two problems about which 'progressive' Australian intellectuals have been unable to think clearly, Pearson argued in 2000. Taking aim at their wrong-headedness, he proposed a principle of welfare reform that would both defend the welfare state from neo-liberal attack and defend Aborigines from the harmful effects of welfare: 'personal and family empowerment' to prevent 'dependency and passivity'.[53]

Here, let me note two features of Pearson's Chifley Lecture. First, he presented his 'welfare reform' proposals as benefiting both 'my mob' and the much wider constituency of 'lower-class' Australians. However, while he sketched the pathological mentality of 'my mob', he offered no such sketch of the mentality of the 'lower-class' Australians who were at risk. It is implicit in Pearson's account that the 'lower-class' Australians are at risk in two ways if welfare reform is badly handled: they might lose eligibility (dismissed as 'bludgers' by those who now prosper in their own employment); or they might develop pathological dependencies (if unreformed eligibility indulges their irresponsibility).

Second, Pearson spent much of his Chifley Lecture characterising the middle class — of which, he acknowledges, he himself is a member. The 'middle stratum that possesses intellectual tools and performs qualified work' consists of the professionals who do 'the qualified work in the production of goods and services' and the intellectuals who uphold 'the cultural, political and legal superstructure'.[54] Pearson seems to present two contradictory propositions about the interests of this 'middle stratum' in a period when the necessity of the welfare state is being reconsidered. On the one hand, the middle class has become an important source of the nation's wealth, and it has bargained successfully for high rewards in the labour market, so that the 'welfare state' (including the regulation of labour markets) has become less important to the material security of the middle class. The middle class increasingly is attracted to non-collectivist means for securing its well-being, leaving the lower-class politically friendless as it faces the neo-liberal argument that a welfare state based on high taxes is an impediment to national prosperity. On the other hand, Pearson suggests that the middle class includes many whose fortunes are closely tied to the welfare state in its current form. He refers to the 'negligent thinkers in the academies and the bureaucracies — the very people who have benefited most from the welfare state'.[55] This middle class has become absorbed in cultural pursuits that 'keep rebellious minds occupied and isolated from the social predicament of the lower classes'.[56] Insofar as this middle class does think about the lower classes, it thinks badly, hanging on to cherished but flawed notions of freedom and responsibility that perpetuate destructive policies. Pearson's examples are policies towards law enforcement and the regulation of alcohol and other substances. 'Academics, bureaucrats and parliamentarians' have become 'the intellectual trustees of the welfare state', but have failed to manage it so that it works for its intended beneficiaries.[57]

Thus there is a tension within Pearson's class analysis of the welfare reform conjuncture. He considers the middle class to be (potentially) selfishly indifferent to the future of the welfare state and to the interests of the most vulnerable strata of Australian society, and he sees the middle class as highly invested in the welfare state in its current perverse form and zealously protective of its own wrong-headed account of the needs of the lower class and of Aborigines. In Pearson's provocative Chifley Lecture in 2000, we see him striving to characterise the mentalities and class interests of two entities: the lower-class supposed beneficiaries of the welfare state (of whom 'my mob' is a distinct sub-set); and the 'middle class' beneficiaries, theorists and trustees of the welfare state. These two problems of historical and political analysis have fascinated Pearson, and he returned to them in his 2010 John Button Oration. Before turning to that piece, we should note Pearson's running commentary on his personal navigation of the rivalry of Labor and the Coalition.

Pearson's admiration for Prime Minister Paul Keating (1991–96) arose from his 1993 negotiations with the Australian government about the native title legislation (for which Pearson and other negotiators had been derided by 'some blackfellas').[58] As he wrote in 1997, Keating 'laid the foundations for Indigenous inclusion in the Australian nation by seizing the opportunity *Mabo* presented to get everything else right'.[59] 'Never before, and likely never again, would Indigenes be invited in from the woodheap to sit at the main table as they did during those Keating years,' he recalled in 2007.[60] At first revolted by Prime Minister John Howard's (1996–2007) leadership, Pearson excoriated the Coalition for what he judged to be a racist election campaign in 1996, and accused Howard of lying about the implications of native title in 1997.[61] Though he conceded that the Liberal Party had sometimes been led by men sympathetic to Aborigines,[62] he found the Howard government divisive and mean 'about immigration, Aborigines and dole bludgers'.[63] Evidently the antipathy was mutual, as Howard was known to regard the Indigenous leadership as 'Labor to the bootstraps'.[64]

However, Pearson soon began to reflect publicly on whether such alienation from a popular conservative Prime Minister was prudent. He asked an ACT Council of Social Services audience in 1997 whether he had burned his bridges.[65] Addressing the Jewish Democratic Society in

1997, he apologised for the 'intemperate remarks' he had made about the Coalition.[66] He described the approach of Howard's first Minister for Aboriginal Affairs, John Herron, as 'refreshing'.[67] The conservative side of Australian politics could be reasoned with, he explained in 2004 — thanking Ron Castan QC for inviting him to see that 'there is more common ground between Indigenous people and people from the Right of Australian politics than conventional political wisdom would have it'.[68] He judged it a strategic necessity to work that common ground: 'The only way to get wide support for Indigenous Australians' aspirations,' he declared in 2004, 'is to first get support from the most conservative people among decent Australians. If you first get the support of the Left, it will become a Left-versus-Right issue.'[69] According to John Howard himself, Pearson's influence among Aboriginal leaders meant that by November 2004 his government had reached a turning point in its relationship with them.[70] By June 2007, Howard was able to count on Pearson's 'understanding' when calculating the politics of the Northern Territory Emergency Response (the 'Intervention'), and he was 'transfixed' by Pearson's ABC Radio rebuttal of Tom Calma's criticism of the Intervention. In rejecting the 'rights at any price' approach, Pearson 'spoke for mainstream Australia as well as many in his own community'.[71]

Pearson has presented himself as a political centrist — a mediator of the polarities of right and left. His political centrism works at two levels: tactical and philosophical. Tactically, he reasons that it is foolish for the Indigenous cause to become aligned with the left: an astute Indigenous leader must find empathy with Australia's conservatives. (Thus his criticism of Windschuttle is, in part, tactical: such history militates against empathic conservatism.) Philosophically, the left has proved to have too limited a vision of Indigenous advancement: social democratic perspectives must be complemented by what liberals and conservatives offer. To make this second, philosophical case was the point of Pearson's Button Oration in October 2010. He argued that Labor's heritage of 'redistributive thinking' was relevant to one part of Indigenous need: for 'social investment' in 'health, education and so on'. Conservative thought was also relevant in that it recognised the need for 'social and cultural norms' of 'mutual responsibilities' and 'mutual respect', and for individuals to feel strong social obligation. Finally, liberal thought gave self-interest its due: the self-interested striving of individuals is 'at the centre of development'. As an outsider to 'the three great philosophical traditions of western social and political thought', Pearson presents himself as their synthesiser, working from his understanding of 'human nature'.[72]

In the Button Oration, Pearson resumes his Chifley Lecture quest to characterise the 'middle class' and 'lower class'. It is a striking feature of this address that the words 'Aboriginal' and 'Indigenous' do not appear; the closest he gets to making the oration a discourse about his 'people' is his occasional passing reference to 'Cape York Peninsula'. He uses the historically unspecific phrases 'the wretched' and 'the disadvantaged', whose 'outlook', he generalises, is an obstacle to their advancement. Perhaps Pearson's Button Oration can be understood as another essay in defining the problems and tasks of his 'people', but it sets aside the particularities of Aboriginal people-hood to make a general argument that all poor people need to become more self-interested. 'Our people have the right to take responsibility' because that is the right of all 'wretched' and 'disadvantaged' people.[73]

In making this point, his foil is again the 'middle class'. In the Button Oration, Pearson's emphasis is on their possessive investment in the welfare state and on their deluded solidarity with the lower class. He seems to have set aside the possibility — canvassed in 2000 — that the middle class might selfishly abandon the poor to the deregulators of markets and downsizers of governments. Pearson urges the middle class to show their understanding of the needs of 'the disadvantaged' not by doing more for them, but by encouraging their self-interest. He does not make any particular policy proposals to illustrate the improved social policy he has in mind — other than to declare: 'We need policies that increase self-regard among the disadvantaged.' If middle-class people have proven so alert to their own interests, he writes, then social justice policy must set in motion 'the numerous engines of self interest that lie dormant in the breasts of the disadvantaged'.[74] He points to a looming issue: the exploitation of natural resources. He warns 'the western environmental left' not to expect the disadvantaged to be restrained in their use of natural resources. His final words in the oration are cryptic, but he seems to identify 'The Greens' as potential opponents of resource exploitation by the poor.

Conclusion: a trajectory from 'people' to class?

I have been tempted to argue that by disciplining his historical imagination with political economy, Pearson has steadily lost focus on the cultural specificity of Indigenous Australian people-hood, in order to dwell on what Indigenous Australians have in common with other poor people in the developed world. Certainly, that is a strong tendency in his thought. However, a contrary tendency is not hard to find in *Up from the mission*. For example, he wrote in 2006:

> The environmental affinity of hunter-gatherers arise from their economy: nature is the source of their sustenance and it is no wonder religion and culture are intimately concerned with the natural world. *These traditions are still strong and relevant today.*[75]

And in 2007:

> [T]he issues that are essential to Indigenous wellbeing *are not all similar* to those affecting the mainstream, who do not have the same socio-economic problems. Government is frequently incapable of properly addressing Indigenous issues, as it is used to servicing the needs of the mainstream.[76]

A degree of uncertainty about the specificity of the Indigenous Australian prospect is a necessary consequence of Pearson's wish to go beyond a discourse of Indigenous rights to consider the political economy of Indigenous adaptation. He emphasises cultural similarity when he formulates the fundamental principle of the 'moral community' that may yet emerge in Australia — summed up in the phrase 'real economy':

> The traditional subsistence economy was very much a real economy. If you didn't work, you starved … In our mission days we lived partly in what I call the institutional modern subsistence economy … If you didn't work, you starved. The whitefella market economy is a real economy. If you don't work, you don't get paid.[77]

To live by the discipline of a 'real economy' has been Pearson's aspiration for his people. His account of Indigenous people-hood thus dwells on what makes them like their fellow Australians as much as on what distinguishes them.

CHAPTER 9

Peter Sutton and the Historical Roots of Suffering

Peter Sutton's *The politics of suffering: Indigenous Australia and the end of the liberal consensus* is a memoir, an ethnography, a policy critique and a history. His views bear on how we might consider Aboriginal people to be a 'people': he sees them as a people with a flawed and debilitating cultural heritage.

Sutton's observations are not only ethnographic, they are historical. In this chapter, I will discuss the three historical perspectives that he brings to contemporary policy debates. First, he labels as 'liberal consensus' a period of Australian Indigenous policy history: 1968–2000. Second, he argues that Indigenous parental authority has been unexpectedly resilient to colonial encroachment, to Indigenous Australians' disadvantage. Third, he questions whether the categories 'Indigenous' and 'non-Indigenous' — useful in ethnography and historical writing — continue to be useful to understanding our contemporary history.

I argue that Sutton's notion of 'liberal consensus' is incomplete, and that he does not clearly distinguish between two ways that the 'liberal consensus' has been significant. Second, I argue that Sutton finds it difficult to assign weight to Indigenous parental authority as a cause of Aborigines' current problems, and he is not clear about what governments should do about it. Third, I conclude that even though he is uncomfortable with the categories assumed by identity politics and public policy discussion, Sutton is too committed to generalising about Indigenous culture and experience to give them up.

The book opens with a vignette of recent social change on Cape York — in particular, the apparent rise in the incidence of homicide, suicide and rape among families known to Sutton 'since the introduction of a regular alcohol supply in 1985'.[1] He then states his thesis:

that a number of the serious problems Indigenous people face in Australia today arise from a complex joining together of recent, that is, post-conquest, historical factors of external impact, with a number of ancient, pre-existent social and cultural factors that have continued, transformed or intact, into the lives of people living today. The main ways these factors are continued is child-rearing.[2]

Thus a concern for children is central to Sutton's book in two ways. The first is that Sutton — drawing on a tradition of psychological anthropology — understands child socialisation to be a determinant of deeply entrenched cultural patterns. This theory of cultural reproduction is relevant to the extent that Indigenous Australians have successfully resisted transformation of their child socialisation practices. The second way in which children matter in *The politics of suffering* is ethical: Sutton questions the priority that some have given to respecting 'cultural differences and racially defined political autonomy' rather than 'a child's basic human right to have love, wellbeing and safety' — a priority that has displaced 'care as the primary determinant of special helping measures for citizens in trouble'.[3] To be sure, children are not the only 'citizens in trouble': the well-being of 'the unborn, infants, children, adolescents, the elderly, and adult women and men' is a neglected priority, according to Sutton.[4] Vulnerable children are nonetheless his recurring example of the disordered ethics that he wishes to challenge.[5]

In keeping with this dual significance of the child, *The politics of suffering* is a work of both social science and ethical advocacy. Sutton challenges his readers to reflect on their own ethical formation as concerned Australians, in particular to reconsider three ways of thinking that we might take for granted: first, categorical thinking that substantiates 'Indigenous/non-Indigenous' and makes sense of individuality in terms of each individual being either Indigenous or non-Indigenous; second, 'cultural relativism'; and third, 'social justice'. Critical of the grip that these three ways of thinking have on our political imagination, Sutton has written a polemical ethnography of recent Australian liberal sensibility. So let me expand a little on his three targets.

First, let's examine the Indigenous/non-Indigenous dichotomy. It is fundamental to Sutton's social philosophy that he seeks 'a better balance between the collective and the personal than we have achieved in recent decades'.[6] Exemplary of the 'personal', as he has experienced it, is the quotidian 'coalface caring business' of service providers in troubled communities.⁷ He himself has been a carer. On Cape York in 1976, he combined fieldwork with 'running a basic [non-profit] food store (the protein was all hunted), and administering the Flying Doctor medical kit' — anthropological compassion later gratefully and publicly acknowledged by Gladys Tybingoompa.⁸ In Chapter 7 of *The politics of suffering*, he extols 'the personal' against the 'corporate' or 'collective' by evoking a series of friendships between anthropologists and informants — relationships that are not intelligible in the categories made available by identity politics. In his final chapter, he criticises 'reconciliation' as a civic ideal founded in a flawed schema of collective 'Indigenous' and collective 'non-Indigenous' agencies.

Turning to 'cultural relativism', if the conceptual alternative that twentieth century anthropology offered to 'race' was 'culture', the ethical antidote that it offered to 'racism' was 'cultural relativism'. As Sutton says, cultural relativism has been 'not merely ... an intellectual or scientific standpoint but also a moral stance, a kind of scientifically underpinned engine of tolerance'.⁹ Sutton is wary of cultural relativism because of its ethical crudity (it makes no distinction between the predatory and the vulnerable members of a culture, its indiscriminate tolerance is not bounded by respect for universal human values). He is clearly annoyed and frustrated by the self-satisfied subjectivities that he sees as characteristic of 'cultural relativism', and his many critical passages on the culture of 'cultural relativism' — if I can put it in that way — have enlivened the reception of his work. Cultural relativism thrives partly on its psychological rewards (he sees it as 'self-redemptive').¹⁰ However, Sutton's philosophical assessment of 'cultural relativism' is not necessarily negative, and it is more subtle than his strictures on cultural relativists would imply: 'Its virtues and vices depend on the context we want to apply it to, and it can't be damned or praised for itself alone, free of context.'¹¹

Third, as well as mocking the ethical simple-mindedness of many adherents of 'cultural relativism', Sutton takes aim at another flawed ethical formation: an over-stated regard for 'social justice' as a matter of 'politics and law'. That concern is also rewarding for those immersed in it; it is 'geared to creating benefits for politically or bureaucratically active adults, in the first instance', it bestows 'political glamour' and it is 'career-enhancing'.¹² Sutton believes that the instruments of a properly ethical concern for Aborigines are not 'politics and law', but actions that work at the level of 'the personal'.¹³

Sutton's critical historical account of what he calls 'the liberal consensus' is that it combined naïve cultural relativism with an optimistic projection of the possibilities of politics and law, and assumed and revalued the categorical distinction Indigenous/non-Indigenous. Sutton suggests that the 'liberal consensus' became influential between 1968 and 1974, and it set the terms of public discussion until 1999–2000. He summarises it thus:

> [Aboriginal] communities should be free of mission or state governance, self-managed through elected councils and relatively autonomous. Land rights would ensure their inhabitants security of tenure and, where possible, a source of income. Traditional culture would be encouraged, not discouraged. Pressures to assimilate to a Euro-Australian way of life were racist and should be curtailed. Liberation, not retraining … would lift people's self-respect and pride, and enable them to embark on a new era in which the quality of their lives would improve. There was an expectation that collective decision-making would be based on a regard for the good of the community. Health would improve through better access to services and a power shift from government health agencies to those who came to form the Indigenous health industry.[14]

This is accurate as far as it goes. However, Sutton has omitted two crucial items in the 'liberal consensus' that emerged in the period 1968–74. One is the doctrine of anti-discrimination. As an avowed aim of assimilation policy, anti-discrimination had many legal and policy manifestations before 1968, including the release of Aborigines from many legislated restrictions on their behaviour, such as withholding the right to vote and to drink alcohol. In the period 1968–74, the achievements of 'anti-discrimination' were largely to do with empowering Aborigines as consumers, with the standardisation of wages and welfare payments to Indigenous Australians. The achievement of formal equivalence in such income entitlements in these years consummated Paul Hasluck's policy of assimilation, a legacy welcomed by those who also held the convictions that Sutton describes as the 'liberal consensus'. One feature of the termination of the 'liberal consensus' is that it has again become respectable to advocate, if only as an 'emergency' measure, racial discrimination in welfare entitlements.

The second idea that Sutton omits from his summary of the 'liberal consensus' is the conviction that the new, post-assimilation mode of

Indigenous advancement would be enabled by public funds flowing through government agencies to Aboriginal organisations that would be set up (under Fraser government legislation in 1976) to provide health, schooling, housing and other essential services. To omit this second item from the 'liberal consensus' renders incomplete — to say the least — Sutton's account of how that consensus came 'undone', for that conviction was always, in one respect, fragile. Whether governments spend too much or too little on assistance to Indigenous Australians has been persistently at issue since the Whitlam government. The question has been polled since the 1960s, and these polls have consistently revealed respondent *dissensus*. Australians have been divided about Indigenous entitlement to financial support. The 'liberal consensus' — in the augmented sense that I suggest is more accurate historically — was thus highly vulnerable to that current of Australian opinion that has long been suspicious of taxpayer-funded state support for vulnerable people. Aborigines have been a prime example for those who view the interventionist welfare state as an expensive mistake. By omitting this taxation/entitlement theme from his account of 'liberal consensus', Sutton has reduced the plausibility of his history, in Chapter 1, of the 'shattered orthodoxy'.[15]

The history of the dissolution of the 'liberal consensus' that Sutton presents in his first chapter is an engaging memoir of his own presence in Queensland communities (from June 1970), as the 'liberal consensus' changed the ways of administration during the years 1968–74. Recalling the solidarities and enmities that these changes occasioned among the non-Aboriginal residents of Cape York, Sutton also offers vignettes of Aboriginal activists, including admiring sketches of the emerging political sophisticates Marcia Langton and Noel Pearson. Comparing 'old and new' Aboriginal activism in the 1990s, he contrasts the 'old' concern for the 'symbolic and rights agenda' with the new, salutory emphasis on 'quality-of-life issues' and appreciation of 'the complex pragmatics of governance'.[16] The pertinence of this emerging agenda, Sutton suggests, was that it focused critical attention on what the 'liberal consensus' had refused to face: that there had been a 'decline in the standard of living and safety'.[17]

However, a growing research literature described these bad conditions, challenging the optimism of the 'liberal consensus'. Sutton describes the impact of this historical narrative — that the ideas and practices of the 'liberal consensus' had inflicted unintended suffering on Indigenous Australians — as 'a fair amount of catharsis' and as a 'wave of unusual honesty and self-examination'.[18] Journalists who had seen the world through the terms of the 'liberal consensus' were ceasing to do so. In this refreshed climate of discussion, 'taboos' on public discussion of 'political morality, personal morality and cultural values' were set aside.[19] In the controversy about the Howard government's Northern Territory Intervention in 2007, principles of 'political rights' were trumped by declarations of humanitarian intent. There is now no 'political consensus on Australian Indigenous policy'.[20] Much later in the book, when discussing whether and in what respects Aboriginal customary law should be recognised, Sutton argues that the 'liberal consensus' has become vulnerable also because the Aboriginal domain that it values has itself been changing. At least, this is what I think he is referring to when he writes that 'wider demographic, cultural and social changes are working to hasten the decline and fall of the kind of strong relativism that informed liberal progressive opinion in the 1970s'.[21]

Two histories are at play in Sutton's story of the successful challenging of the 'liberal consensus': a narrative of the declining influence of a set of ideas (the 'liberal consensus'); and a narrative of the degrading impact of policies favoured by the 'liberal consensus' on Aboriginal communities. He puts more effort into setting out the first history, an evocative tale of people he has met and political scenes in which he has participated. In addressing the second history, he does not clearly distinguish two propositions: that the 'liberal consensus' inhibited our public recognition that conditions on some Aboriginal communities are very bad and not improving; and Noel Pearson's thesis that the application of the 'liberal consensus' to public policy *caused* the degradation of the conditions of life of these Aboriginal communities.

The first proposition is persuasive: reading Sutton enables me to see how my hopes framed in terms of the 'liberal consensus' have led me to highlight the potential of Indigenous agency; when confronted by instances of Indigenous stupidity, greed, mental illness, treachery, violence, laziness and apathy, it was tempting to treat these qualities as marginal and/or as the fading legacies of colonisation. It has been refreshing to be able to acknowledge, publicly, that the difficulties of realising the hopes promoted by the 'liberal consensus' point in part to unmet Indigenous responsibilities and to cultural and historical explanations of flawed Indigenous agency. However, readers will be disappointed if they expect Sutton to expound the argument that the application of the 'liberal consensus' to public policy *caused* 'the downward spiral since the 1970s' — the Pearson thesis that has played so well in the press since 2000. Sutton implies *some* sympathy for the Pearson thesis, though his formulations are notably cautious ('many agreed that this was an important part of the truth', and 'there was an apparent correlation between the progressiveness of policy and the degree of community disaster').[22]

Sutton's history differs significantly from Pearson's: unlike Pearson, Sutton suggests that Indigenous authority structures have been resilient, and he sees them now as causes of distress and suffering. As Sutton tells the story, there was a 'breakdown in social control in a number of Aboriginal settlements' as state and church withdrew or redesigned their authority in the period 1968–74. I understand him to qualify his account of state and church withdrawal when he suggests that the administration of goods and services in Aboriginal communities has remained 'functionally, not politically, by non-Indigenes' — not necessarily officials of state or church, to be sure.[23] At the same time as non-Indigenous authority was receding and/or changing its forms, access to alcohol improved (and Sutton recalls his own hospitality on Cape York). According to the 'liberal consensus', the destiny of resurgent Aboriginal authority was to deal effectively with these new circumstances. What Aboriginal authority was there?

Unlike Pearson — who offers us an account of diminishing adult Aboriginal authority — Sutton emphasises the continuity of Aboriginal routines of child socialisation, while lamenting their effects. However, his account of Aboriginal parental authority is indirect, piecemeal and scattered throughout the book. He briefly mentions household 'matriarchy' as a newly significant formation. Looking wider, to the place of kinship, he implies that surviving Aboriginal custom was strong enough to make it difficult to establish the legitimacy, in Indigenous eyes, of incorporated Aboriginal organisations with codes of responsibility that could contradict obligations to kin. At the same time, he assures us, many Indigenous people have embraced modern ways, including formal organisations. His main point about Indigenous authority in the era of 'liberal consensus' is that it was able to resist colonial influence: it has proven robust, and the forms of its persistence worry him. For example, in the Western Desert it remains realistic for Aboriginal people to fear that they will be 'strangled for religious misbehaviours'.[24] The persistence of customary Indigenous authority is mainly to be found, he says, in the ways that parents raise children. The effect of persisting approaches to child-rearing becomes a central topic, running through Chapter 3: 'some very deeply seated and old cultural conceptions of power, obligation and economy' have determined how Aborigines have responded to the circumstances of the late twentieth century.[25]

Sutton is committed to the view that child socialisation contributes massively to the reproduction of Indigenous culture. In some Indigenous families, he suggests, the socialisation process has recently so miscarried that it has produced young adults who can be effective in terms of neither Indigenous nor non-Indigenous expectations. Some contemporary adults can function in Indigenous society but, unlike their own parents who had long contact with white employers, missionaries or officials, they lack the cognitive and emotional skills to go beyond the regional Aboriginal domain. Some young people have been socialised to drink alcohol in destructive ways. Sutton is worried that where Indigenous child socialisation processes persist, they reproduce maladaptive behaviour. He chides adherents of the 'liberal consensus' for being blind to the significance, in determining Indigenous disadvantage, of such cultural factors as egalitarian social organisation, power structures that encourage dependency, family loyalties, certain beliefs about the causes of illness, minimal hygiene practices, demand sharing and the rejection of accumulation, use of physical force in disputes, fatalism and a sense of an unchanging world.[26] Children still learn these patterns of culture, and Sutton argues that what they learn disables their engagement as adults with the wider Australian society and sometimes with their own.[27]

In underlining these cultural factors as real and persistent determinants of behaviour, Sutton is correcting what he sees as the blindness of the 'liberal consensus' to cultural explanations of Aboriginal disadvantage. Accepting that corrective, we are nonetheless left with the question: are these major or minor determinants of persistent Indigenous disadvantage? This is a difficult question to answer in a generalised way, as Sutton rightly points out, but it is not a question that he can evade. Weighing the causal importance of surviving pre-colonial culture, and thus its relevance to government intervention, is difficult. While Sutton urges those whom he criticises to pay more attention to the effects of persistent cultural patterns, this is a challenge that he himself can defer, as long as he preoccupies himself with the idiocies of the 'liberal consensus'. It is surprising to me (though evidently gratifying to some reviewers) that the 'liberal consensus' as a stupid structure of perception and feeling occupies so many scornfully worded pages in Sutton's book. As long as non-Indigenous self-delusion is Sutton's theme, he can rub our liberal noses in problematic features of Indigenous culture, without saying *how important* these features are in determining what Indigenous people do and without being clear about what — if anything — governments must now do.

Perhaps the best that can be achieved by way of an explanatory model is to say that certain contemporary circumstances have interacted with certain inherited dispositions to produce damaging patterns of behaviour. When Sutton commented on Gillian Cowlishaw's critiques of his work in 2005, he suggested that wherever limited colonisation had left much of the Indigenous socialisation process intact, it was not plausible to explain violent behaviour primarily as a response to imposed colonial conditions. Rather, the violence, he argued,

> is rooted much more immediately in the dynamic local polity of competitive interpersonal and gender relationships, in a cultural world where jealous rage is not normally suppressed during child socialisation, where berserks are legitimated childhood reactions to thwarted desires, where, under recently sedentary conditions, dispersal is no longer the favoured option during conflict, and where drugs, especially alcohol, act as disinhibitors for strong emotions. In other words, it is rooted much less in realms of broader social control and colonial resistance, with their loaded hints of collective good, and much more in the struggle of the person.[28]

Consistent with this account, Sutton's powerful review of archaeologies, histories and ethnographies of violence among Aborigines (Chapter 4 of *The politics of suffering*) suggests that male violence against women 'is found at its most extreme in communities that have remained closest to their cultural traditions, and where alcohol is available in quantity'.[29] He adduces his Aurukun data to illustrate such a place (though he does not compare Aurukun with a community with access to alcohol that has not remained close to its cultural traditions). Of all the elements in the 'liberal consensus' that could be reassessed as damaging mistakes, the legislated end of restrictions on Aborigines' access to alcohol emerges in Sutton's book as the most consequential misjudgment. Paternalistic and discriminatory though they may have been in intention and effect, the laws, institutional structures and patterns of settlement that restricted the liberty to drink were beneficial to Aborigines. We can't go back to those days, writes Sutton. However, he is sceptical of the current 'collectivist' solutions to the alcohol abuse problem, such as zoning communities as grog-free and restricting retail supply. The solutions that interest him are characteristically in 'the struggle of the person', and in the helpful dyad: he commends one-to-one talks between patients and their doctors as prompts to self-reform.

Sutton's wariness of the collective and the corporate is consistent with his suspicion of histories that assume the centrality of government policy in the determination of Indigenous well-being. Consider the logic of Sutton's emphasis on the persistence of cultural factors in his history of Indigenous Australia since the 1960s. To the extent that they are the major reason for persistent Indigenous disadvantage, then the causal importance of other factors is diminished. Perhaps the revised modes of government and church presence, approved by the 'liberal consensus', were not so important? Perhaps no imaginable configuration of polity and economy would have saved Aborigines from their maladaptive cultural patterns. Or perhaps we need to distinguish among the policies approved by the 'liberal consensus', weighing the causal importance of different policies and highlighting those that interacted powerfully and perversely with features of Indigenous culture. Policies that had the effect of improving Indigenous access to alcohol emerge in Sutton's account as particularly important.

Sutton gives us good reason for wanting a causal model that is clear about the relative weights of Indigenous culture and non-Indigenous policy in the generation of misery: such a model is relevant to our assessment of what, if anything, changes in government practices could achieve. Reading his chapter on health policy gave me the sense that Sutton is troubled by the question of the relevance of government. On the one hand, he says Indigenous culture is much less accessible to deliberated manipulation and critical self-reflection than government policies. On the other hand, he alludes to the possibility of 'remov[ing] by appropriate interventions' unhygienic customary practices, and he attributes real health benefits and lasting behavioural change to some of the practices enforced under assimilation.[30] He acknowledges the possibility that external initiatives to promote changes in Aboriginal behaviour will resonate with 'traditional Aboriginal values', and thus be accepted.[31] To assign great causal significance to entrenched, socialised Indigenous culture is not necessarily to diminish one's hopes regarding what governments may do. Sutton's emphasis on cultural determinants could nonetheless nurture that worm of doubt within the 'liberal consensus' to which I drew attention above: if what governments do or provide is of little consequence, why spend so much 'tax-payers' money' on public provision?

Sutton generally seems to be more interventionist than such welfare state sceptics: he would direct more expenditure to health promotion — that is, to adult education for behavioural change.[32] He goes so far as to say that 'the cycle of childhood socialisation needs to be re-geared' — a metaphor that does not illuminate the imagined mechanism of social engineering.[33] However, he has no proposals to make about schooling, and (remarkable in a book so concerned with child socialisation) the term 'education' does not appear in his index.

In a 2005 paper, Sutton explained that his underlying policy preference was for 'a fundamental reversal of interventionism'. As he explained:

> I support greater intervention where there is, for example, an unmet need to protect vulnerable individuals. This need has been increasing in recent decades, and interventionist strategies have been increasingly a matter of demand from Aborigines, not just from members of the wider society. But in the longer term I consider it false to assume that more intervention will remove the underlying factors at work. In that sense I question the present vast intervention of an officially maintained and publicly funded organisational racial separatism. That includes being in favour of a gradual withdrawal of non-essential services from settlements and institutions which, without it, would have to make more of their own way in the world, perhaps even sink or swim.[34]

Sutton is not a policy nihilist, but an advocate of the broad thrust of recent Commonwealth government policies towards remote and very remote Indigenous communities: questioning subsidised spatial separation and encouraging population concentration, and promoting engagement with the mainstream labour market. To the extent that such policies give rise to more 'vulnerable individuals', this policy stance could exacerbate Sutton's ambivalence towards state 'intervention' into Indigenous lives. Opportunities for 'coal-face caring' may proliferate.

Sutton closes his book with a critique of reconciliation that, while suggestive and thought-provoking, is bedevilled by a tension that runs through the whole book. As I pointed out above, in his critique of social justice/politics/law, Sutton wishes to revalue the personal and to question the collective or corporate as vectors of action and feeling. The categorical habits of Australia's contemporary languages of social analysis and civic concern arouse his suspicion repeatedly throughout the book: needs for care, he protests, will not be grasped through narratives of colonial history ordered in the generalised terminology of identity politics. Conflicts, solidarities and grievances are matters of local configuration — scenes deeply susceptible to the projects and personalities of the individuals present. This ontology of the local is integral to Sutton's anthropological humanism. 'Reconciliation' thus strikes him as a particularly ill-conceived project because, via national apologies and possibly reparations, it seeks to bring into a condition of empathy two nationwide *categories* of Australians. The project tends to institutionalise the categories, he argues, as much perpetuating as overcoming their estrangement:

> The official creation of this parallel universe of Indigenous/non-Indigenous functions, committees, boards and programs creates a career structure such that those who want to tread this ladder of success are easily wedded to the continuance of racial division, and indeed to the status of victimhood that prompted the compensatory acts in the first place. If one's career is wedded to suffering and its compensation, then there cannot be an easily accepted endpoint for special status as victim. Victimhood thus becomes, for many, the family business, a business of status as well as of economics.[35]

What's more, he goes on to say, such a project cannot work emotionally. Insofar as 'reconciliation' is emotional work, it is 'a state of being between persons, or a resolution of issues within one's consciousness' that is independent of the measured gaps between the two statistical entities: Indigenous and non-Indigenous Australia.

At this point, while continuing to discuss emotions, Sutton changes his argument. From asserting — credibly — that there cannot be empathy between gross statistical entities, only empathy between individual human beings, he shifts to saying that there are huge emotional differences between Aborigines and other Australians. That is, having just critiqued categories, he reinstates them to remark that Aborigines and other Australians have 'quite opposed ways of responding with the feelings': 'The visceral intensity of a remote Aboriginal settlement is almost impossible to describe. It is also pretty well invisible to the casual outside visitor, until the lid blows off. There are cross-cultural limits to empathy, and thus to real mutual recognition.'[36] Thus one of Sutton's most powerful reasons for disbelieving in 'reconciliation' is his experience of the radical emotional difference of Aborigines: it stands 'in the way of better mutual acceptance'.[37]

Sutton puts his personal experience front and centre of his frequently autobiographical book, and those who have praised *The politics of suffering* in reviews have, correspondingly, evoked the author's grieving witness as an assurance of the book's integrity. However, while the narrative appeal of his witness arises from his ability to evoke particular moments and individuals, the argumentative force of these accumulating vignettes is that they tell us about a generalised Aboriginal condition — that is, about 'Aborigines' as a category. Categorical thinking is integral to his book, even if its credibility is secured by Sutton's stories of particular places and people. It is clear from reviews, with their concern to evoke Sutton as a man who was 'there', at troubled Aurukun, that the persuasiveness of *The politics of suffering* rests partly on our willingness to accept that Sutton's witnessing of particular places at particular times is a reliable source of knowledge of Indigenous Australia and of its relationship with non-Indigenous Australia. Certain versions of categorical thinking may strike Sutton as implausible and artificial, and well may he say that formal reconciliation 'politicizes and collectivizes the very things that need to be dealt with by individuals'.[38] Nonetheless, his book demonstrates the limited relevance to Sutton himself of such an atomising paradigm of relatedness. He is deeply committed to a generalised model of Indigenous sociality, based largely on what he has found, as a field-worker, in many remote and very remote Aboriginal communities. *The politics of suffering* has been welcomed or refused in the terms on which he offered it: generalising representation of some abiding, widespread and troubling characteristics of Indigenous Australia.

CHAPTER 10

The Coombs Experiment

This chapter explores the implications of a phrase that has been recurrent in the writings of certain policy intellectuals: the 'Coombs experiment'. However, let's begin by considering what we might call 'the Yates experiment'.

In his PhD candidature at Charles Darwin University, Peter Yates has been investigating Central Australian Aborigines' economic development.[1] He asks: What happens when Western Desert Aborigines are given an opportunity to participate in commercial food production? Mr Yates is a Director of Outback Bushfoods, and his paper shows how, through that company, Aboriginal people became suppliers of bush tomatoes and wattle seeds. Aboriginal people have a very long history of gathering these two foods in the wild, and Outback Bushfoods has tried to mobilise their knowledge and skill in a commercially relevant way. When dry conditions made it difficult to gather wild-grown bush tomatoes in the volume required, the company experimented in horticulture. The bush tomatoes grew well, but Aboriginal women who had been happy to gather them in the wild were reluctant to pick a sown crop. Yates offered the explanation that it did not seem right to these women to get bush tomatoes in that way:

> Bush tomatoes, as with everything else in the world, are supposed to be *made* through ceremony, not grown by people, so it is possible that rather than tapping into and resonating with the past, these captive plants may have seemed to the women to challenge the proper order of the world ...[2]

As he writes, 'the bushfoods industry is inherently a cross-cultural enterprise'.[3] The different world views of the Aboriginal workers and the food processors who sought their gathered bush tomatoes made it difficult for them to combine in a chain of production–supply–further production. Yates' action research project discovered

> just how deep are those cultural divides. For Aboriginal people, the idea that their traditional foods could be a mere commodity is almost beyond comprehension. To them, these are not just foods: they are bound up in stories of creation, in kinship, and in multiple layers of personal and collective memory ...[4]

Government as experiment

The significance of this story is that it is about the experimental production of knowledge. What did Peter Yates discover? He discovered cultural difference. His discovery illustrates the familiar idea that Aboriginal and non-Aboriginal people may participate differently in the world that they share. According to Yates, the relevant difference on this occasion was cosmological — a difference in basic assumptions about the nature of matter itself and about the human relationship to non-human matter. Yates may not be right; it may rather be that the women resisted the industrialisation of their labour time.[5] No matter which account we find plausible, we can agree that Yates and his Aboriginal collaborators enacted what we can understand to be cultural difference. Yates combined things that had not often been combined before: some Aboriginal people who could gather bush tomatoes, some food processing firms that could turn bush tomatoes into a retail commodity, land on which bush tomatoes could grow, an irrigated farm block where they could grow. This assemblage of people, plants, land and irrigation pipes interacted in a certain way, and Yates observed and reported their interaction. By producing an instance of cultural difference, he produced new knowledge — however debatable his interpretation may be — about the cross-cultural complexity of such assemblages of people, plants, land and technology.

What Peter Yates did is exemplary of the contemporary government of remote Australia. That is, his research illuminates what can happen when you contrive new assemblages of people and things, and then observe what those assemblages actually do — how they actually work or don't work. If we observe carefully and report/interpret plausibly how those assemblages of people and things do and don't work together, or how they work in ways that we did not expect, then we are doing two things simultaneously. We are engaging in both government and knowledge production. The process of government is inherently and unavoidably experimental — and it produces knowledge, if we care to notice it. In remote Australia, the government of people is the arrangement of new assemblages of people and things — often on new scales and for unprecedented intervals of time — in order to see how those assemblages work. The project of government is an ongoing series of little experiments (and sometimes big ones) such as that of Peter Yates: to enact sameness and to enact difference, and to see in what contexts Aboriginal people and non-Aboriginal people are like each other and unlike each other.[6] Of course, as the Yates example demonstrates, every account that one can give of an experimental assemblage is a contestable interpretation — especially when the report offers 'culture' as an explanation.

If we can agree that the government of remote Australia is an ongoing project of exploratory testing of the relative significance of human sameness and cultural difference between Aboriginal and non-Aboriginal Australia, then we might cautiously use the word 'hypothesis' to refer to the expectations that launch any intervention — whether to grow bush tomatoes or to grow outback towns — into Aboriginal Australia. We need not suppose that the policy intellectual is a perfectly rational hypothesis-tester: such a figure would be difficult to find in the history of either science or public policy. Such an ideal type is nonetheless heuristically helpful. In maintaining that government can be a process of conjectural practice and reflection on intended and unintended outcomes, I wish to emphasise the cognitive or learning dimensions of political activity, including public policy. In claiming government to be — whether we like it or not — 'experiment', I see government as a partly non-intentional production of new knowledge: reflection on it may contribute to the shaping of further action.

Thus I am attracted to the perspective offered by Henry Mintzberg and by Albert O Hirschman: each has advocated a neutral, inquiring perspective on unintended consequences. Mintzberg's studies of governments and corporations revealed to him that strategic thinking is not confined to 'planning' but includes lots of post-hoc reflection on what has unexpectedly emerged from action.[7] Hirschman — whose work has been preoccupied with the unintended consequences of 'development' programs — invites us to accept 'unintended consequences' as normal and as beneficial. He takes 'strong objection to the misuse' of the phrase 'unintended consequences' in policy debates.[8] Polemical usage transforms it into a perverse effect and proclaims that any attempt to bring about reform produces exactly the opposite effect. I consider this way of arguing a betrayal of the idea of unintended consequences because it cancels the open-endedness (the open-endedness to a variety of solutions) and substitutes it by total predictability and fear.[9]

'Experiment' — a pejorative term?

Among critics of the 1970s policy experiments in the management of land and labour in remote Aboriginal Australia, HC Coombs looms as a perversely generative figure, as the arch-'separatist', the mastermind of 'exceptionalism'. Coombs is alleged to have persuaded governments to allow and to encourage Aboriginal Australians — at least those in remote and very remote regions — to refuse the socialisation that is offered by conventional schooling and to pursue only those models of economic development that are compatible with their continuing customary associations with kin and country.

Geoffrey Partington initiated this iconic invocation of the Coombs name in 1996, in his book *Hasluck versus Coombs: white politics and Australia's Aborigines* — a comparison of two policy philosophies and their guiding geniuses.[10] Partington argues that Coombs had over-stated Aborigines' alienation from capitalist Australia, projecting on to them his own socialist leanings.[11] Following Partington, it has become popular among some writers to label as 'Coombsian' a whole era of Indigenous policy. On 22 July 2010, my search on 'Coombs' on the Bennelong Society's website yielded seventeen references, each highlighting his influence in the formation of policies of which the writers (Keith Windschuttle, Geoffrey Partington, Gary Johns, Peter Howson and Ray Evans) were critical. 'The Coombs experiment' has become a talisman of naïve leftist arrogance. For example, Helen Hughes and Jenness Warin referred to 'the Coombs socialist experiment' in their *A new deal for Aborigines and Torres Strait Islanders in remote communities*, and Warin refers to Coombs again in *Why the trade in girls and other human rights abuses remain hidden*.[12] The phrase also occurs in Hughes' opinion pieces submitted to newspapers to capture interest in *A new deal for Aborigines*. In the *Courier-Mail* on 1 March 2005, Hughes wrote:

> The deprivation of remote communities is the result of a 30-year socialist experiment with the lives of Aborigines and Torres Strait

Islanders. The Coombs, Brandl and Snowdon (*A certain heritage*) program for a utopia of traditional hunter-gatherer communities, culminating in a nation independent of the rest of Australia, was supported by *Mabo* and subsequent judgments that transferred large areas of land to communal ownership.[13]

The 'Coombs experiment' has been supported by government expenditure, she went on to say — and she added: 'Any group subject to the Coombs experiment, regardless of ethnicity, would have shocking health and would be subject to alcoholism, other substance abuse and violent behaviour.'[14] Hughes applauded the Howard government's announcement that it would review CDEP and land tenure policies. On the same day, in the *Australian Financial Review*, Hughes expressed the hope that the Howard government was about to dismantle 'the Coombs experiment in remote Australia'.[15] Again, she characterised the 'experiment' as enabling 'Aborigines to revert to living in remote hunter-gatherer communities, that would eventually culminate in a "nation" independent of the rest of Australia'.[16]

In April and May 2007, there was another ripple of comment on 'the Coombs experiment'. The ABC Radio National *Counterpoint* program devoted its 23 April 2007 edition to a discussion of Coombs between Paul Comrie-Thomson, Michael Duffy, Warren Mundine and Gary Johns.[17] The program opened with an archived quotation from Coombs himself that implicitly cast doubt on Helen Hughes' account of Coombs as seeking separate Aboriginal nationhood. In 1980, Coombs had said his work had been to pursue what he understood as the goal of Aborigines, who accepted 'that they were part of Australian society and wanted to be that way, but they wanted to be a distinctive part with their own identity'.[18]

In comment, Gary Johns said that he understood Aborigines to have a variety of aspirations, and that any who wished to maintain their own identity would find it easier to do so in 2007 than they would have in 1980. Neither Johns nor Warren Mundine spelled out what they understood to have been Coombs' policies; rather, their point was that any policies that Coombs had shaped had left people in a condition of poverty and poor health. Mundine sketched his corrective: 'getting a proper economy, getting Aboriginal people to play a better role within the economy of the Australian community, and that is only through education, only through building a private sector and using land that can be built up as assets to get Aboriginal people into a better economic standing'.[19] Gary Johns said that he understood Aborigines as wanting 'a real job and a real role', and not working within a publicly subsidised 'Indigenous economy'.[20]

Paul Comrie-Thomson then commented: 'Nugget Coombs would have been opposed to that. He was quite opposed to what he called capitalist society and in some ways thought that fitting into that society was a betrayal of the Aboriginal people.'[21] Gary Johns then described Coombs as 'quaint', as 'very sixties' and as a 'socialist who wanted to run a centralised sort of economy'.[22] He went on to say that Aborigines had been 'duped' by such Green, left, mine-hating anti-capitalists as Coombs. Comrie-Thomson continued this negative characterisation of Coombs and of credulous Aborigines by claiming that 'he was quite opposed to [Aborigines] even learning English'.[23] After quoting Coombs describing traditional Aboriginal child socialisation, Comrie-Thomson suggested that Coombs' influence on schooling in remote regions was continued by 'romantic' teachers who found work difficult in remote schools, left after a short time and were replaced by other 'romantic' teachers.[24] Johns added that Wadeye community, with 'youths roaming around there playing merry havoc', was where 'Nugget's dream has come true'.[25]

Soon Helen Hughes penned another op-ed piece for the *Australian Financial Review* that used 'the Coombs experiment' as a foil:[26]

> The shameful conditions in the 'homelands' have been created by well meaning separatist policies associated with the Coombs socialist experiment that have continued the more than 200 year tradition of treating Indigenous Australians as being different from other Australians.[27]

Clearly, for a number of commentators, the idea that the policies advocated by Coombs were 'experiments' is scandalous — enough to warrant our negative appraisal of both the policies and the man. We need not be horrified that a program of government action is an experiment. Experiment is intrinsic to government. If we wish to evaluate a policy, it is of no help to know that the policy had the character of an 'experiment', and if we characterise Coombs as having an 'experimental' stance towards the policies that he studied and advocated, we acknowledge his intelligence.

Coombs' influence

Between 1967 and 1976, Coombs chaired the Council for Aboriginal Affairs — a policy advisory group that was especially, though not exclusively, interested in Commonwealth policy towards Northern Territory Aborigines. From 1976 until his withdrawal from public life in 1995, Coombs used his affiliation with the Australian National University as a base from which to continue his policy advocacy, adding a vision for the Kimberley to his Northern Territory preoccupations. He was undoubtedly influential in the Commonwealth's gradual embrace of a land rights policy in the Northern Territory, though in the formulation of the Land Rights Bill itself, he was not nearly as influential as Edward Woodward, Gerard Brennan and Barrie Dexter. Coombs was particularly influential in the Commonwealth's adoption of CDEP grants as an alternative to rendering individuals eligible for unemployment benefits from 1977. He was also one of many who sought ways for remote Aboriginal education to become more bicultural. However, Coombs was notably *not* influential in other reforms. In 1973 he advised Whitlam against setting up the Department of Aboriginal Affairs, for he was an advocate of what today is known as administrative 'mainstreaming'. He was sceptical of the series of national elected assemblies established by the Whitlam, Fraser and Hawke governments, arguing that these initiatives solicited the premature formation of a national Indigenous political elite. When the Keating government responded to the High Court's *Mabo* judgment in 1993, Coombs warned that the *Native Title Act* was likely to be, in effect, a sophisticated instrument for extinguishing native title. Coombs' support for Indigenous self-determination did not necessarily align him with people who were promoting the idea of Aboriginal sovereignty: one of the purposes of the treaty for which Coombs campaigned in the early 1980s was to *extinguish* Aboriginal sovereignty, on just terms.[28]

Perhaps the CDEP scheme is the best example of a clear connection between Coombs' field research, his policy creativity and his policy impact. Yet his pride in that scheme can best be described as pragmatic. I recall dining in a foursome with Coombs in the Darwin's Asian Gateway restaurant in 1994. Our two companions made an extended attack on CDEP, using arguments with which Coombs was both familiar and in some agreement. His response, after a friendly but vigorous debate, was to remind us of the economic and cultural circumstances of remote Aboriginal communities and to ask his two critics to suggest a better policy than CDEP. They conceded that, for all its faults, CDEP was the best option for the time being. Our meal ended in a mood of untriumphal political consensus. I wish that those who now evoke Coombs as a misguided policy dogmatist had been at our table to see for themselves the nature of Coombs' political convictions. They were in the best sense experimental and pragmatic.

A Darwinian view of history

A clue to understanding this intellectual and political demeanour is Coombs' forgotten interest in Charles Darwin's view of history. At the time that Coombs was thinking his way into 'Aboriginal affairs' — the late 1960s — he was also reading ethology — the scientific study of the biology of human behaviour. Ethology arose from comparative zoology in the 1930s and 1940s, though the discipline can be traced back to Charles Darwin's 1872 monograph *The expression of emotions in man and animals*. Ethology thinks about human behaviour in the ways that it resembles the behaviours observed in other species. It can pose to human behaviour the question that Darwin's theory of evolution poses to any biological phenomenon: how functional is this or that pattern of 'human nature' in the environment in which it occurs? Ethology can thus share in evolutionary theory's pitiless vision of human history as a small chapter in Nature's history. Ethology can make sense of the competition between and within species to occupy a given order of the world. It can contemplate the competitive destruction of one human way of life or the competitive success of another. From the viewpoint of the theory of evolution, human history is a series of intentional or unintentional experiments in human innovation: some give adaptive advantage, while others fail.

Coombs' scientific sensibility made him curious about human adequacy, and he showed in a 1969 paper, 'Science and the future of man: the role of the social scientist', that he was capable of taking a detached view of the prospects of Australians' adaptive success. The occasion of his address was the Felton Bequest's seventieth birthday symposium for Sir Macfarlane Burnet, *Man and His Science*, on 15 September 1969.[29] Burnet was not only a molecular biologist and immunologist, he was also an exponent of socio-biology, and that was Coombs' way to connect with this occasion. Thinking aloud about Aborigines' past and future from the perspective of evolution, Coombs' address is both the most 'ethological' and the least known of Coombs' writings on Aboriginal affairs. When he published a book of his first ten years of essays and lectures on Aboriginal affairs — *Kulinma* — he omitted his Burnet Symposium paper.[30]

Coombs began by arguing that ethology was 'a link between the observational and experimental biological sciences and the behavioural and social sciences concerned with man himself'.[31] Ethology promised to be 'an integrated chain of sciences of man — sciences which would study aspects of his existence from the bio-chemistry of sub-cellular units within his body, through to the developing cultures of multi-racial communities'.[32] Ethology told Coombs that human nature had evolved, and that 'the scope for learned behaviour is limited by the need to adhere to the basic inherited pattern' that had 'survival value'.[33] Therefore, it was possible for human behaviour to be poorly adapted to environments that had recently and rapidly changed. Drawing attention to human adaptive capacity, Coombs strove to avoid a too-deterministic account. 'There can be no doubt that for the species highest in the evolutionary scale, and particularly for man, learned behaviour and culturally determined behaviour are increasingly important compared with that more completely genetically determined such as that of insects and other such species.'[34] However, even for humans, 'the scope for learned behaviour is limited by the need to adhere to the basic human pattern'.[35]

Coombs then turned to the case of Aborigines. They had evolved over the millennia into a rather different kind of human being from the European colonists who now blithely expected them to turn into waged and salaried employees and small businessmen. He urged that policy take into account such deep differences within human nature. Coombs thus evoked the highly evolved distinct nature of the Aboriginal branch of humanity in order to question the hubris of assimilation policy. In this critical move, Coombs can be likened to such ethological critics of the human sciences as Robin Fox. In his early 1970s essay 'Anthropology as a vocation', Fox was scornful of what he characterised as a 'liberal' ideological formation within the behavioural sciences that had dismissed neo-Darwinian science. Liberals' belief in 'progress, reform, the perfectibility of man — or at least his social improvement' had led them to see as reactionary any approach to human behaviour that gave causal weight to inheritance, to 'human nature'.[36] In Fox's view, there was a naive pact between certain assumptions about government and modern behavioural science: both placed their faith in the malleability of humans and both were indifferent to the profoundly evolved and stubbornly determinative significance of the behavioural patterns that have enjoyed evolutionary success. In a very specific sense, we may label as 'conservative' Fox's critique of liberal optimism in government and the human sciences. Coombs' doubts about 'assimilation' in 1969 were in this sense 'conservative' doubts.

Coombs' argument from an ethological understanding of Aborigines' predicament contributed to his rethinking of Australian policies towards Aborigines. Australian Aborigines had evolved culturally and psychologically to fit certain environmental demands. However, their environment and thus these demands had recently been altered radically by colonisation. Aborigines were now threatened by a 'disparity between the environment they must now live in and that for which their capacities have in the past been developed'.[37] In particular, European compulsion had had three effects on Aborigines:

(a) his mutual relationship with the land and the natural environment is destroyed;
(b) the 'cleverness' with which evolution endowed him ceases to have survival value, and 'industriousness', which in the past has been of neutral or negative significance, is regularly demanded of him;
(c) the natural and ritualistic outlets for his aggression are lost with his divorce from the land and the atrophy of his tribal and ceremonial life.[38]

Add the impact of diseases, European aggression and a sense of 'hopelessness and despair', and it was no wonder that Aborigines had come close to extinction since the British had overrun their habitat.[39]

Coombs was not attracted by pessimistic scenarios, and so he pointed to a fortunate feature of Aborigines' nature that would give them a chance. This evolved capacity for Aborigines' 'wise passiveness' had proved adaptive 'in a situation where aggression had proved futile'.[40]

In the winter of 1969, Coombs thought that he saw in Australians a new resolve to treat Aborigines with respect. If based on study of the evolved nature of Aboriginal people, a reformed approach to Indigenous affairs policy could be a 'living test of the usefulness of ethology'.[41] Taking the lessons of ethology, policy-makers must now study Aboriginal nature and its relationship with a radically modified environment. Policy-makers must learn 'enough of the inherited capacities and culturally modified behaviour of the Aboriginal people so as intelligently and humanely to make a place for them in our society'.[42] The inherited patterns of Aboriginal behaviour that made them different from Europeans would have to be studied in order to find out 'what opportunities and handicaps do these differences present for them in the task of coming to terms with our competitive and acquisitive world'.[43]

However, Aborigines would not be the only objects of the policy-oriented ethology recommended by Coombs. The inherited patterns of non-Aboriginal behaviour would have to be studied too, for it was the responsibility and the opportunity of non-Aboriginal Australians 'to ease the path of these our fellows and to profit from the richness of their culture and experience'.[44] Aborigines and non-Aborigines would each have to work out the extent to which they could adapt to the challenge posed by the other.

Learning from experiment

Coombs' 1969 foray into ethology helps to ground my invitation to rethink the phrase 'the Coombs experiment'. What makes the term 'Coombs experiment' gratuitously polemical is that those who advocate alternative policies to those advocated by Coombs do not acknowledge that the enactment of their proposals would also be an experiment. It would be an experiment in the two ways that Coombs distinguished in his 1969 paper. On the one hand, any policy directed towards Indigenous Australians implies certain hypotheses about the behavioural dispositions of Indigenous Australians: hypotheses about what Aborigines can change in the short term and what is too deep-seated in their evolved nature to be changed in a brief period. On the other hand — and equally important — any suite of policies addressed to Indigenous Australians is an assertion about what is malleable, and what is essential and non-negotiable, in the ways of non-Aboriginal Australians. To remove the pejorative connotations of 'experiment', we can admit that Indigenous policy is a tradition of experimental interventions on Indigenous and non-Indigenous patterns of behaviour. To acknowledge that Coombs' Indigenous policy ideas were 'experimental' is not to impugn his heartlessness, but to acknowledge his intellectual humility.

Caricatures of Coombs have become reactionary bling — cheap ornamental devices sported by a few revisionist policy intellectuals, a prop for their political hubris. Competent biography is my antidote: Coombs often feared for the experiment in self-determination that he was advocating.

In November 1969, addressing a meeting of the Society of Friends in the comfortable Sydney suburb of Wahroonga, Coombs described Aboriginal political culture as he understood it. He said that Aboriginal people had not yet developed decision-making procedures to apply to some of the matters that were now confronting them:

> Problems which arise out of their new social situation — relationships with Europeans, the conduct of community affairs, even keeping the camp tidy — present difficulties. There does not seem to be any traditional way for them to act socially. It is therefore exceedingly difficult for them to confront a highly organised society such as our own. Their traditional structure gives nobody clear authority to speak for them and they find it hard to evolve ways of choosing such persons.[45]

These thoughts drew upon a year of thinking and discussion about the possible evolution of remote Aboriginal political institutions. Earlier in that year, Coombs had begun to sketch the political forms through which Yolngu might be able pursue their joint interests. In March 1969, he circulated a paper called 'Social aspects of the Yirrkala problem', in which he outlined a form of association that would enable Yolngu to determine collectively the forms of economic development on their land. There would be a museum, an art and craft centre, a language study facility and a motel for tourists interested in Aboriginal culture. A trust made up of Elders would supervise these facilities, clans would register as lodges or friendly societies, and Rotarians might possibly be persuaded to offer Yolngu managerial advice. At his suggestion, Yirrkala would become a village, and there would be a Yirrkala Community Society to engage in enterprises ancillary to the bauxite mine. Royalties from the mine, paid into a Yirrkala Trust Fund, would help to finance these developments. Through William Stanner, Coombs circulated these plans to anthropologists at the Australian National University, asking for comment. By September 1969, Coombs' Yirrkala plan was in its third draft. However, Stanner warned Coombs that what he was sketching would impose greatly on Yolngu. Better to wait and to listen, Stanner counselled, and to try to come to a better understanding of the pattern of local authority among Yolngu.

Stanner was visiting the Gove Peninsula while Coombs was explaining to his Wahroonga audience why Aborigines found collective political action beyond their traditional concerns difficult. Upon his return, he told Coombs that he was just beginning to understand how firmly Yolngu were adhering to their traditions, and how shocked and alienated they were by the beginnings of the bauxite mine. He was highly critical of the demands that Coombs' Yirrkala Village scheme would make on Yolngu, and he predicted that Yolngu would protect themselves from the novelties visited upon them by dispersing to their homelands in the Arnhem Land

Reserve. At best, Stanner advised, Coombs' ideas about Yirrkala political development were 'experimental and promissory'.[46] By the beginning of 1970, the Council for Aboriginal Affairs was thus divided in its assessment of how to model the adaptive development of Yolngu in North-East Arnhem Land.

At that moment, they learned that Yolngu were taking the collective action that Stanner had predicted: many of them were dispersing from Yirrkala. Coombs' hypothesis — that adaptive social and political effort by Yolngu would focus on Yirrkala and intensify as formalised associations — had been falsified. Yolngu had voted with their feet. To Coombs' surprise, their capacity for a collective response to impending change took the form of becoming less 'collective'. After learning more about the Yolngu dispersal, Coombs reassessed what he thought he knew about remote Indigenous people's aspirations and resilience. No longer did he promote his Yirrkala Village scheme; instead, he made himself the theorist and apologist of the outstation movement. After visiting other remote regions where Aborigines were decentralising, he wrote a paper that became his 1974 presidential address to the Anthropology section of ANZAAS.[47]

Experiments in the formalisation of Indigenous political capacities were again on the reform agenda when the Whitlam government drafted the Bill for Aboriginal land rights in the Northern Territory. The Bill gave statutory design to the Central and Northern Land Councils, which had arisen in 1973–74 to serve the Woodward Royal Commission's need for advice from Aboriginal land-owners, anthropologists and lawyers. What permanent shape should the land rights statute now give these bodies? There were issues of scale and responsibility to ponder, yet — apart from South Australia's 1966 experiment in a statewide land trust — there was no heritage of policy to draw upon. In 1975, Coombs and Stanner knew that Yolngu thought that the Northern Land Council covered too large an area; Yolngu wanted more and smaller Land Councils, such as an Eastern Arnhem Land Council. In a draft report on Arnhem Land, Coombs and Stanner endorsed the idea of a regional land council for Yolngu, and they ventured that perhaps there should be several regional Land Councils within Central Australia too. Their colleague in the Council for Aboriginal Affairs, Barrie Dexter, resisted publicising this idea; as secretary of the Department of Aboriginal Affairs, Dexter worried that the Coombs/Stanner/Yolngu argument would fuel criticism of the already controversial Land Rights Bill. Coombs and Stanner saw his point, and they accepted his compromise that the Bill should include a mechanism for allowing regional Land Councils to form whenever they could make a political case to the minister for breaking away from the Northern or Central Land Councils. Coombs and Stanner also accepted a feature of the Bill about which Yolngu had been critical: that the Land Councils should distribute royalties from mining, with benefits going wider than the clans on whose land a mine stood. Finally, Coombs and Stanner agreed that the large Land Councils, rather than smaller regional bodies, be entrusted with the task of negotiating with companies and governments on behalf of traditional owners. In short, Coombs and Stanner put aside much of what Yolngu had said to them about the design of the institutions of the new land rights regime. Persuaded by Dexter, they agreed in the winter of 1975 to institutional innovations that they knew many Yolngu would question. That is, they allied themselves with a governmental project — the *Aboriginal Land Rights (Northern Territory) Act* — that they knew to be a challenge to Indigenous capacities for adaptation and political innovation. That was their wager, their hypothesis to be tested by enacting their design; they could not know that they were right. They were complicit in the conducting of an experiment — any recognition of Indigenous rights is an experiment in the formation of new political subjects, collective actors without precedent.

Coombs subsequently had reason to think that Yolngu had been right in their misgivings about the size of the Land Councils. In *Obliged to be difficult*, I tell some stories about Coombs' unsuccessful effort in 1977 and 1978 to mediate between the newly formed Northern Land Council and the Aboriginal traditional owners in the Alligator Rivers region over the development of uranium mines. I also give an account of Coombs' consultancy, in 1982–83, about the redesign of the Central Land Council. That consultancy is a good example of an intelligent appraisal of an experiment, an inquiry into what can be learned from experience, one that never gives up on the human capacity to deal thoughtfully with acknowledged problems.

What is radical?

Helen Hughes' phrase 'socialist experiment' implies that Coombs' approach to Indigenous policy was radical. Informed by what I have explained so far, an alternative view is possible: impressed with a sense of the evolved 'wise passivity' of Aborigines, Coombs sought correctives to the radical hubris of 'assimilation'. Assimilation policies continued and intensified the radically disruptive impact of colonisation, as Paul Hasluck — historian and politician — explained to the ANZAAS Conference in 1959:

> Looked at from one point of view, the weakness of the old aboriginal society and of the present-day groups of aborigines is an advantage. The more it crumbles the more readily may its fragments by mingled with the rest of the people living in Australia. Looked at from another point of view, the disappearance of aboriginal society leaves the aboriginal person with limited capacity to assert himself or to service his own interests.[48]

Hasluck's admission of risk is a mark of his intellectual honesty: he was ambivalent about his own radical agency, aligned as it was with colonisation's destructive trajectory. He did not live long enough to consider Noel Pearson's argument (Chapter 8) that the climax of assimilation — the formal equality of Indigenous entitlement in the late 1960s/early 1970s — became colonisation's most destructive historical conjuncture, at least in the remote regions. Taking Hasluck's and Pearson's theses together, we have the context of Coombs' Darwinian epiphany in 1969: that there was enough surviving social order among Aborigines and Torres Strait Islanders to warrant the government's careful nurturing of the as yet unextinguished collective capacity of Indigenous Australians to assert themselves and to service their own interests. Coombs sought to slow things down, to give time and space for Indigenous Australians to make choices about which elements of European-Australian culture to embrace and about how quickly they would embrace them. More a conservative than a 'radical', Coombs advocated continuity, and perhaps over-estimated its possibility. He wanted Aboriginal adults to be empowered to maintain some authority over the socialisation of their children.

My re-labelling of Coombs as a 'conservative' is itself open to qualification if we consider that one of the persistent values in Coombs' policy advocacy is 'choice' — a central item in the vocabulary of liberalism. Thus in 1983 (with Brandl and Snowdon) he advocated that 'Aboriginal communities should have the right to choose to have control over the schooling of their children: of the building, the school organisation, the curriculum and the choice of teachers';[49] and in 1994 he advocated an Aboriginal education policy that would 'guarantee to every Aboriginal community the right of choice for its children between a government school, a private or religious-based school, or an independent Aboriginal school responsible to the community it serves'.[50] This upholding of the parental right of choice is a version of liberalism on which Julia Gillard and Tony Abbott could agree.

However, the liberal emphasis on choice is open to competing inflections when we come to the question of who or what is doing the choosing. The matter for policy debate now is: who do we imagine to be the choosing agent? What is the 'self' in self-determination? I see three possible choosing agents: the individual, the family/household and the community. All three will usually be in play, to some degree.

The underlying structure of political debate about Indigenous policy in recent years can be conceptualised as a consideration about how Indigenous individuals, Indigenous households/families or Indigenous communities should combine to be the 'self' that chooses the combination of strategies for Indigenous flourishing. Mal Brough, minister in the Howard government, thus helped to define a policy direction when he stated in 2006 that governments had for too long 'focused on the collective Aboriginal community at the expense of considering the needs and aspirations of the individuals and families that make up those communities'.[51]

If there was something distinctive, valuable and open to intelligent debate in Coombs' policy thinking, I suggest it was the emphasis that he placed on local communities as political agents. In his hope that Indigenous communities would evolve into agents of collective choice and action, Coombs was at his most experimental. That is, his vision of self-determination rested on a hypothesis that Indigenous Australians who had only recently lived as nomadic hunter-gatherers could be like non-Indigenous Australians in at least one respect: their capacity for local corporate action and municipal cohesion.

In the eyes of some observers, the Coombs hypothesis of an emergent Indigenous capacity for local self-government has been disproven. So what might replace that hopeful vision? Whatever the answers to that question, I urge the authors of the new policies on the labour market, municipal government, land tenure and homelands to admit that imposed, accelerated change is just as experimental as the raft of Coombsian 'autonomy' policies that policy revisionists have condemned. The new policies advocated by those who condemn 'the Coombs experiment' are experimental in that they implicitly hypothesise that underneath apparent differences between Indigenous and non-Indigenous approaches to working, governing and associating, there is a latent commonality of potential to be waged workers, to be entrepreneurial land-owners, to be home-owners, to be small businessmen and women and to be town-dwellers. They urge governments to act as if that hypothesis — their neo-liberal social imaginary — were true.

I can't be sure that this revisionist hypothesis of an emergent commonality of Indigenous and non-Indigenous aspirations and social forms is false. However, I am sure that the only way to test this hypothesis is by acting as if it were true and then examining how much damage and how much good those actions do. Innovations in policy are never without risk. Settler colonial societies do not have any instruction manuals when they seek to deal with the consequences of their colonisation of Indigenous people: all policies that nations such as Australia pursue towards Indigenous people are unavoidably experimental, and their intended and unintended consequences have to be faced with intellectual honesty and political courage, and without sentimental demonisation of the policy intellectuals and Indigenous people who have supported them.[52]

In telling these stories of Coombs' changes of mind, I wish to counter Peter Sutton's recent characterisation of Coombs as given to 'idealistic but unrealistic fantasy'.[53] Drawing in part on my writing about Coombs, Sutton concludes that Coombs

> seemed able to accommodate a profound contradiction, namely the view that Aboriginal people would find it feasible to maintain major cultural and social structural patterns from their traditional past while at the same time pursuing economic and other forms of modernisation in bureaucratic and corporate ways derived from industrial society.[54]

Complicit with the prevailing caricature of Coombs, Sutton's reasoning here took liberties with the reader. Let's examine Sutton's assumptions that, first, we can distinguish easily between reality and fantasy and, second, there is a clear difference between Coombs' qualities of mind (his ability to accommodate contradiction) on the one hand, and the reality external to Coombs' mind (that a less contradictory cast of mind than Coombs' would have apprehended clearly) on the other. Against both of Sutton's assumptions, I suggest a more historically nuanced view that *the reality with which Coombs was dealing was itself contradictory and was amenable to different ways of performing it.* Aborigines were manifesting both 'traditional' and 'modern' inclinations. Another way to say this is that, in remote Australia, among the realities that government is constantly investigating — whether government cares to admit this or not — are the realities of similarity and difference. We can see Coombs as experimentally working within these realities. Thus it was 'realistic' for Coombs to interact with these realities, to engage in practical explorations of their dynamics, the unpredictable configuration of behaviours and dispositions (which we sometimes tendentiously label 'traditional' and 'modern'). It is not so much that Coombs was unable to manage a contradiction in his mind (by a more disciplined effort to think consistently); it was more that he saw no alternative but to inhabit, in his political practice, the contradictions in a complex social reality. Within the epistemology implied by Sutton, a political engagement is open to the evaluative question of whether it was based on a rational appreciation of reality. I suggest that a more adequate epistemology allows that Coombs inhabited a reality with contradictory tendencies, a scene open to competing readings and to interventions that contributed to diverse emergent configurations of the customary and the imposed. He could be surprised and at times rebuffed by this reality's dynamics.

These episodes in Coombs' policy advocacy teach us that the design of Indigenous political institutions is both a troubling and an unavoidable task in public policy. The trouble occasioned by Indigenous political innovation is endless. It is productive trouble, and we would be foolish to seek to avoid it. The episodes I have narrated and on which Sutton has commented were essays in Coombs' political humility and hope.

Is Aboriginal autonomy sustainable?

The idea has become potent that Indigenous Australians have revealed themselves to be too 'dysfunctional' to be self-determining political subjects. Indeed, in our ever-improving ability to measure the condition of contemporary Aboriginal people, we have become better informed about the breadth and depth of mental health problems, of psycho-social pathologies manifest in suicide, the abuse of alcohol and other substances and family violence, including sexual abuse of children. Ah Kit's term 'dysfunctional' can be illustrated very easily. The literature on Indigenous psycho-social morbidity was synthesised to great effect by Rosemary Neill in her 2002 book *White out*. It was reasonable for her to ask whether people so disabled have sufficient emotional resources for the emotionally demanding processes of politics.

One of the differences between Coombs' time and ours is that it did not occur to him to ask that question, whereas we can no longer avoid it. Some anthropologists recently have speculated that Aboriginal society has changed very rapidly since Coombs interacted, forty years ago, with Elders in the Northern Territory who had spent their childhood in worlds scarcely changed by colonial contact. Jeremy Beckett has recently noted:

> Looking at Aboriginal society, one finds some critical changes: sedentarism, increased social density, and an explosion of the under-15 age cohort have all pulled Aboriginal society out of shape, into a different shape which has to some degree stabilised in recent years. What kind of culture is really being reproduced in Aboriginal communities? One suspects that the teachers and role models are not only, or even mainly, the elders, who are by now sickly and outnumbered. One finds few answers to this question in the literature. Moreover, even if pornographic videos are banned, Aboriginal people in the present are exposed to global media, sports and music, matters to which anthropologists have started to pay attention only in recent times.[55]

Marcia Langton has suggested that anthropology is reeling from 'the shock of the new', including 'the rapid demographic change in the Aboriginal population of the last half century'.[56] Australianist anthropology, she continues,

> is much influenced by the ethnographies of an Aboriginal world governed by a gerontocracy and supported by hunter-gatherer economies and ways of life. This world no longer exists in much of Australia, and where these institutions survive, they are compromised and altered by welfare dependency, modern consumerism and a range of conditions associated with a rapid transition to modernity.[57]

The research literature of academic anthropology has tended to neglect generational differences, according to Langton, yielding a misleadingly 'gerontocratic' model of Aboriginal society.[58]

In Coombs' work, the possibility of what I am calling here psychosocial pathology came up only once, as far as I know, and that was in *A certain heritage*, the book he co-authored with Warren Snowdon and Maria Brandl in 1983. Brandl, Coombs and Snowdon suggest that 'Aboriginal socialization processes are adequate so long as they are not subject to outside interference'.[59] They maintain that when those processes were interfered with (sometimes inadvertently), the result was 'non-traditional conflicts and confusions within Aboriginal society, and misunderstandings between Aboriginal society and the wider community', giving rise to such 'problems or symptoms of problems' as petrol-sniffing, alcohol abuse and gambling.[60] They warn of 'conflict and uncertainty' in the minds of students subject to the 'hidden curriculum' of Australian schooling, unless that schooling is designed by Aboriginal parents.[61] Their hypothesis is that psycho-social morbidity is an effect of inappropriate external intervention into an otherwise healthy cultural domain.

In Peter Sutton's *The politics of suffering*, psycho-social pathology is no longer a threatening possibility but a given fact, a condition whose genesis Sutton seeks to illuminate by highlighting what he considers to be a neglected contributor to malaise: Aboriginal culture itself. He argues that Aboriginal child-rearing practices have been much more robust than we have supposed; far from being under threat from modern practices of state and market, they have not been threatened enough, and their persistence keeps producing values and dispositions that ill-equip Aboriginal people for living in contemporary Australia. Aboriginal socialisation used to produce persons and relationships that worked well in a hunter-gatherer economy, Sutton argues, but those same socialisation practices produce persons and relationships that are inappropriate to the world in which all Aborigines now find themselves. The persistence of Aboriginal tradition, he suggests, contributes significantly to Aborigines' psycho-social pathology.

It is interesting to compare Sutton's view of Aboriginal socialisation processes with that offered nearly 30 years ago by Brandl, Coombs and Snowdon. Both write of Aboriginal socialisation practices as intact and continuing — at least in remote regions. Both propose that there is a tension between traditional Aboriginal socialisation practices and the regimes of value and personality that go with the normal workings of state institutions and labour markets. And both say that what is at stake in the playing out of this tension is the psycho-social well-being of Aboriginal Australians. Where Sutton differs from Brandl, Coombs and Snowdon is in his assumptions about the fundamental architecture of Australian society. For Brandl, Coombs and Snowdon, settler colonial society was an incomplete hegemony, and it was possible for them to imagine Australian institutions redesigned so that they left space for Aboriginal people.

This returns us to Coombs' brief public exploration of a 'Darwinian' perspective on colonial history, and in particular to his challenge to non-

Aboriginal to adapt intelligently to the persistent and inescapable presence of Aboriginal civilisation within the nation. What, in practice, could such adaptations include? Coombs indeed saw potential for non-Aboriginal adaptation. The historical geography of colonisation meant that there was literally space for Aboriginal difference to flourish — vast 'unalienated' regions, increasingly under Aboriginal title, over which Aboriginal people were re-dispersing themselves as outstations of homelands. These territories could be a distinct socio-cultural space too, argued Brandl, Coombs and Snowdon, as long as public policy was wise enough to adapt the routines of education and of labour to the practices and values of Aboriginal people living on their own land. And — not least — Coombs saw in Australia's federal constitution considerable scope for adaptation. In a 1985 essay reflecting on the 'treaty' campaign, he wrote:

> There does not seem any real constitutional difficulty, at least in respect of groups of communities geographically marginal or external to the Australian mainland, in their being offered a status as a Commonwealth territory or territories with a form of self-government ... There is already a variety of such Commonwealth Territories with various degrees of autonomy.[62]

Whether or not one considers this to be a good idea, the inescapable Darwinian question is: Was there any necessity for Australian institutions to adapt in these ways to the continuing presence of Aboriginal ways? Would Australia's survival be at risk were Australia not to experiment with ways of accommodating a persistently different Aboriginal way of life?

In Coombs' and Darwin's thinking, there was such pressure to adapt — an evolved imperative for societies to develop their moral community. In Chapter 5 of *The descent of man*, 'On the development of the intellectual and moral faculties during primeval and civilised times', Darwin argues that humans may adapt to the changing demands of their environments not only through changes in their bodies and physical capabilities — as continuing animal species do — but also (and much more so) through the intelligent redesign of their technologies, including their political technologies, their institutions and the ideals that sustain such institutions. 'Sympathy, fidelity and courage', he inferred, had proven to be adaptive human qualities, and a sense of honour — our love of praise, our dread of blame — was for Darwin a causally significant, primeval human mechanism in the evolution of human altruism.[63] Societies lacking an institutionalised moral commitment to solidarity were, in his view, unlikely to flourish:

> Ultimately our moral sense or conscience becomes a highly complex sentiment — originating in the social instincts, largely guided by the approbation of our fellow men, ruled by reason, self-interest, and in later times by deep religious feelings, and confirmed by instruction and habit.[64]

If Coombs was exploring, with conviction, the implications of a Darwinian understanding of evolved Indigenous nature and its adaptive potential, he was also publicly probing non-Indigenous sensibility — that is, thinking aloud what might induce non-Indigenous Australians to strengthen the fragile moral roots of their nationhood. This was one of his themes in 1979 when, in a series of three addresses, he began to advocate a treaty between Australia and its Indigenous peoples. He put it to Australians that their nationhood — their codes of social solidarity — was deeply impaired by their domination of Aborigines: without a treaty, their nationhood was morally shallow and increasingly subject to hostile international scrutiny.[65] He campaigned for an agreed extinguishment of Aboriginal sovereignty on just terms. Just as, for Darwin, advanced societies were advanced because they honoured and institutionalised certain codes of social solidarity, so for Coombs, Australians' social cohesion required fundamental repair of its moral foundations. Acquiring its land base by conquest and incorporating Aborigines by coercion had put Australia in jeopardy. In this perspective (unconvincing to many Australians), the adaptation of Australian institutions to Aborigines' difference would not be gratuitous kindness but an evolutionary necessity. Darwin and Coombs were both evolutionary moralists of community and civilisation.

In contrast to Coombs, Peter Sutton, in his *Politics of suffering*, does not explore the adaptive potential of non-Aboriginal Australians, for he is working with a much more homogeneous model of contemporary Australia. In this model — as plausible as that of Coombs — the disappearance of the hunter-gatherer economy and the more recent fading of the colonial surrogates of the hunter-gatherer economy — the missions and pastoral stations of remote Australia — have effectively extinguished a viable Aboriginal domain into which it would be appropriate to continue to socialise children in the old ways. Even the most remote Aborigines have lost their autonomy over the last four decades — in this way of thinking about Australia — and the erstwhile zones of autonomy evoked by Brandl, Coombs and Snowdon have soured into enclaves of a hopeless, mutually destructive sociality — the milieu represented in such films as *Samson and Delilah* and *Toomelah*. Indeed, had Sutton addressed the work of Brandl, Coombs and Snowdon explicitly, he might have said:

> You may have been right, around 1980, to point to the vulnerability of the remote Aboriginal domain to the alien structures of learning, working and social control that were pressing on it; but you were wrong to think that anything could be done, by way of wiser public policy and institutional design, to defend that domain as a space in which Aboriginal traditions of child-rearing and relatedness would continue to be appropriate. That zone of relative autonomy has deteriorated and is disappearing; its continuity must cease to be an assumption of public policy.

So we are now faced with two conflicting hypotheses about the signi-ficance of continuing neo-traditional socialisation practices among remote-region Aborigines. Reflecting field experience in remote Aboriginal Australia in the 1970s, and in critical reaction to Hasluck's assimilationism, the Coombs hypothesis led us to public policies about land tenure, labour markets, outstation infrastructure and schooling that aimed to maintain much of the neo-traditional Aboriginal domain. The Sutton hypothesis derives credibility from its author's field experience over the last 40 years, and also from our greater capacity for measuring what we now call 'the gaps' between Indigenous and non-Indigenous well-being. The Sutton hypothesis — that the relatively autonomous domains of remote Aboriginal Australia are fast disappearing and that what remains of them now handicaps Indigenous integration — recapitulates Hasluck's view in the 1950s that, while Aboriginal identity and culture might persist in limited ways (similar to Scots heritage, as Hasluck suggested), Aboriginal 'society' was doomed, if not already extinguished.

Conclusion

If we can avoid conflating our account of Coombs the man with our evaluation of the policies that he advocated, then we will be showing more intellectual subtlety than many of Coombs' recent critics. Some policy critics have mingled their critical reflection on land rights and CDEP policies — a necessary activity — with a gross caricature of the author of one of these policies: the 'socialist', romantic, fantastic, anti-capitalist, anti-mining, centralist experimenter HC Coombs. They have thus done two disservices to our understanding. They have caricatured Coombs — and, as his biographer, I have urged my factual correctives. More serious is their disservice to our understanding of government itself — particularly of government as an activity of knowledge-production. I have argued in this chapter that we should not be shamed by the word 'experiment', and I have illustrated the experimental character of Coombs' policy activism. He always worked from a horizon of limited knowledge and frail conjecture; for me to show that he did so is perhaps the best contribution that I can make, as his biographer, to a discussion of our current policy dilemmas.

The Coombs experiment has been a chapter in a longer experiment that British people initiated by colonising this continent; that longer experiment is a continuing self-interested exploration of the ways in which Aboriginal and non-Aboriginal Australians are similar and different. Every project of government — from growing bush tomatoes to creating 'Territory growth towns' — enacts hypotheses about Aboriginal becoming: their latent and emergent similarity to non-Aborigines, their latent and emerging differences from non-Aborigines. The question is whether we will acknowledge the experimental nature of our policy hunches by adopting a thoughtful, open-minded approach to the intended and unintended consequences of these interventions. Here I am going beyond the question of whether our policies will be evidence-based. It has been well established in the philosophy of science that evidence is 'theory-laden'. It thus makes sense to ask: What intellectual and administrative practices have constituted what we now count as policy-relevant evidence? One feature of the 'evidence' that we should not take for granted is that government agencies rarely share responsibility for data collection with those they are monitoring. Sullivan points to what could be done if Indigenous organisations were taken more seriously: 'Funded and regulated by government (and carried out by community organisation), client appraisals, surveys, community juries and relational contracting can be used to develop trust between the parties.'[66]

Using statistics collected by government agencies, the COAG National Indigenous Reform Agreement has set out in detail the 'evidence' that governments will use to assess their efforts to 'Close the Gaps'. In the evidentiary framework of 'Closing the Gaps', we can see the contemporary influence within Australian governments of assuming the truth of the

Hasluck/Sutton hypothesis of a fatally stricken 'Aboriginal society'. The statistical apparatus of the National Indigenous Reform Agreement is a reassertion, in an apparently objective idiom, of this assumption. 'Closing the Gaps' assumes that there are ultimately no differences between Indigenous and non-Indigenous aspirations. We are thus diverted from an alternative notion of social justice that has an honourable liberal lineage: social justice as the right of minority peoples to choose the ways in which they engage with majorities — even if those choices include continuing material deprivation. Our public policy thinking at the moment is dominated by a fixation on equality of outcome, to the effective exclusion of considering how to allow Indigenous Australians choices in their mode of engagement. Let me give three examples of the way the proposed measurement of 'Closing the Gaps' begs or obscures the question of Indigenous choice.

The Reform Strategy indicators for 'economic participation' include data on participation in CDEP. However, because there is no such thing as a non-Indigenous rate of participation in CDEP, it is not clear what the measurement of CDEP participation has to do with a strategy of 'closing the gaps' — unless we assume that the goal of Closing the Gaps is to phase out all CDEP participation, in the belief that CDEP participation is not 'really' a form of economic participation. We should not prejudge the benefits of CDEP. Its social utility should be matter of ongoing reviews that are sensitive to the context of each scheme,[67] and to the changing ways that 'work' and 'employment' are understood by CDEP's Indigenous clients as meaningful and desirable.[68] CDEP may have been a beneficial component of what Jon Altman has been theorising as the remote 'hybrid economy'.[69] It should be neither defended or condemned — as for the most part it has been — on the basis of holistic models of the Australian or Aboriginal social orders.

The unit of analysis for reporting statistics about 'closing the gaps' is to be the jurisdiction — that is, each of the six States and two Territories. To report by jurisdiction, however, makes it difficult to see regional differences within jurisdictions and thus to consider 'outcome' in the context of regionally differentiated opportunity and aspiration. A jurisdiction-based grammar for portraying disparity implies that the aspirations and opportunities of urban Aborigines are to be viewed in the same way as the aspirations and opportunities of people in remote communities — as if each State/Territory has its calculable 'average' Indigenous person or household. We need indicators of well-being that allow regional distinctions to emerge. If, for technical reasons, such disaggregation is difficult, then we must be cautious in our use of the data we have.

Finally, within the magnificent statistical grid that now makes disparity between Aborigines and non-Aborigines visible, there are no statistical indicators of the strength or weakness of a variable that the authors of the framework describe in the following words: '*Effective engagement* with Indigenous communities is critical to ensuring that Indigenous people's needs and aspirations are built into the planning and implementation of initiatives agreed by COAG.'[70] That is, while the Reform Strategy has operational definitions of education, health and employment that make it possible to measure 'gaps' between Indigenous and non-Indigenous Australians, 'it is difficult to establish numerical indicators of governance'.[71] Yet 'governance and leadership' is recognised by the Council of Australian Governments (COAG) as one of seven 'strategic areas for action'.[72] I do not doubt that many in government are working on this 'variable'.[73] However, because no measuring instrument makes it statistically visible as a disparity, the reporting of social justice as the closing of quantified gaps tends to fail to mention the quality of political engagement between Australian governments and Indigenous peoples. This implicit demotion of the political variable contributes to what Sullivan calls 'a changing policy consensus, about how Aboriginal people, their settlements, communities and service organisations are to be imagined within the overarching polity of Australian governance'.[74]

The Closing the Gaps paradigm of social justice is thus equipped with an acute instrument for measuring certain disparities according to certain assumptions. But this is a theory-laden instrument; it embodies ways of thinking about well-being that are valid within a certain perspective but not exhaustive of possible ways of thinking about well-being. The Closing the Gaps policy and its reflexive apparatus are a benign Cyclops — a one-eyed giant, an experimental juggernaut of goodwill, possessing only a partial capacity to reflect on the results of its experiments.

THE APPEAL OF QUANTIFICATION

CHAPTER 11

The Australian Reconciliation Barometer and the Indigenous Imaginary

> Aboriginal people who not so long ago were represented as newly emancipated and enfranchised, struggling proudly through their own institutions to march towards a new dawn both modern and exotic, are now represented as culpable by their own aberrant behaviour of the appalling conditions that, despite the good will and considerable expense of the public, they persist in perpetuating.[1]

To the extent that Sullivan's description of a shift in public perception is credible, could Reconciliation Australia inadvertently be contributing to it? In June 2010, Reconciliation Australia released the second edition of its four-part study, the Australian Reconciliation Barometer. The product of research by Auspoll, the Barometer has been set up to 'measure the progress of recon-ciliation between Indigenous and non-Indigenous Australians'.[2] The first surveys were conducted in 2008, and they will be repeated every second year. On my reading, the terms of the Barometer reinforce a public perception of Indigenous incapacity.

There is much to welcome in the Barometer. It breaks new ground in the campaign for 'reconciliation' by constituting the two parties to 'reconciliation' as two comparable publics: the 'general community' and the 'Indigenous'. As well as asking questions of a representative national sample (n=1220 in 2010), in which Indigenous Australian respondents would be only a tiny few (20–30 respondents), Auspoll solicited an 'Indigenous' sample (n=704 in 2010). This is a welcome recognition of the 'Indigenous public'.

In a June 2010 media release, Reconciliation Australia highlighted certain findings:

- Some 87 per cent of all Australians believe the relationship between Indigenous and non-Indigenous Australians is important and 48 per cent say it is improving.
- Some 58 per cent of Indigenous people think that the Australian parliament's 2008 apologies to the Stolen Generations have improved the relationship.
- Around 67 per cent of general community respondents assess their 'knowledge about Indigenous culture' as 'fairly low' or 'very low'.
- Around four out of five 'Australians' believe it is important to know more about Indigenous history and culture and are open to learning more.
- Only 9 per cent of all Australians feel that trust between the two groups is good — we still don't trust each other.
- A high proportion of both the general community and the Indigenous samples believe that there is much prejudice between Indigenous and non-Indigenous Australians.
- Few Australians trust media representations of Indigenous Australians: only 9 per cent of Indigenous people and 16 per cent of the general population do so.
- Approximately 59 per cent of all Australians believe in the special place of Indigenous people, connection to the land and family relationships, but only 44 per cent say Indigenous people are open to sharing their culture.
- Some 91 per cent of Indigenous Australians believe past policies still affect Indigenous people.[3]

In its media release, Reconciliation Australia said very little to interpret these items of information.

In this chapter, I will offer my interpretation of the data generated by Auspoll. I will argue that the questions posed by the Reconciliation Barometer imply that 'reconciliation' is largely a project to overcome two problems: Indigenous socio-economic disadvantage, as measured by Australia's official statistics ('closing the gaps'); and non-Indigenous Australians' negative views of Indigenous Australians. I will further suggest that it is difficult to pursue 'reconciliation' when it is framed in these terms because one understanding of 'Indigenous disadvantage' — that it is exacerbated by a lack of Indigenous responsibility — reinforces rather than undermines many non-Indigenous Australians' negative perceptions of Indigenous Australians. Worse — and largely by omission — the Barometer itself fails to imagine Indigenous agency, political capacity and responsibility in positive terms. Thus, in the Barometer, the attributes of people-hood are overshadowed by the representation of Indigenous Australians as a disadvantaged population.

Before discussing the Auspoll findings in detail, it is necessary to pause to consider two key words: 'relationship' and 'reconciliation'.

The many meanings of reconciliation

There continues to be a struggle over the meaning of 'reconciliation'. Angela Pratt's content analysis of parliamentary speeches between June 1991 and December 2000 distinguishes nine senses:

1. recognition of Indigenous-specific rights
2. not recognising Indigenous-specific rights
3. should not be about guilt for past wrongs
4. practical improvements to Indigenous life chances
5. recognition of Indigenous, history, culture, heritage
6. relational and/or attitudinal
7. 'people's movement'/'grass-roots'.
8. a general sense of goodwill, including national unity
9. cynicism of reconciliation as 'politically correct'.[4]

The questions asked by the Reconciliation Barometer effectively mobilise senses 4–8 — that is, the Barometer did not test the public's opinions about Indigenous-specific rights (1 and 2), and it did not explore the public's sense of guilt (or rejection of guilt) (3); nor did it explore the public's cynicism about 'reconciliation' as an imposed 'political correctness' (9).

Behind the different senses of 'reconciliation' is a word whose complexity is rarely noticed: 'relationship'. When the Barometer refers to 'the relationship between Indigenous and non-Indigenous Australians', the term 'relationship' has at least three possible meanings:

1. *The statistical relationship between two measured entities:* the similarity/difference between the value of a variable measured in one population and the value of the same variable measured in the other population. For example, the Barometer can tell us the size of the difference between the answers that the Indigenous and the general community samples gave to the question: 'As an Australian, I feel proud of Indigenous culture'. While 97 per cent of Indigenous people agreed with this proportion,

only 50 per cent of the general community sample agreed with it. There was a similar difference in responses to a similar proposition: 'Australia has a richer culture because of our Indigenous heritage'. Nine out of ten (91 per cent) of Indigenous respondents agreed, but only 56 per cent of the general community did so. Large minorities of the general community — 37 per cent and 29 per cent respectively — neither agreed not disagreed with these two propositions.[5] One way to understand the Barometer as a diagnostic of 'relationships' would be to target these non-committal respondents — to induce them to declare their pride in Indigenous heritage as a component of Australian culture. This is an example of the way in which a poor relationship between Indigenous and non-Indigenous Australians could plausibly be represented as a 'gap' between the measured value of a variable found in two measured publics — a statistical gap to be 'closed' so that non-Indigenous Australians 'equal' Indigenous Australians in the proportions taking pride in Aboriginal culture.

2. *The interpersonal relationships between indigenous individuals and non-Indigenous individuals.* There are a number of items in the Barometer that evoke this sense of 'relationship' — for example, a question about whether you would feel comfortable if a member of your family married an Indigenous person, and a question about whether you wanted to have more contact with Indigenous people. One of the problems with such questions in the Barometer, as I will explain below, is that they are asymmetrical: the questions about relating to an Indigenous person are not always matched by questions about relating to a non-Indigenous person. The result is a subtle elision of Indigenous agency.

3. *The political relationship between the 'Australian people' (the nation) and the Indigenous peoples of Australia (Aborigines and Torres Strait Islanders).* The Barometer has little to say about this 'relationship'. Although the study constitutes an 'Indigenous public' methodologically, it does not explicitly entertain other ways in which Indigenous Australians as a whole could be politically represented and thus enter into a political relationship with the structures (the Commonwealth parliament, the main political parties) that represent those in the general community sample. However, the study does include a question that refers to the relationship between Indigenous and non-Indigenous political leaders, and this implies a political 'relationship' and not just an interpersonal one. The study missed an opportunity when it omitted to ask what respondents thought of the idea that Indigenous Australians were

entitled to represent themselves through some formal body when dealing, as 'peoples', with the Australian nation-state.

Without saying what is meant by 'the relationship', the Barometer asked respondents if they agreed that 'the relationship between Indigenous and other Australians is important for Australia'.[6] Almost all (99 per cent) of the Indigenous sample, and 87 per cent of the general community sample agreed that 'the relationship' is important. The survey then asked respondents what they thought of the relationship between Indigenous people and other Australians. More than half of the general community sample (57 per cent) thought the relationship to be 'fairly poor' or 'very poor'; and slightly more than half the Indigenous sample (53 per cent) thought this. Respondents from both groups were slightly more critical of the condition of 'the relationship' in 2010 than the respondents in 2008 had been. Only half of the general community sample (50 per cent) had thought the relationship to be 'fairly poor' or 'very poor' in 2008. Of the Indigenous sample about the same proportion (49 per cent) had held this view in 2008.[7] About half (49 per cent) of the general community and 56 per cent of the Indigenous sample thought that 'the relationship' in 2010 was improving.[8]

In what ways did people in 2010 think the relationship was poor or very poor? The Barometer explored at least two distinguishable dimensions of relationship quality. One had to do with such material (in)equalities as have been the focus of the slogan 'Closing the Gaps'. The other highlights attitudinal variables such as perceived trust. I will deal with each of them — the material and the attitudinal — in turn.

Perception of the relationship as material (in)equality

One question referred to the statement that 'Indigenous people are mostly disadvantaged and live on the edge of mainstream society'. In the general community, 48 per cent agreed. Among Indigenous respondents, 66 per cent agreed.[9]

Another question asked people whether they agreed that 'Being born Indigenous makes it harder for an individual to achieve in Australia today'. In the general community, 45 per cent agreed; among Indigenous respondents, 61 per cent agreed. Among those who agreed with this proposition about it being 'harder ... to achieve', there were some who strongly agreed. The strongly agreeing endorsement of the 'Being born Indigenous ...' statement was weaker in the general community (8 per cent of total responses) than among the Indigenous sample (21 per cent of the total responses).[10]

Another question asked people to compare Indigenous and non-Indigenous 'access to opportunities'.[11] In the general community, 42 per cent thought Indigenous access to opportunities was 'better or the same as others'. However, when the Barometer nominated specific dimensions of well-being, Indigenous people were judged by high proportions of the general community respondents to be worse off than non-Indigenous:

- *Housing:* 68 per cent
- *Education:* 74 per cent
- *Employment:* 77 per cent
- *Health:* 78 per cent.[12]

Indigenous Australians' perceptions of Indigenous people's dimensions of disadvantage were almost universal. Only 17 per cent of the Indigenous sample thought Indigenous access to opportunities was 'better or the same as others'. And for specific dimensions of disadvantage, almost the entire Indigenous sample saw Indigenous Australians as disadvantaged:

- *Housing:* 90 per cent
- *Education:* 90 per cent
- *Employment:* 92 per cent
- *Health:* 92 per cent.[13]

The survey posed one other question about socio-economic inequality: knowledge of the life expectancy gap. In the general community, 69 per cent thought there was a life expectancy gap of twelve years or more (which I take to be a clear perception of disadvantage); 91 per cent of the Indigenous sample thought the gap was twelve years or more.[14]

In short, when the general community was asked about *specific* dimensions of socio-economic disadvantage, very large majorities agreed with the view that Indigenous Australians were disadvantaged. Among Indigenous Australians, the perception of Indigenous disadvantage, when posed in terms of specific dimensions, was almost universal. However, when the issue of Indigenous disadvantage was put in structural terms — the questions about 'being born Indigenous' and Indigenous 'access to opportunity' — a smaller proportion of the general community than the Indigenous endorsed the idea: 42 per cent of the general community sample did not agree with the proposition that Indigenous Australians had inferior 'access to opportunities'; Indigenous Australians' systemic or structural disadvantage was conceded by a bare majority of the general community (54 per cent).[15] As well, there seems to be growing resistance among Indigenous Australians to the idea that they constitute a community of fate — that is, that they share a condition of structural or systemic disadvantage. In 2008, 35 per cent of Indigenous strongly agreed that 'being born Indigenous makes it harder for an individual to achieve in Australia today'; in 2010, the proportion strongly agreeing with that proposition had fallen to 21 per cent, and the proportion of Indigenous unwilling to endorse the statement grew from 34 per cent in 2008 to 39 per cent in 2010.

What causes inequalities?

In their perceptions of Indigenous disadvantage as a problem that reconciliation must overcome, people perceived causes and solutions in different ways. On this vital theme, the Barometer was both disappointing and illuminating. It is disappointing that that the Barometer did not ask respondents whether they thought that there was such a thing as 'disadvantage' among non-Indigenous Australians, and so did not ask people about the causes and remedies of 'disadvantage' among non-Indigenous people. Thus we have no way of knowing whether the respondents' answers about Indigenous disadvantage exhibit their views about disadvantage that is specific to Indigenous Australians or their views about social disadvantage in general. It may be that many people who perceive Indigenous Australians as disadvantaged apply the same explanations and propose the same solutions for all 'disadvantaged' people — whether the 'disadvantaged' are 'Indigenous' is, in this perspective, irrelevant. That the Barometer did not explore this possibility perhaps arises from the strength within Reconciliation Australia of the assumption that the current condition of Indigenous Australians owes much to their specific historical experience as victims of colonisation and its associated heritage of racism. Perhaps it did not occur to the designers of the Barometer to find out how many Australians do not share this assumption.

The Barometer offered respondents nine factors that could be 'important in creating Indigenous disadvantage', and it allowed respondents to agree with as many of these prompted explanations as they wished. It was characteristic of the Indigenous respondents that nearly all of them considered all factors to be important. The following factors were considered important by 90 per cent or more of the Indigenous sample:

- alcohol and substance abuse (95 per cent)
- lack of confidence and self-esteem of Indigenous people (91 per cent)
- lack of respect for Indigenous people (96 per cent)
- discrimination (95 per cent)
- poor access to health and education services (95 per cent)
- race-based policies of the past (94 per cent)
- inadequate living conditions (96 per cent)
- ineffective government programs and policies (95 per cent).[16]

Among Indigenous respondents, the only factor to rate a *relatively* low endorsement as important was 'lack of personal responsibility (among Indigenous people)', and this was still judged important by more than four out of five (83 per cent).

The general community was a little more reluctant to rate any of these factors as 'important', but the ratings were still high — with a range of 70–90 per cent agreeing that each of the nine suggested factors was important. We should remember that not all of the people responding to this question about the causes of disadvantage agree with its premise that Indigenous people are disadvantaged. Perhaps the most interesting feature of the general population sample's responses is the difference between the highest rated factor, 'alcohol and substance abuse' (90 per cent), and the lowest, 'ineffective government programs and policies' (70 per cent). Roughly the same proportion of Indigenous Australian (83 per cent) and general community respondents (82 per cent) thought 'lack of personal responsibility' was an important factor.[17]

The survey allowed people to differentiate between saying a factor was 'important' and saying it was 'very important'. With one exception, general community ratings of factors as 'very important' ranged between 28 and 45 per cent. The exception was 'alcohol and substance abuse' (rated as very important by 70 per cent). We can infer that among general community respondents the idea that 'alcohol and substance abuse' explains much of Indigenous disadvantage is particularly strong. Any initiative to redress disadvantage, whether by government or other agent, would have to say it was addressed to 'alcohol and substance abuse' in order to be taken seriously by the general community. When the Indigenous sample was asked to distinguish between 'important' and 'very important', all nine factors that rated 'important' were rated 'very important' by most Indigenous Australians (a range of 61–80 per cent). The two factors with the highest 'very important' rating by Indigenous Australians (both 81 per cent) were 'poor access to health and education services' and 'discrimination'.

Are Indigenous people responsible?

That the 'disadvantaged' should be held personally responsible for their fate is one of the more contentious ideas of our times. The Barometer tests the strength of that idea in both the general community and the Indigenous public. 'Lack of personal responsibility' was thought to be 'very important' by 48 per cent of the Indigenous public in both 2008 and in 2010. In the general community, the notion became more popular — from 39 per cent in 2008 to 45 per cent in 2010, still slightly less than for the Indigenous proportion.

The Barometer includes data that we could interpret as relevant to the issue of the perceived readiness of Indigenous Australians to take responsibility for their own well-being. That is, the Barometer asked respondents to attribute certain qualities to Indigenous and to non-Indigenous Australians; here I focus on those qualities that have something to do with being 'responsible': the qualities 'disciplined', 'hard working' and 'good at working together to address the problems that confront them'.

When asked the question 'Are Australians "disciplined"?' 41 per cent of the general community respondents thought that Australians tended to be 'disciplined', while 32 per cent of Indigenous thought Australians to be 'disciplined'. When asked 'Are Indigenous Australians "disciplined"?' 13 per cent of general community respondents thought Indigenous Australians tended to be 'disciplined', while 36 per cent of Indigenous respondents thought Indigenous Australians tended to be 'disciplined'. That is, in neither sample did a majority attribute 'discipline' to itself, and each sample was less likely to attribute 'discipline' to the 'other' than to itself.

Are other Australians and Indigenous Australians 'hard working'? The general community very commonly esteem 'other Australians' (i.e. themselves, mostly) to be 'hard working' (68 per cent), but fewer of the general community (19 per cent) saw 'hard working' as an 'Indigenous' quality. A substantial majority of Indigenous Australians saw both themselves (74 per cent) and 'Australians' (60 per cent) as 'hard working'.[18]

Unfortunately, the survey did not ask the question: 'Are Australians good at working together to address the problems that confront them?' For some reason, Auspoll asked this question — about political capacity to take responsibility — only about 'Indigenous Australians'.[19] The result was hardly a vote of confidence in Indigenous political capacity. A bare majority of Indigenous Australians (53 per cent) attributed this quality to themselves (with 21 per cent in strong agreement). Only one in five

(22 per cent) of general community respondents agreed that this was a quality of Indigenous Australians, with only 3 per cent 'strongly' agreeing. These data suggest that there is little faith in Indigenous political capacity, even among Indigenous Australians themselves. However, it is difficult to interpret this lack of faith: had the general community been asked, perhaps few would have rated Australians' collective political capacity highly. By omitting to ask about Australians' perceived ability to work together 'to address the problems that confront them', the Barometer falls into the trap of assuming that only Indigenous political capacity is problematic. In this respect, the Barometer seems unwittingly complicit with a general community assessment, with a very low proportion attributing Indigenous Australians with such 'responsibility' qualities as 'hard working' and 'disciplined'.

Public policy and the scope for individual action

'Reconciliation' is presented by the survey as a responsibility in two ways:
- *political*: for governments to adopt the laws and policies conducive to reconciliation, and for Indigenous and non-Indigenous leaders to 'cooperate'
- *individual*: for individuals to act in some way that promotes reconciliation.

The Barometer collected data not long after the Australian parliament's Apology in February 2008.[20] Both samples thought that the Apology was important for Indigenous people (78 per cent of the general community, 97 per cent of Indigenous Australians), and smaller but still large proportions of both samples also thought that the Apology had been 'important for relations between Indigenous people and other Australians' (65 per cent of the general community, 91 per cent of Indigenous Australians).[21] Both samples included majorities who saw that the relationship was partly a matter of respect and not simply one of material (in)equality.

Notwithstanding the respondents' evident sensitivity to the 'symbolic' aspects of 'reconciliation', the question of socio-economic disadvantage remains powerfully present within many people's understanding of 'reconciliation'. The Barometer asked respondents about others' responsibility for relieving 'disadvantage'. Perhaps the government was the implicit agent in many respondents' minds when they were asked whether they agreed that 'Some Indigenous people need specific help to reach equality with other Australians'.[22] This proposition was almost universally supported (92 per cent) by Indigenous Australians, and widely supported

(72 per cent) by the general community. Would these levels of support have been less had the statement specified that the 'help' was to be in the form of government programs? It would be interesting to know.

Another question asked people whether they agreed that 'The government should put measures in place to help Indigenous people in specific ways'. The Indigenous sample very strongly supported such a view (92 per cent agreement), and 57 per cent of the general community agreed.[23] Note that the first statement says that those to be helped were 'some Indigenous people', the second says that 'Indigenous people' would be helped. It is difficult to know which of the two differences in wording (specifying that the government was the source of help, or allowing the help to go to all, not merely 'some', Indigenous people) explains the lower general community support for the second proposition. Nonetheless, it is clear that in both samples the idea had majority support that government has some kind of responsibility to deal with the disadvantage of Indigenous people.

However, the survey also revealed widespread doubts about the efficacy of past government action. For example, there was a popular view that 'race-based policies' had been harmful in the past.[24] Indigenous Australians held almost universally to the view that this was an important factor in creating Indigenous disadvantage (94 per cent 'important', 77 per cent 'very important'). The general community was less likely to blame 'race-based policies in the past' (75 per cent 'important', 39 per cent 'very important'). However, these percentages are high; clearly, history has taught Australians that 'race-based' policies may be harmful. A large majority of general community respondents (70 per cent) agreed that 'ineffective government programs and policies' have helped to create Indigenous disadvantage, and 33 per cent said this was a very important factor.[25] Nearly all in the Indigenous sample (95 per cent) agreed (77 per cent 'very important') that 'ineffective government programs and policies' helped to create Indigenous disadvantage.[26] A similar question asked for respondents' assessment of 'past programmes designed to address Indigenous disadvantage'.[27] A relatively high proportion of the general community (16 per cent) did not have a view, but 96 per cent of the Indigenous sample had a view, and it was largely negative — 67 per cent said 'fairly unsuccessful' or 'very unsuccessful'. A majority (57 per cent) of the general community respondents agreed with this negative verdict on 'past programmes designed to address Indigenous disadvantage'.

There is a paradox here. The Indigenous sample more strongly supported the views that past policies had not been successful and that race-based policies had been a factor in causing Indigenous disadvantage, yet at the same time the Indigenous sample supported more strongly than the general community the idea that 'The government should put measures in place to help Indigenous people in specific ways'. History has taught Indigenous Australians that governments can do them great harm in their 'race-based' policies; however, their expectations and hope remain high that governments can do them good. But by what kind of policies could governments do good? Would they need to be 'race-based'? This term has many possible meanings that the Barometer does not attempt to explore.

If not the government, then who can act effectively?

The Barometer questioned respondents about their willingness and ability to 'help disadvantaged Indigenous people'. The data are poignant. The Barometer asked people whether they agreed with the statement 'I would like to do something to help disadvantaged Indigenous people'.[28] It also measured agreement with the statement 'I know what I can do to help disadvantaged Indigenous people'. In both samples, there was a significant gap between the proportion of respondents saying that they wanted to help and the proportion who said they knew what help to give. This difference was 17 per cent in the general community (33 per cent wanting to help, 16 per cent knowing what help to give); and 18 per cent in the Indigenous sample (93 per cent wanting, 75 per cent knowing).[29] That is, the general community and the Indigenous samples had similar proportions of people (almost one in five) who did not know how to help Indigenous Australians when they wanted to help. The Barometer tested the strength of people's commitment to helping by asking whether they strongly agreed with the two statements. In the general community, the gap between strongly wanting (4 per cent) and strongly knowing how (2 per cent) to help disadvantaged Indigenous Australians was small (2 per cent), but among Indigenous Australians the gap between strongly wanting (65 per cent) and strongly knowing how (39 per cent) was quite high (26 per cent).[30] In short, the Barometer has uncovered a significant problem of what we might call 'baffled willingness to help' disadvantaged Indigenous people, and that problem seems to be greater in the Indigenous sample. There thus seems to be a widespread hope that governments will know how to act on 'disadvantage', when many individuals are baffled by the question of what they themselves could do about it.

Do Indigenous actions matter?

Attitudinal dimensions of 'the relationship' were important to those who designed the Barometer. Do Indigenous and non-Indigenous Australians trust each other? People were not asked about their own level of trust and whom they trusted, but they were asked about their opinion of others' level of trust.[31] Some 81 per cent of those in the general community and 91 per cent of Indigenous respondents thought that other Australians had a fairly low or very low level of trust for Indigenous Australians, while 81 per cent of respondents in the general community sample and 85 per cent of the Indigenous respondents thought that Indigenous Australians had a fairly low or very low level of trust for other Australians. That is, at least four out of five Australians believe that that there is low trust between Indigenous Australians and other Australians. There are no significant 'gaps' between Indigenous and non-Indigenous Australians in their opinions about the low level of trust.

People were not asked whether they were 'prejudiced', but they were asked to estimate others' levels of prejudice.[32] The general community sample thought there was a lot of prejudice: 71 per cent thought that the prejudice of non-Indigenous Australians towards Indigenous Australians was 'fairly' or 'very' high; and 72 per cent of general community thought that Indigenous Australians' prejudice against other Australians was 'fairly' or 'very' high. A higher proportion of the general community saw 'very high' prejudice in Indigenous attitudes (26 per cent) than in 'Australian' attitudes (20 per cent). The Indigenous sample also thought there was a lot of prejudice: 93 per cent of Indigenous Australians thought Australians to be fairly or very highly prejudiced towards them, and 74 per cent of Indigenous Australians thought Indigenous Australians to be highly prejudiced towards other Australians. Indigenous Australians saw 'very high' prejudice (53 per cent) among other Australians. However, we should note that Indigenous respondents also see their own people as highly prejudiced, and one in five (19 per cent) Indigenous respondents thought Indigenous prejudice towards other Australians was 'very high'. Again, these questions did not measure 'prejudice', but people's opinions about the occurrence of prejudice. There do not seem to be great gaps between the two publics in their opinions about the extent of prejudice in Australia. We nearly all seem to agree that we are nation of prejudiced people when it comes to the Indigenous/non-Indigenous relationship.

Does Reconciliation Australia still hold out hope that individuals can act in trusting and unprejudiced ways? The promotion of such hope would seem to be central to its mission, but the Barometer's approach to the interpersonal dimension of reconciliation so far shows an asymmetrical view of responsibility for trusting, unprejudiced actions. The Barometer asks what non-Indigenous Australians might or might not do with or for Indigenous Australians, but it does not ask Indigenous Australians about what they might or might not do with or for non-Indigenous Australians.

The Barometer discovered the extent of agreement with the statement 'I would feel fine if I had a child who decided to marry an Indigenous person': 55 per cent in the general community, 91 per cent of Indigenous Australians.[33] However, the Barometer did not seek responses to the statement 'I would feel fine if I had a child who decided to marry a non-Indigenous person' — a scenario that a great many Indigenous Australian parents confront. Do Indigenous Australians welcome or fear such intimate associations with non-Indigenous Australians?

Similarly the Barometer asked respondents 'What level of contact would you like to have with Indigenous people in the future?' In the general community, 61 per cent said 'frequent' (15 per cent) or 'occasional' (46 per cent); among Indigenous Australians, 94 per cent desired 'frequent'.[34] The Barometer did not ask whether respondents desired more contact with non-Indigenous Australians than they currently had — surely a relevant piece of information about Indigenous Australians.

The Barometer asked whether, in the previous twelve months, a respondent had 'built personal relationships with Indigenous people'. In the general community, 15 per cent reported they had done so; among Indigenous Australians, the proportion was 86 per cent. The Barometer did not ask whether respondents had 'built personal relationship' with non-Indigenous people. Why not? Nor did the survey ask whether a respondent, in the previous twelve months, had 'reconsidered your views about non-Indigenous Australia'. It asked only whether respondents had reconsidered their views about Indigenous Australia.[35] By such omissions, the Barometer implies that while the interpersonal aspects of reconciliation are open to the initiatives (indeed, are the responsibilities) of non-Indigenous Australians, the reciprocal efforts of Indigenous Australians are not worth asking about.

Conclusion

The Barometer is interesting not only as social science — telling us something about Australians' perceptions of reconciliation — but also as an intervention by Reconciliation Australia into our understandings of 'reconciliation'. In this chapter, I have argued that in Reconciliation Australia's 'Barometer' there is an implicit agenda for improving 'the relationship'.

First, the Barometer shows little concern for reconciliation of nation to 'peoples'. The Barometer does not investigate popular attitudes to the idea that Aborigines and Torres Strait Islanders are peoples with collective rights that should be expressed in laws and institutions, negotiated between the nation and its Indigenous peoples. Indeed, the Barometer risks entrenching the idea that Australia's Indigenous peoples lack the collective political capacity for such negotiation. That is, the Barometer asks a question about Indigenous political capacity, and it reveals widespread doubts among both publics about such Indigenous capacities, but it poses no such question about the political capacity or statesmanship of non-Indigenous Australians. Indigenous political capacity is problematic, the Barometer implies, but the non-Indigenous political framework is beyond investigation or evaluation. When possible governmental initiatives towards Indigenous people are evoked, the measures are described in terms of the socio-economic inequality that they would reduce: 'measures to reach equality in ... health, education, life expectancy, employment, housing etc.'[36] Thus the Australian nation-state is imagined in terms of the *socio-economic* inequalities that its policies might address, not as a set of political institutions that arguably embody *political* inequality. This is a narrow conception of Australia's policy horizons. And within this narrow horizon there are still two issues left unexplored: do the two publics perceive current government policies as 'race-based'? And do they think such policies help or hinder 'reconciliation'?

Second, the Barometer points to scope for constructive actions by non-Indigenous individuals, but it implies that the scope for action by Indigenous individuals is of little interest. Although the Barometer documents a widespread belief (in both publics) that Indigenous people are untrusting and prejudiced, it does not try to measure the Indigenous willingness or capacity to act constructively towards non-Indigenous Australians. It is as if 'reaching out' to the Other is something that non-Indigenous people are required to do and expected to be capable of doing — while these dispositions and capacities among Indigenous people are of no consequence. In this way, the Barometer fails to imagine new forms of Indigenous agency as contributing to 'reconciliation'.

Third, and grounding the above two points, the idea of Indigenous disadvantage looms very large in the Barometer's conception of what is wrong with 'the relationship'. The strength of this association between 'Indigenous' and 'disadvantage' is such that there is no investigation of Indigenous and non-Indigenous views about non-Indigenous people who are socio-economically disadvantaged. Thus we get no comparative perspective on the view that is measured as prominent among general community respondents: that Indigenous Australians are not systemically lacking in opportunity, not handicapped from birth by racial discrimination. Are general community views about Indigenous disadvantage different from general community views about all disadvantaged people? We need to know. The tendency to associate being Indigenous with being disadvantaged is also in diabolical affinity with the subtle elision of the possibility of Indigenous agency, noted above.

Thus the 'relationship' problem in Australia is implied to consist largely (though not exclusively) of two matters: helping Indigenous Australians to overcome their socio-economic disadvantage, and persuading non-Indigenous Australians to come to a positive view of Indigenous Australians. These two specifications of what 'the relationship' is about are in tension with one another. When the Barometer evokes the topic 'Indigenous disadvantage', it cannot help evoking, at the same time, features of Indigenous Australians that are not so likeable, such as their widely attributed failure to take responsibility for themselves.

Notes

Introduction

1. Chapter 1 is a revised version of Rowse (1998).
2. Chapter 3 incorporates passages from Rowse (1999) and Rowse (2002).
3. This chapter incorporates passages from Rowse (2005b).
4. This chapter is a slightly revised version of Rowse (2007).
5. Chapter 11 is a substantially revised version of Rowse (2009).
6. Weiner (2006: 18–19).

Chapter 1: Recognising 'Peoples' and 'Populations'

1. McGregor (2011).
2. Australian Law Reform Commission (1986).
3. Povinelli (2006: 157).
4. Quoted in Engle (2010: 80).
5. Pearson (2007: 55).
6. Dodson (2012).
7. Smith (1980: 219).
8. Smith (1980: 27).
9. Smith (1980: 44). In the 1981 Census, the question was again revised, but only slightly: 'Is the person of Aboriginal or Torres Strait Islander origin?'
10. Rowse and Smith (2010).
11. Borrie (1975: 455).
12. Taylor (2002: 9).
13. Sanders (2002, 2007).
14. Taylor (2007: 71).
15. Taylor (2007: 71).
16. Thorburn (2007a: 85).
17. Taylor (2002: 2).
18. Martin (2002: 21).
19. Taylor (2002: 4).
20. For an Alice Springs case study related to the problems of household formation, see Rowse (1988).
21. Martin (2002: 20–1).

NOTES

22. Quoted in Morphy (2007a: 107).
23. Morphy (2007b: 171).
24. Martin et al. (2002: 98).
25. Morphy (2007b: 167).
26. Morphy (2007a: 103).
27. Martin et al. (2002: 100).
28. Morphy (2007a: 111).
29. For a longer account of the CAEPR commentaries on the Census, see Rowse (2011).
30. In these two points, I follow Taylor (2009) and Prout (2011).
31. McGregor (2011: 118).
32. Quoted by McGregor (2011: 92).
33. Downing (1971); Loveday (1989).
34. *Milirrpum v Nabalco Pty Ltd* (1971) 17 FLR 141 at 268.
35. South Australian Parliament 1967, p. 13, emphasis added.
36. Finlayson (1999: 7).
37. Australian Law Reform Commission (1986, para. 43).
38. Ritter (2009: 172–6).
39. Quoted in Strelein (2006: 125).
40. Quoted in Strelein (2006: 129), emphasis added.
41. Pearson (2009: 119), emphasis added.
42. Pearson (2009: 118).
43. Strelein (2006: 130).
44. Glaskin (2003: 78).
45. Merlan (2006: 101).
46. Merlan (2006: 98).
47. Martin (2009: 108–9).
48. Loos and Keast (1992: 286–7).
49. Rowley (1971: 417).
50. Cited in Rowse (2000: 132).
51. For a critical account of the notion of 'dysfunctionality', with particular reference to the recent work of Peter Sutton, see Lattas and Morris (2010). In the same collection, Francesca Merlan summarises the data on child abuse and offers vignettes from her own field work: Merlan (2010).
52. Ritter (2009: 64).
53. Ritter (2010: 202).
54. Ritter (2009: 65).
55. Blagg (2008: 167), emphasis added
56. Blagg (2008: 168).
57. Blagg 2008:153–4).
58. Blagg (2008: 154).
59. Blagg (2008: 159).
60. Blagg (2008: 166).
61. Blagg (2008: 169).
62. Blagg (2008: 174).
63. Blagg (2008: 174).

64. Blagg (2008: 174).
65. Blagg (2008: 154).
66. Blagg (2008: 159).

Chapter 2: Hasluck and Elkin

1. Hasluck (1959a).
2. Hasluck (1959b).
3. Hasluck (1959b).
4. Hasluck (1959b).
5. Hasluck (1959b).
6. Hasluck (1959b).
7. Hasluck (1959a).
8. Hasluck (1959a).
9. Hasluck (1959a).
10. Hasluck (1959b).
11. Hasluck (1959a).
12. Hasluck (1959b), emphasis added.
13. Hasluck (1959b).
14. For recent, detailed accounts of Hasluck's attempts to eschew racial terminology, see Gray (2011: 116–23) and McGregor (2011: 81–8).
15. Australian Archives (ACT) A452 Item 57/3943 'Statement of Citizenship Status', Commonwealth and States Conference on Native Welfare, Canberra, 3–4 September 1951.
16. Hasluck (1959b).
17. The institutional entrapment of reforming administrators of Aboriginal welfare is the theme of Anna Haebich's (2005) insightful study of Western Australia's SG Middleton.
18. Hasluck (1959a).
19. Hasluck (1959b).
20. Hasluck (1959b).
21. Hasluck (1959b).
22. Hasluck (1959b).
23. Wise (1985: 230–1).
24. Wise (1985: 231), citing Elkin (1959).
25. Wise (1985: 232).
26. Berndt (1962: 88).
27. Berndt (1962: 82).
28. Berndt (1962: 83).
29. According to McGregor (2011: 98–118), the term 'integration' was sometimes used by critics of government policy and practice as if 'integration' offered something different. McGregor argues that both 'assimilation' and 'integration' were used so loosely that it is not possible for the historian now to attribute a distinct vision of the nation and of government programs to those who proposed 'integration'. I suggest that the uneasiness around 'assimilation' and the poorly articulated sense that 'integration' was an alternative may be taken as symptomatic of the tension between what I

am calling (with my own post-hoc vocabulary) 'juridical' and 'sociological' liberalisms.
30. Fenton (1984: 113).
31. For a brief account of this theme in Australian social science in the 1950s and 1960s, see Rowse (2005a).
32. Russell McGregor (2001, 2002) has sensitively explored Elkin's ambivalence about assimilation. For an older account of Elkin's context, see Rowse (1978: 147–76).
33. Hasluck (1988: 130).
34. Elkin (1951: 16).
35. Hasluck (1988: 93).
36. Rowley (1971: 417).

Chapter 3: Strehlow Damns Coombs

1. Strehlow (1947).
2. Strehlow (1956, 1961).
3. Strehlow (1974a).
4. Strehlow (1974b).
5. Strehlow (1971a).
6. Strehlow (1971a).
7. Strehlow (1986, 1987a, 1987b).
8. Strehlow (1986: 2), emphasis in original.
9. Strehlow (1986: 4).
10. Strehlow (1986: 4).
11. Strehlow (1987a: 3).
12. Strehlow (1987a: 1).
13. Strehlow (1987a: 3).
14. Strehlow (1987a: 4).
15. Strehlow (1987b: 1).
16. Strehlow (1965).
17. Strehlow (1965: 8).
18. Strehlow (1965: 9).
19. Strehlow (1965: 9).
20. Strehlow (1965: 9).
21. Strehlow (1965: 9).
22. Strehlow (1965: 9).
23. Northern Territory Legislative Council (1965: 4).
24. Strehlow (1971b).
25. Strehlow (1971c).
26. Strehlow (1969: 211).
27. As quoted in AIAS Annual Report (1973: 9).
28. Edwards (1975: 119).
29. Strehlow (1973).
30. I give a slightly longer account of this discussion in Rowse (2002: 300–2).
31. Strehlow (1958: 10).
32. Strehlow (1958: 12).

33. Strehlow (1958: 12–13).
34. Strehlow (1961: 12).
35. Strehlow (1961: 31).
36. Strehlow (1961: 34), my emphasis.
37. Strehlow (1961: 35), my emphasis.
38. *Advertiser* (Adelaide), 11 January 1961, emphasis added.
39. 'The Situation of Aboriginal Australians', unpublished paper of the Council for Aboriginal Affairs, 7 July 1971, Dexter Papers, file 29/3, AIATSIS Library.
40. Strehlow (1947: 6).
41. Coombs (1972: 142).
42. Coombs (1972: 144).

Chapter 4: 'The Whole Aboriginal Problem in Microcosm'

1. South Australia House of Assembly (henceforth SAHA), 13 July 1966, p. 478.
2. South Australian Parliament, 1967, p. 13.
3. South Australian Parliament, 1967, p. 11.
4. SAHA, 4 August 1966, p. 889.
5. There were: 7827 acres of 'unmanned' reserves; 17,700,655 acres of 'manned' reserves (of which 17,676,800 was North-West Reserve); and 1,701,760 acres of missions ('manned') — a total Aboriginal estate of 19,410,242 acres.
6. South Australian Aboriginal Affairs Board (1967: 1).
7. Raftery (2006: 130).
8. Berndt and Berndt (1951: 168–9).
9. Berndt and Berndt (1951: 169).
10. Berndt and Berndt (1951: 190).
11. SAHA, 13 July 1966, p. 479.
12. South Australian Parliament, 1967, p. 14.
13. South Australian Parliament, 1967, p. 20.
14. South Australian Parliament, 1967, p. 20.
15. South Australian Parliament, 1967, p. 33.
16. South Australian Parliament, 1967, p. 34.
17. South Australian Parliament, 1967, p. 34.
18. South Australian Parliament, 1967, p. 34.
19. Parliament of Australia, 'Report from the Select Committee on Voting Rights of Aborigines', p. 4.
20. SAHA, 20 July 1966, pp. 606–7.
21. SAHA, 9 August 1966, p. 923.
22. SAHA, 2 August 1966, p. 798, emphasis added.
23. SAHA, 2 August 1966, p. 803.
24. SAHA, 2 August 1966, p. 803.
25. SAHA, 2 August 1966, p. 808.
26. South Australian Parliament, 1967, pp. 14–15.
27. South Australian Parliament, 1967, p. 29.

28. South Australian Parliament, 1967, p. 30.
29. South Australian Parliament, 1967, p. 30.
30. SAHA, 2 August 1966: pp. 808–9, 810.
31. SAHA, 2 August 1966, p. 811
32. SAHA, 2 August 1966 p. 811
33. SAHA, 4 August 1966 p. 886
34. South Australian Parliament, 1967, p. 31; SAHA, 2 August 1966, p. 803.
35. South Australian Parliament, 1967, p. 25.
36. South Australian Parliament, 1967, p. 25.
37. SAHA, 26 July 1966, p. 658.
38. SAHA, 26 July 1966, p. 663.
39. SAHA, 2 August 1966, p. 799.
40. South Australian Parliament, 1967, p. 13.
41. South Australian Parliament, 1967, p. 21.
42. SAHA, 15 November 1966, p. 3046.
43. SAHA, 15 November 1966, p. 3048.
44. SAHA, 2 August 1966, p. 801.
45. SAHA, 2 August 1966, p. 802.
46. South Australian Parliament, 1967, p. 31.
47. South Australian Parliament, 1967, p. 14.
48. South Australian Parliament, 1967, p. 35.
49. South Australian Parliament, 1967, p. 32.
50. South Australian Parliament, 1967, p. 21.
51. South Australian Parliament, 1967, p. 20.
52. South Australian Parliament, 1967, p. 21.
53. South Australian Parliament, 1967, p. 33.
54. South Australian Parliament, 1967, p. 19.
55. South Australian Parliament, 1967, p. 14.
56. South Australian Parliament, 1967, p. 20.
57. SAHA, 9 August 1966, p. 922.

Chapter 5: The Politics of Enumerating the Stolen Generations

1. The term 'Stolen Generations' originated in a short study by Peter Read (1981). Three historical expositions have amplified, elaborated and complicated his story: HREOC (1997); Haebich (2000); and Haebich and Mellor (2002).
2. Host and Milroy (2001) is a fine example of such scholarly combativeness.
3. Senate (2000: 17).
4. Senate (2000: 20).
5. Senate (2000: 26).
6. Stanner (1970: vi–ix).
7. Read (2003).
8. Kruger and Waterford (2007: 309).
9. Kruger and Waterford (2007: 309).
10. HREOC (1997: 36).
11. HREOC (1997: 37).

12. HREOC (1997: 37).
13. Kamien (1978: 169).
14. Herron (2000: 13–18).
15. Herron (2000: 18).
16. Quoted in *The Koori Mail*, 19 April 2000, p. 4, emphasis added.
17. Manne (2001: 26–7).
18. Manne (2001: 27).
19. Blake (1998); Evans (1999).
20. Blake (1998: 52).
21. Evans (1999: 94).
22. Copland (2005: 18).
23. 'In Queensland, certain periods of time favoured removing "half-caste" children to mainstream child welfare institutions whilst at other times this was deemed an unnecessary cost to the state and they were sent to Aboriginal settlements and missions with their parents.' (Copland 2005: 339). 'Queensland favoured a system of removing Aboriginal children together with their parents for a large part of the period from 1910 to the early 1970s.' (Copland 2005: 344).
24. Windschuttle (2009).
25. Copland (2005: 306).
26. Haebich (2000: 174).
27. Windschuttle (2009: 603).
28. Copland (2005: 308).
29. Hegarty (2003).
30. Windschuttle (2009: 603).
31. Copland (2005: 108).
32. Copland (2005: 100).
33. Copland (2005: 108).
34. Copland (2005: 105).
35. Copland (2005: 104).
36. Copland (2005: 106).
37. Copland (2005: 105).
38. Copland (2005: 106). Copland cites the Queensland government submission to the HREOC inquiry, reporting 2024 children removed between 1908 and 1971 (a shorter period than in Copland's study). He comments that it 'had 1000 fewer children removed and 400 less children separated from their parents than found in [his own] study' (Copland 2005: 42–3, 304).
39. Copland (2005: 324).
40. Copland (2005: 324).
41. Copland (2005: 329).
42. Copland (2005: 329).
43. Copland (2005: 329).
44. Copland (2005: 324).
45. Read (1981,1999, 2003); Edwards and Read (1989).
46. Read (1999: 27), emphasis added.
47. Copland (2005: 337).
48. Broome (2005: 96–7, 215).

49. Windschuttle (2009: 77–8).
50. Windschuttle (2009: 80).
51. Windschuttle (2009: 82).
52. Windschuttle (2009: 82–3).
53. Windschuttle (2009: 83).
54. Windschuttle (2009: 88–9).
55. Windschuttle (2009: 93–4, 96).
56. Edwards and Read (1989: ix); see Read (1999: 26) for his clarification that he and Edwards did not think of these people as 'separations'.
57. Herron (2000: 14).
58. Read (1999 [1981]: 67).
59. Read (1999: 26), emphasis in original.
60. Dexter (2008: 79), emphasis added.
61. Read (1999: 74).
62. Dodson (2003: 32, 39–40).
63. For a recent account of the technical and political factors determining the rewording of the Census 'race' question from 1961 to 1971, see Rowse and Smith (2010).
64. Read (1999: 29, 47).
65. Read (1999: 67).
66. Read's emphasis on descent thus converges with what Kirsty Gover (2010) recently has argued to be the distinctive idiom of contemporary Indigenous political thought in the Anglophone settler societies — Australia, Canada, New Zealand and the United States.

Chapter 6: The Changing Cultural Constitution of the Indigenous Sector

1. Sullivan (2011: 55).
2. Sullivan (2011: 77). Readers should note that although Patrick Sullivan and I largely agree in our accounts of 'the Indigenous sector', his use of that category is significantly narrower than mine, insofar as he also refers to these organisations as the 'Aboriginal not-for-profit sector'; in my conception of the Indigenous sector, an organisation may well adopt a business plan that generates a surplus of revenue over expenditure, a benefit that the organisation might return to its members.
3. Martin (2003: 1).
4. Smith (2002: 9) — that is, about 4000 bodies.
5. Smith (2008: 80).
6. Smith (2002: 29).
7. Reilly et al. (2007: 127).
8. Reilly et al. (2007: 165–6).
9. Reilly et al. (2007: 154).
10. Corrs et al. (2002: 18).
11. Corrs et al. (2002: 9).
12. Corrs et al. (2002: 7).
13. Corrs et al. (2002: 15).
14. Swansson (2010: 5).

15. Loveday (1989).
16. Howard (1990: 275).
17. Niezen (2003: 209).
18. Lange (2008: 323–4).
19. Lange (2008: 326).
20. Lange (2008: 327).
21. De Ishtar (2011: 76).
22. De Ishtar (2011: 77–8).
23. De Ishtar (2011: 81).
24. De Ishtar (2011: 78).
25. Morphy (2007c: 97). Brigg and Murphy (2011) rely heavily on this paper but draw largely negative conclusions about current Indigenous governance training.
26. Morphy (2007c: 97).
27. Morphy (2007c: 98).
28. Morphy (2007c: 98).
29. Morphy (2007c: 102).
30. Smith (2008: 101).
31. Smith (2008: 103).
32. Thorburn (2008: 348).
33. Altman (2008: 194).
34. Altman (2008: 177).
35. Ivory (2008: 253–6).
36. Thorburn says that people now have a repertoire of identities: 'pre-contact or traditional) (language, clan/country and kin), "station times", and now "community". None necessarily take[s] precedence over any other, but [they] rather co-exist and over time begin to reinforce (or undermine) one another within particular "community" reifications, some of which have been juridified within organisational structures.' (2007b: 11). This is similar to Ben Smith's (2008) point about Cape York political identities.
37. Merlan (1997: 150).
38. Glaskin (2007) gives a vivid instance of how West Kimberley people, as they adjust to native title success, change their norms of reckoning their obligations to one another.
39. Cowlishaw (1999: 296).
40. Cowlishaw (1999: 258).
41. Martin (1997: 23).
42. Smith (2002: 8).
43. Fingleton (1996: 90).
44. Martin (2009) — using the implementation of a mining agreement as a case study — continues the arguments of Martin (2003). Sullivan's recent book is aimed at the 'contemporary recognition of rights [that requires] the construction of Aboriginal societies as separate, distinct, classical and primordial' (Sullivan 2011: 84). He seeks to shift attention from 'essential cultural identity' to a 'needs-based approach' (2011: 16). Both authors insist on historicising the diverse modernising projects of contemporary Indigenous Australians.

NOTES

45. Martin (2003: 10), emphasis added.
46. Martin (2003: 11), emphasis added.
47. Martin (2003: 9).
48. Martin (2003: 9), emphasis added.
49. Martin (2003: 9), emphasis added.
50. Martin and Finlayson (1996: 5).
51. Martin and Finlayson (1996: 6).
52. Martin and Finlayson (1996: 8).
53. Finlayson (1998: 10).
54. Finlayson (1997: 5, 7).
55. Smith (2002: 25).
56. Smith (2002: 24).
57. Smith (2002: 25).
58. Smith (2002: 28).
59. Smith (2002: 23), emphasis added.
60. Sanders (2004: 15).
61. Sanders (2004: 19).
62. Sanders (2008: 285).
63. Smith (2007: 31); see also p. 43 for her account of the Western Central Arnhem Regional Authority (WCARA) model for 'networked governance'.
64. Smith (2007: 46).
65. Smith (2008: 79–80).
66. Marsh (2012: 12–19).
67. Marsh (2012: 12).
68. Marsh (2012: 29).
69. Dillon and Westbury (2007).
70. Smith (2008: 28–9).
71. Smith (2008: 50).
72. Michel, Gerritsen and Thynne (2010: 8).
73. Michel et al. (2010: 19).
74. Morton Consulting Services (2009: 11).
75. Morris, Callaghan and Walker (2010: 24).
76. Dillon and Westbury (2007: 190).
77. Martin (2009); in the same volume, see Levitus's (2009) specification of the functional requirements of one kind of Indigenous sector organisation: the royalty holder and distributor.
78. Dodson and Smith (2003: 15).
79. Dodson and Smith (2003: 14–15).
80. Dodson and Smith (2003: 16).
81. Dodson and Smith (2003: 16–17).
82. Dodson and Smith (2003: 17).
83. Dodson and Smith (2003: 18).
84. Dodson and Smith (2003: 19).
85. Martin (2003: 12).
86. Martin (2003: 11).
87. Attwood and Markus (2004: 94).
88. Dodson and Smith (2003: 15).

Chapter 7: The Ambivalence of Helen Hughes

1. Hughes (2007: 64–5).
2. Hughes (2007: 65–6).
3. Hughes (2007: 64, 66, 187).
4. Hughes (2007: 143).
5. Hughes (2007: 3).
6. Hughes (2007: 3 and Tables 2.1 and 2.3).
7. Hughes (2007: 23).
8. Hughes (2007: 85).
9. Hughes (2007: 3).
10. Hughes (2007: 85).
11. Hughes (2007: 181).
12. Hughes (2007: 40).
13. Hughes (2007: 103).
14. Hughes (2007: 118).
15. Hughes (2007: 12–13, 70, 90).
16. Hughes (2007: 70).
17. Hughes (2007: 181).
18. Hughes (2007: 165).
19. Hughes (2007: 167).
20. Hughes (2007: 162–4).
21. Hughes (2007: 164).
22. Hughes (2007: 164)
23. Hughes (2007: 160, 173).
24. Hughes (2007: 162).
25. Hughes (2007: 162).
26. Hughes (2007: 163).
27. Hughes (2007: 162).
28. Hughes (2007: 84).
29. ATSISJC (2007: 141).
30. ATSISJC (2007: 144, 145, 147).
31. Hughes (2007: 84).
32. Hughes (2007: 37).
33. Hughes (2007: 95).
34. Hughes (2007: 127).
35. Hughes (2007: 128).
36. Hughes (2007: 154).
37. Devine (2005: 49), emphasis added.
38. Hughes (2007: 36).
39. Hughes (2007: 72).
40. Hughes (2007: 77), emphasis added.
41. Hughes (2007: 123).
42. Hughes (2007: 184).
43. Hughes (2007: 41).
44. Hughes (2007: 14).
45. Hughes (2007: 48, 46).

46. Hughes (2007: 29, 46).
47. Hughes (2007: 66).
48. Hughes (2007: 56).
49. Hughes (2007: 187).
50. Hughes (2007: 143).
51. Hughes (2007: 110).
52. Hughes (2007: 119–20).
53. Hughes (2007: 107).
54. Hughes (2007: 96).
55. Hughes (2007: 97).
56. Hughes (2007: 52).
57. Hughes (2007: 62).
58. Hughes (2007: 66).
59. Hughes (2007: 144, 161, 146).
60. Hughes (2007: 89).
61. Hughes (2007: 87).
62. Hughes (2007: 56, 86, 173).
63. Hughes (2007: 64, 51).
64. Hughes (2007: 56).
65. Hughes (2007: 56).
66. Hughes (2007: 139, 186).
67. Hughes (2007: 69, 139, 22).
68. Hughes (2007: 160).
69. Hughes (2007: 160).
70. Hughes (2007: 23).

Chapter 8: 'If We are to Survive as a People…'

1. Pearson (2009: 327).
2. The opening paragraphs of *Our right to take responsibility* (2000) were an exception. See Pearson (2009: 144).
3. Pearson (2009: 366).
4. Pearson (2009: 358–9).
5. Pearson (2009: 327).
6. Pearson (2009: 386).
7. Pearson (2009: 42).
8. Pearson (2009: 41).
9. Pearson (2009: 44).
10. Pearson (2009: 44).
11. Pearson (2009: 47).
12. Pearson (2009: 38).
13. Pearson (2009: 34).
14. Pearson (2009: 143).
15. Pearson (2009: 149).
16. Pearson (2009: 327).
17. Pearson (2009: 189).
18. Pearson (2009: 59).

19. Pearson (2009: 117).
20. Pearson (2009: 237).
21. Pearson (2009: 351).
22. Pearson (2009: 154).
23. Pearson (2009: 158).
24. Pearson (2009: 158).
25. Pearson (2009: 329).
26. Pearson (2009: 158).
27. Pearson (2009: 189).
28. Pearson (2007: 60); Pearson (2009: 159).
29. Pearson (2007: 61).
30. Pearson (2009: 232).
31. Pearson (2009: 233).
32. Pearson (2009: 241).
33. In Rowse (2006 and 2010), through reading four autobiographies published in the wake of the 'Hindmarsh Island Affair', I have attempted to discern the differentiated formation of Ngarrindjeri historical consciousness.
34. For example, Wilson (1998).
35. Pearson (1986: 7–8).
36. Pearson (1986: 27).
37. Pearson (1986: 33–4).
38. Pearson (1986: 34).
39. Pearson (1986: 61–2). In 2008, reflecting on the Australian parliament's apology to the Stolen Generations, Pearson hailed Schwartz as 'a hero to me and to my people': see Pearson (2009: 383).
40. Pearson (1986: 102).
41. Pearson (1986: 38).
42. Pearson (1986: 39).
43. Pearson (2007: 15).
44. Pearson (2009: 26).
45. Pearson (2007: 13).
46. Pearson (2009: 33–4).
47. Pearson (2009: 34).
48. Pearson (2009: 235).
49. Pearson (2006).
50. Pearson (2009: 183–4).
51. Pearson (2009: 185).
52. Pearson (2009: 188).
53. Pearson (2009: 194).
54. Pearson (2009: 190).
55. Pearson (2009: 195).
56. Pearson (2009: 192).
57. Pearson (2009: 195).
58. Pearson (2009: 134).
59. Pearson (2009: 76).
60. Pearson (2009: 251).
61. Pearson (2009: 61–7, 91).

62. Pearson (2009: 67).
63. Pearson (2009: 67, 73).
64. Pearson (2009: 75).
65. Pearson (2009: 70).
66. Pearson (2009: 86).
67. Pearson (2009: 77).
68. Pearson (2009: 98).
69. Pearson (2009: 99).
70. Howard (2010: 282).
71. Howard (2010: 283–4). Note Marcia Langton's comment that Pearson was 'not involved' in 'the development of the NT Intervention approach'. He was telephoned once or twice by Howard, 'but was largely unaware of the approach being developed (and its heavy borrowing from his own thinking and initiatives in Cape York) until it became public' (Langton 2010: 94).
72. Pearson (2010).
73. Pearson (2010).
74. Pearson (2010).
75. Pearson (2009: 351), emphasis added.
76. Pearson (2009: 365), emphasis added.
77. Pearson (2009: 155).

Chapter 9: Peter Sutton and the Historical Roots of Suffering

1. Sutton (2009: 1).
2. Sutton (2009: 7).
3. Sutton (2009: 10–11).
4. Sutton (2009: 10).
5. Also the theme in Langton (2010).
6. Sutton (2009: 164).
7. Sutton (2009: 11).
8. Sutton (2009: 24, 32).
9. Sutton (2009: 144).
10. Sutton (2009: 11).
11. Sutton (2009: 162).
12. Sutton (2009: 10–12).
13. Sutton (2009: 12).
14. Sutton (2009: 17).
15. Sutton (2009: 17).
16. Sutton (2009: 31).
17. Sutton (2009: 31).
18. Sutton (2009: 33, 41).
19. Sutton (2009: 35).
20. Sutton (2009: 40).
21. Sutton (2009: 160).
22. Sutton (2009: 49, 55).
23. Sutton (2009: 56).
24. Sutton (2009: 79).

25. Sutton (2009: 64).
26. Sutton (2009: 85).
27. Recent ethnography of child-rearing among Pitjantjatjara (Eickelkamp 2011) supports Sutton's impression of continuity in the formation of remote Aboriginal person-hood, but judges that this is socially integrative (with kin and community). Eickelkamp cites Sutton but does not directly respond to his argument that such socialisation will maladapt Pitjantjatjara people to contemporary Australian society.
28. Sutton (2005: 39).
29. Sutton (2009: 101).
30. Sutton (2009: 122, 132).
31. Sutton (2009: 133, 136–7).
32. Sutton (2009: 141); see also Sutton's op-ed piece in *The Australian*, 30 September 2009.
33. Sutton (2009: 143).
34. Sutton (2005: 40).
35. Sutton (2009: 205).
36. Sutton (2009: 206).
37. Sutton (2009: 207).
38. Sutton (2009: 209).

Chapter 10: The Coombs Experiment

1. Yates (2009: 47–56).
2. Yates (2009: 49).
3. Yates (2009: 50).
4. Yates (2009: 50).
5. For a recent ethnographic study of conflicting orientations to the labour process in the remote Aboriginal context, see McRae-Williams and Gerritsen (2010). Drawing on EP Thompson, Richard Broome (1994) argues that in the nineteenth century cultural difference in orientations to work was one of the factors determining Aborigines' relationship to the labour market.
6. One of the most important of those assemblages is the school. For an account of the difficulty of treating the school as a site for the experimental production knowledge about the difference/sameness of Aboriginal and non-Aboriginal worlds, see Lea (2010).
7. Mintzberg and Waters (1985).
8. Hirschman (1998: 93).
9. Hirschman (1998: 93).
10. Partington (1996).
11. Partington (1996); see also Rowse (1996) for a critique, and Partington's response in Partington (1997).
12. Hughes and Warin (2005: 14–15); Warin (2007: 11).
13. *Courier-Mail*, 3 March 2005.
14. *Courier-Mail*, 3 March 2005.
15. *Australian Financial Review*, 1 March 2005.
16. *Australian Financial Review*, 1 March 2005.

NOTES

17. *Counterpoint*, ABC Radio National, Transcript, 23 July 2007.
18. Coombs quoted on *Counterpoint*, ABC Radio National, Transcript, 23 July 2007.
19. *Counterpoint*, ABC Radio National, Transcript, 23 July 2007.
20. *Counterpoint*, ABC Radio National, Transcript, 23 July 2007.
21. *Counterpoint*, ABC Radio National, Transcript, 23 July 2007.
22. *Counterpoint*, ABC Radio National, Transcript, 23 July 2007.
23. A false claim. See Coombs (1994: 191), and Coombs, Brandl and Snowdon (1983: 181), where the authors *complain* that English is not yet taught well enough to many Aboriginal pupils.
24. *Counterpoint*, ABC Radio National, Transcript, 23 July 2007.
25. *Counterpoint*, ABC Radio National, Transcript, 23 July 2007.
26. *Australian Financial Review*, 26 May 2007.
27. *Australian Financial Review*, 26 May 2007.
28. For an extended account of Coombs' policy advocacy that fleshes out each of the moments to which this paragraph refers, see Rowse (2000).
29. Coombs (1969: 329–37).
30. Coombs (1978).
31. Coombs (1969: 329).
32. Coombs (1969: 329).
33. Coombs (1969: 329).
34. Coombs (1969: 331).
35. Coombs (1969: 331).
36. Fox (1973: 13).
37. Coombs (1969: 331).
38. Coombs (1969: 332).
39. Coombs (1969: 332).
40. Coombs (1969: 332).
41. Coombs (1969: 331).
42. Coombs (1969: 332).
43. Coombs (1969: 332).
44. Coombs (1969: 332).
45. Quoted in Rowse (2000: 33).
46. Quoted in Rowse (2000: 82).
47. Coombs (1978: 131–49)
48. Hasluck (1959b).
49. Coombs, Brandl and Snowdon (1983: 388).
50. Coombs (1994: 189).
51. Cited in Sullivan (2011: 75). The minister was speaking to the National Institute for Governance, University of Canberra on 5 December 2006.
52. In their recent essay 'Very risky business: the quest to normalise remote-living Aboriginal people', Jon Altman and Melinda Hinkson (2010: 188) consider the risks of forcing 'remote living Indigenous people into the mainstream'. Their principal argument is that the new policies demand that an 'ego-centred worldview' displace a social order in which Aboriginal cosmology remains 'an organising principle for the relations between

people, other living things and the environments they inhabit' (2010: 190). Individual responsibility would become more important at the expense of a sense of mutual responsibility; kinship would become a private concern rather than being the most important framework in which to understand social connection. The consequences (which they say may be intended or unintended) that they fear are that for many Aborigines income will decrease, unemployment will increase, home mortgages will become an unsustainable financial burden, welfare entitlements will be more conditional, and the social infrastructure of region-specific 'hybrid economies' will disappear. A rigorous use of the concept 'risk' would consider what might happen if the 'mainstreaming' policies to which they object were *not* pursued. The authors cite — but do not evaluate — the risks associated with not applying the 'mainstreaming' policies of the Howard government when initiating the Northern Territory Intervention.
53. Sutton (2009: 52).
54. Sutton (2009: 52).
55. Beckett (2010: 42–3).
56. Langton (2010: 92).
57. Langton (2010: 92).
58. Langton (2010: 95), though see Merlan (1997) for an account of generational differences among Jawoyn perspectives on land.
59. Coombs, Brandl and Snowdon (1983: 146).
60. Coombs, Brandl and Snowdon (1983: 148).
61. Coombs, Brandl and Snowdon (1983: 170).
62. Coombs (1985: 298).
63. Darwin (2004: 155).
64. Darwin (2004: 157).
65. Rowse (2000: 177–8).
66. Sullivan (2011: 82). The Australian Bureau of Statistics has been experimenting in partnerships with Aboriginal organisations. See Taylor (2009) and Prout (2011) for ideas about redesigning indicators of Indigenous wellbeing.
67. Povinelli (2010: 22).
68. Austin-Broos (2010: 143–5); Peterson (2010: 254–6); McRae-Williams and Gerritsen (2010).
69. Altman (2001, 2007, 2010).
70. COAG (2009: A-31).
71. SCRGSP (2011: 11.1).
72. SCRGSP (2011: 13).
73. Reading Chapter 11, 'Governance and leadership' (SCRGSP 2011) leaves a strong impression that this 'building block' is taken seriously by a large cohort of researchers, educators, government officials and Indigenous leaders.
74. Sullivan (2011: 105); see also pp. 103–7 for a critique of the evidence base of the National Indigenous Reform Agreement.

NOTES

Chapter 11: The Australian Reconciliation Barometer and the Indigenous Imaginary

1. Sullivan (2011: 74).
2. Stolper and Hammond (2010: 5).
3. Reconciliation Australia (2011).
4. Pratt (2005: 34, Figure 2.1).
5. Stolper and Hammond (2010: 44).
6. Stolper and Hammond (2010: 23).
7. Stolper and Hammond (2010: 25).
8. Stolper and Hammond (2010: 24–5).
9. Stolper and Hammond (2010: 32).
10. Stolper and Hammond (2010: 53).
11. Stolper and Hammond (2010: 35).
12. Stolper and Hammond (2010: 35).
13. Stolper and Hammond (2010: 35).
14. Stolper and Hammond (2010: 55).
15. Stolper and Hammond (2010: 35).
16. Stolper and Hammond (2010: 50–1).
17. Stolper and Hammond (2010: 50–1).
18. Stolper and Hammond (2010: 30–1).
19. Stolper and Hammond (2010: 34).
20. Stolper and Hammond (2010: 18).
21. Stolper and Hammond (2010: 61).
22. Stolper and Hammond (2010: 57).
23. Stolper and Hammond (2010: 58).
24. Stolper and Hammond (2010: 50).
25. Stolper and Hammond (2010: 41–2).
26. Stolper and Hammond (2010: 41–2).
27. Stolper and Hammond (2010: 60).
28. Stolper and Hammond (2010: 65).
29. Stolper and Hammond (2010: 65).
30. Stolper and Hammond (2010: 65).
31. Stolper and Hammond (2010: 27).
32. Stolper and Hammond (2010: 26).
33. Stolper and Hammond (2010: 28).
34. Stolper and Hammond (2010: 42).
35. Stolper and Hammond (2010: 66).
36. Stolper and Hammond (2010: 59).

References

Official publications

Aboriginal and Torres Strait Islander Social Justice Commissioner (ATSISJC) 2007, *Social Justice Report 2006*, ATSISJC, Canberra.

Australian Human Rights and Equal Opportunity Commission (HREOC) 1997, *Bringing them home: report of the National Inquiry into the Separation of Aboriginal and Torres Strait Islander Children from Their Families*, Commonwealth Government, Canberra, April, viewed 29 April 2012, <http://www.hreoc.gov.au/social_justice/bth_report/report/index.html>.

Australian Institute of Aboriginal Studies 1973, *Annual Report 1972–73*, AIAS, Canberra.

Australian Parliament 1961, *Report from the Select Committee on Voting Rights of Aborigines*, Commonwealth Government, Canberra.

Australian Law Reform Commission 1986, *Recognition of Aboriginal Customary Laws*, Report no. 31, ALRC, Canberra, viewed 29 April 2012, <http://www.alrc.gov.au/publications/report-31>.

Council for Aboriginal Affairs (CAA) 1971, 'The situation of Aboriginal Australians', unpublished paper, 7 July, Dexter Papers, file 29/3, AIATSIS Library, Canberra.

Council of Australian Governments (COAG) 2009, *National Indigenous Reform Agreement (Closing the Gap)*, viewed 29 April 2012, <http://www.coag.gov.au/coag_meeting_outcomes/2009-07-02/docs/NIRA_closing_the_gap>.

Northern Territory Legislative Council 1965, *Report of the Select Committee on the Native and Historical Objects and Areas Preservation Ordinance 1955–60*, Commonwealth Government Printer, Darwin.

Productivity Commission, Steering Committee for the Review of Government Service Provision (SCRGSP) 2011, *Overcoming Indigenous Disadvantage: Key Indicators 2011 Report*, Productivity Commission, Canberra.

Senate Legal and Constitutional Affairs Committee 2000, *Healing: a legacy of generations*, Commonwealth Government, Canberra.

South Australian Aboriginal Affairs Board 1967, *Report of the Aboriginal Affairs Board for the Year Ended 30th June, 1966*, SA Parliamentary Paper 20, in *Proceedings of the SA Parliament*, Vol. 2, South Australian Government, Adelaide.

South Australian Parliament 1967, *Report of the Select Committee of the Legislative Council on the Aboriginal Lands Trust Bill, 1966* (together with minutes of proceedings and evidence with appendices (1967) SA PP 98, 1966–67, second session of the 38th Parliament, 28 September–21 November 1966, South Australian Government, Adelaide.

REFERENCES

Books and articles

Altman, JC 2001, *Sustainable development options on Aboriginal land: the hybrid economy of the 21st century*, CAEPR Discussion Paper no. 226, Centre for Aboriginal Economic Policy Research, Australian National University, Canberra.
—— 2007, 'Alleviating poverty in remote Indigenous Australia: the role of the hybrid economy', *Development Bulletin*, no. 72, March, pp. 47–51.
—— 2008, 'Different governance for difference: the Bawinanga Aboriginal Corporation', in *Contested governance: culture, power and institutions in Indigenous Australia*, eds J Hunt, D Smith, S Garling & W Sanders, CAEPR Research Monograph no. 29, ANU ePress, Canberra, pp. 177–203.
—— 2010, 'What future for remote Indigenous Australia? Economic hybridity and the neoliberal turn', in *Culture crisis: anthropology and politics in Aboriginal Australia*, eds J Altman & M Hinkson, UNSW Press, Sydney, pp. 259–80.
Altman, J & Hinkson, M 2010, 'Very risky business: the quest to normalise remote-living Aboriginal people', in *Risk, responsibility and the welfare state*, eds G Marston, J Moss & J Quiggin, Melbourne University Publishing, Melbourne, pp. 185–211.
Attwood, B & Markus, A (eds) 2004, *Thinking Black: William Cooper and the Australian Aborigines League*, Aboriginal Studies Press, Canberra.
Austin-Broos, D 2010, 'Quarantining violence: how anthropology does it', in *Culture crisis: anthropology and politics in Aboriginal Australia*, eds J Altman & M Hinkson, UNSW Press, Sydney, pp. 136–49.
Beckett, J 2010, 'National anthropologies and their problems', in *Culture crisis: anthropology and politics in Aboriginal Australia*, eds J Altman & M Hinkson, UNSW Press, Sydney, pp. 32–44.
Berndt, CH 1962, 'Mateship or success: an assimilation dilemma', *Oceania*, vol. 33, no. 2, pp. 71–89.
Berndt, R & Berndt, C 1951, *From Black to White in South Australia*, FW Cheshire, Melbourne.
Blagg, H 2008, *Crime, Aboriginality and the decolonisation of justice*, Hawkins Press, Sydney.
Blake, T 1998, 'Deported … At the sweet will of the government: the removal of Aborigines to reserves in Queensland 1897–1939', *Aboriginal history*, vol. 22, pp. 51–61.
Borrie, W 1975, *Population and Australia: a demographic analysis and projection, vol. 2*, AGPS, Canberra.
Brigg, M & Murphy, L 2011, 'Beyond captives and captors: settler-Indigenous governance for the twenty-first century', in *Unsettling the settler state: creativity and resistance in Indigenous settler-state governance*, eds S Maddison and M Brigg, Federation Press, Sydney, pp. 16–31.
Broome, R 1994, 'Aboriginal workers on south-eastern frontiers', *Australian Historical Studies*, vol. 26, no. 103, pp. 202–20.
—— 2005, *Aboriginal Victorians: a history since 1800*, Allen & Unwin, Sydney.
Coombs, HC 1969 'Science and the future of man: the role of the social scientist', paper presented at the Felton Bequest symposium 'Man and his Science', in honour of the 70th birthday of Sir Macfarlane Burnet, Melbourne, *Australasian Annals of Medicine*, vol. 18, no. 4, pp. 329–37.
—— 1972, 'Decisions by Aborigines', *Anthropological Forum*, no. 3, pp. 136–45.
—— 1978, *Kulinma: listening to Aboriginal Australians*, Australian National University Press, Canberra.
—— 1985, 'Where do we go from here?', in J Wright, *We call for a treaty*, Fontana, Sydney, pp. 284–307.
—— 1994, *Aboriginal autonomy*, Cambridge University Press, Melbourne.

Coombs, HC, Brandl, MM & Snowdon, WE 1983, *A certain heritage: programs for and by Aboriginal families in Australia*, Centre for Resource and Environmental Studies, Australian National University, Canberra.

Copland, M 2005, 'Calculating lives: the numbers and narratives of forced removals in Queensland 1859–1972', PhD thesis, Griffith University.

Corrs Chambers Westgarth 2002, *A modern statute for Indigenous corporations: reforming the Aboriginal Councils and Associations Act*, Final report of the Review of the *Aboriginal Councils and Associations Act*, Office of the Registrar of Aboriginal Corporations, Canberra, December, viewed 20 November 2011, <http://www.orac.gov.au/publications/legislation/final_report.pdf>.

Cowlishaw, G 1999, *Rednecks, eggheads and blackfellas: a study of racial power and intimacy in Australia*, Allen & Unwin, Sydney.

Darwin, C 2004 [1879], *The descent of man*, Penguin, Harmondsworth.

De Ishtar, Z & the Women Elders of Kapululangu Aboriginal Women's Law and Culture Centre 2011, 'The ways of Walawalarra: Kapululangu's two-way governance', in *Unsettling the Settler State: Creativity and Resistance in Indigenous Settler-State Governance*, eds S Maddison and M Brigg, Federation Press, Sydney, pp. 68–82.

Devine, F 2005, 'A conversation with Helen Hughes', *Quadrant*, December, pp. 48–50.

Dexter, B 2008, 'Stanner: reluctant bureaucrat', in *An appreciation of difference: WEH Stanner and Aboriginal Australia*, eds M Hinkson & J Beckett, Aboriginal Studies Press, Canberra, pp. 76–86.

Dillon, M & Westbury, N 2007, *Beyond humbug: transforming government engagement with Indigenous Australia*, Seaview Press, Adelaide.

Dodson, M 2003, 'The end of the beginning: re(de)finding Aboriginality', in *Blacklines: contemporary critical writing by Indigenous Australians*, ed M. Grossman, Melbourne University Press, Melbourne, pp. 25–42.

Dodson, M & Smith, D 2003, *Governance for sustainable development: strategic issues and principles for Indigenous Australian communities*, CAEPR Discussion Paper 250, Centre for Aboriginal Economic Policy Research, Australian National University, Canberra.

Dodson, P 2012, 'Mahatma Gandhi Inaugural Oration', University of New South Wales, 30 January, typescript.

Downing, JH 1971, 'Consultation and self-determination in the social development of Aborigines', in *A question of choice: an Australian Aboriginal Dilemma*, ed. RM Berndt, UWA Press, Perth, pp. 61–90.

Edwards, C & Read, P (eds) 1989, *The lost children*, Doubleday, Sydney.

Edwards, R (ed) 1975, *The preservation of Australia's Aboriginal heritage*, Australian Institute of Aboriginal Studies, Canberra.

Eickelcamp, U 2011, 'Changing selves in remote Australia? Observations on Aboriginal family life, childhood and "modernisation"', *Anthropological Forum*, vol. 21, no. 2, pp. 131–51.

Elkin, AP 1951, 'Aborigines and the Ministers' Welfare Council', *Australian Quarterly*, vol. 23, no. 4, pp. 9–20.

—— 1959, 'Assimilation and integration', address to the ANZAAS Congress, Perth, Elkin Papers, Fisher Library, University of Sydney, Box 108, item 1/17/3.

Engle, K 2010, *The elusive promise of Indigenous development*, Duke University Press, Durham, NC.

Evans, R 1999, '"Steal away": the fundamentals of Aboriginal removal in Queensland', *Journal of Australian Studies*, vol. 23, no. 61, pp. 83–95.

Fenton, S 1984, *Durkheim and modern sociology*, Cambridge University Press, Cambridge.

Fingleton, J 1996, *Final report: Review of the Aboriginal Councils and Associations Act 1976* (vol. 1), Australian Institute of Aboriginal and Torres Strait Islander Studies, Canberra.

REFERENCES

Finlayson, J 1997, *Native title representative bodies: The challenge of strategic planning*, CAEPR Discussion Paper 129, Centre for Aboriginal Economic Policy Research, Australian National University, Canberra.

—— 1998, *New and emerging challenges for native title representative bodies*, CAEPR Discussion Paper 167, Centre for Aboriginal Economic Policy Research, Australian National University, Canberra.

—— 1999, 'Northern Territory land rights: purpose and effectiveness', Discussion Paper 180, Centre for Aboriginal Economic Policy Research, Australian National University, Canberra.

Fox, R 1973, 'Anthropology as a vocation', introductory essay in his *Encounters with Anthropology*, Harcourt Brace Jovanovich, New York.

Glaskin, K 2003, 'Native title and the "bundle of rights" model: implications for the recognition of Aboriginal relations to country', *Anthropological Forum*, vol. 13, no. 1, pp. 67–88.

—— 2007, 'Claim, culture and effect: property relations and the native title process', in *The social effect of native title*, eds BR Smith & F Morphy, CAEPR Research Monograph, no. 27, ANU ePress, Canberra, pp. 59–77.

Gover, K 2010, *Tribal constitutionalism*, Oxford University Press, New York.

Gray, S 2011, *Brass discs, dog tags and finger scanners: the Apology and Aboriginal protection in the Northern Territory 1863–1972*, Charles Darwin University Press, Darwin.

Haebich, A 2000, *Broken circles*, Fremantle Arts Centre Press, Fremantle.

—— 2005 'Nuclear, suburban and black: Middleton's vision of assimilation for Nyungar families', in *Contesting Assimilation*, ed. T Rowse, API Network, Perth, pp. 201–20.

Haebich, A & Mellor, D (eds) 2002, *Many voices: reflections on experiences of Indigenous child separation*, National Library of Australia, Canberra.

Hasluck, PMC 1959a, 'Are our Aborigines neglected?' unpublished paper presented at PSA Service, the Lyceum, Sydney on 12 July, Box 80, item 294, papers of AP Elkin, Fisher Library, University of Sydney.

—— 1959b, 'Some problems of assimilation' unpublished paper presented to Section F (Anthropology) of ANZAAS in Perth, 28 August 1959, Box 80, item 295, papers of AP Elkin, Fisher Library, University of Sydney.

—— 1988, *Shades of darkness*, Melbourne University Press, Melbourne.

Hegarty, R 2003, *Bitter sweet journey*, University of Queensland Press, Brisbane.

Herron, J 2000, Federal government submission to the Senate Legal and Constitutional Committee Inquiry into the Stolen Generation, typescript held in the Library of the Australian Institute of Aboriginal and Torres Strait Islander Studies.

Hirschman, AO 1998, *Crossing boundaries: selected writings*, Zone Books, New York.

Host, J & Milroy, J 2001, 'The Stolen Generation: John Herron and the politics of denial', *Studies in Western Australian History*, no. 22, pp. 141–67.

Howard, A 1990, 'Cultural paradigms, history, and the search for identity in Oceania', in *Cultural identity and ethnicity in the Pacific*, eds J Linnekin & L Poyer, University of Hawaii Press, Honolulu, pp. 259–80.

Howard, JW 2010, *Lazarus rising: a personal and political autobiography*, Harper Collins, Sydney.

Hughes, H 2007, *Lands of shame*, Centre for Independent Studies, Sydney.

Hughes, H & Warin, J 2005, *A new deal for Aborigines and Torres Strait Islanders in remote communities*, Centre for Independent Studies, Sydney.

Ivory, B 2008, 'Indigenous leaders and leadership: agents of networked governance', in *Contested governance: culture, power and institutions in Indigenous Australia*, eds J Hunt, D Smith, S Garling & W Sanders, CAEPR Research Monograph no. 29, ANU ePress, Canberra, pp. 233–62.

REFERENCES

Kamien, H 1978, *The dark people of Bourke*, Australian Institute of Aboriginal Studies, Canberra.

Kruger, A & Waterford, G 2007, *Alone on the soaks: the life and times of Alec Kruger*, IAD Press, Alice Springs.

Lange, C 2008, 'Incorporating cattle: governance and an Aboriginal pastoral enterprise', in *Contested governance: culture, power and institutions in Indigenous Australia*, eds J Hunt, D Smith, S Garling & W Sanders, CAEPR Research Monograph no. 29, ANU ePress, Canberra, pp. 313–30.

Langton, M 2010, 'The shock of the new: a postcolonial dilemma for Australianist anthropology', in *Culture crisis: anthropology and politics in Aboriginal Australia*, eds J Altman & M Hinkson, UNSW Press, Sydney, pp. 91–115.

Lattas, A & Morris, B 2010, 'The politics of suffering and the politics of anthropology', in *Culture crisis: anthropology and politics in Aboriginal Australia*, eds J Altman & M Hinkson, UNSW Press, Sydney, pp. 61–87.

Lea, T 2010, 'Indigenous education and training: what are we here for?' in *Culture crisis: anthropology and politics in Aboriginal Australia*, eds J Altman & M Hinkson, UNSW Press, Sydney, pp. 195–211.

Levitus, R 2009, 'Aboriginal organisations and development: the structural context', in *Power, culture and economy: Indigenous Australians and mining*, eds J Altman & D Martin, CAEPR Research Monograph no. 30, ANU ePress, Canberra, pp. 73–98.

Loos, N & Keast, R 1992, 'The radical promise: the Aboriginal Christian cooperative movement', *Australian Historical Studies*, no. 99, pp. 286–301.

Loveday, P 1989, 'Local governance in Aboriginal communities', in *That community government mob; local government in small Northern Territory communities*, ed. J Wolfe, Australian National University North Australia Research Unit, Darwin, pp. 13–35.

Manne, R 2001, *In denial: the Stolen Generations and the right*, Australian Quarterly Essay no. 1, Black Inc, Melbourne.

Marsh, I 2011, *The Evolution of Governance in Remote Australia: From Centralised to Contextualised Approaches?* report for remoteFocus, November, viewed 28 March 2011, <http://www.desertknowledge.com.au/remoteFocus>.

Martin, D 1997, *Regional agreements and localism: a case study from Cape York Peninsula*, CAEPR Discussion Paper 146, Centre for Aboriginal Economic Policy Research, Australian National University, Canberra.

—— 2002, 'Counting the Wik: the 2001 Census in Aurukun, Western Cape York Peninsula', in *Making sense of the Census*, eds DF Martin, F Morphy, WG Sanders & J Taylor, CAEPR Research Monograph 22, ANU ePress, Canberra, pp. 13–28.

—— 2003, *Rethinking the design of Indigenous organisations: the need for strategic engagement*, CAEPR Discussion Paper 248, Centre for Aboriginal Economic Policy Research, Australian National University, Canberra.

—— 2009, 'The governance of agreements between Aboriginal people and resource developers: principles for sustainability', in *Power, culture and economy: Indigenous Australians and mining*, eds J Altman & D Martin, CAEPR Research Monograph no. 30, ANU ePress, Canberra, pp. 99–126.

Martin, D & Finlayson, J 1996, *Linking accountability and self-determination in Aboriginal organisations*, CAEPR Discussion Paper 116, Centre for Aboriginal Economic Policy Research, Australian National University, Canberra.

Martin, D, Morphy, F, Sanders, W & Taylor, J 2002, 'The Indigenous enumeration strategy: an overview assessment and ideas for improvement', in *Making Sense of the Census*, eds DF Martin, F Morphy, WG Sanders & J Taylor, CAEPR Research Monograph, no. 22, ANU ePress, Canberra, pp. 95–102.

REFERENCES

McGregor, R 2001, 'From Old Testament to New: AP Elkin on Christian conversion and cultural assimilation', *Journal of Religious History*, vol. 25, no. 1, pp. 39–55.

—— 2002, 'Assimilationists contest assimilation: TGH Strehlow and AP Elkin on Aboriginal policy', *Journal of Australian Studies*, no. 75, pp. 43–50.

—— 2005, 'Assimilation as acculturation: AP Elkin on the dynamics of cultural change', in *Contesting Assimilation*, ed. T Rowse, API Network, Perth, pp. 169–83.

—— 2011, *Indifferent inclusion: Aboriginal people and the Australian nation*, Aboriginal Studies Press, Canberra.

McRae-Williams, E & Gerritsen, R 2010, 'Mutual incomprehension: the cross-cultural domain of work in a remote Australian Aboriginal community', *International Indigenous Policy Journal*, vol. 1, no. 2, Article 2, viewed 20 November 2012, <http://ir.lib.uwo.ca/iipj/vol1/iss2/2>.

Merlan, F 1997, *Caging the rainbow: places, politics and Aborigines in a Northern Territory town*, University of Hawaii Press, Honolulu.

—— 2006, 'Beyond tradition', *Asia Pacific Journal of Anthropology*, vol. 7, no. 1, pp. 85–104.

—— 2010, 'Child sexual abuse: the Intervention trigger', in *Culture crisis: anthropology and politics in Aboriginal Australia*, eds J Altman & M Hinkson, UNSW Press, Sydney, pp. 116–35.

Michel, T, Gerritsen, R & Thynne, I 2010, *Northern Territory scoping study*, Australian Centre of Excellence for Local Government (ACELG), Sydney, viewed 21 December 2011, <http://www.acelg.org.au/library.php?id=mostRecent>.

Mintzberg, H & Waters, JA 1985, 'Of strategies, deliberate and emergent', *Strategic Management Journal*, vol. 6, no. 3, pp. 257–72.

Morphy, F 2007a, 'The transformation of input into output: at the Melbourne Data Processing Centre', in *Agency, contingency and Census process*, ed. F. Morphy, CAEPR Research Monograph no. 28, ANU ePress, Canberra, pp. 101–12.

—— 2007b, 'Uncontained subjects: "population" and "household" in remote Aboriginal Australia', *Journal of Population Research*, no. 24, pp. 163–84.

—— 2007c, 'The language of governance in a cross-cultural context: what can and can't be translated', *Ngiya: Talk the Law*, vol. 1, pp. 93–102.

Morris, R, Callaghan, R & Walker, B 2010, *Rural-remote and Indigenous local government: Western Australian scoping study report*, Australian Centre of Excellence for Local Government (ACELG), Sydney, viewed 29 November 2011, <http://www.acelg.org.au/library.php?id+mostRecent>.

Morton Consulting Services Pty Ltd 2009, *Capacity-building needs of non-amalgamated councils: 2009 scoping study*, Australian Centre of Excellence for Local Government (ACELG), Sydney, viewed 29 November 2011, <http://www.ACELG.org.au/library.php?id+mostRecent>.

Niezen, R 2003, *The origins of Indigenism: human rights and the politics of identity*, Berkeley, CA: University of California Press.

Partington, G 1996, *Hasluck versus Coombs: White politics and Australia's Aborigines*, Quaker's Hill Press, Sydney.

—— 1997, 'Riposte: Geoffrey Partington replies to Tim Rowse', *Meanjin*, no. 56, pp. 439–46.

Pearson, N 1986, 'Ngamu-ngaadyarr, Muuri-bunggaga and Midha Muni in Guugu-Yimidhirr history = dingoes, sheep and Mr Muni in Guugu-Yimidhirr history: Hope Vale Lutheran Mission 1900-1950', thesis (BA hons), University of Sydney, NSW (AIATSIS Library).

—— 2006, 'Hope Vale lost', *The Weekend Australian*, 17–18 February.

—— 2007, 'White guilt, victimhood and the quest for a radical centre', *Griffith Review 16: Unintended consequences*, Winter, pp. 34–72

—— 2009, *Up from the mission: selected writings*, Black Inc, Melbourne.
—— 2010, 'Nights when I dream of a better world: moving from the centre-left to the radical centre of Australian politics', The 2010 John Button Oration, viewed 29 November 2011, <http://johnbuttonprize.org.au/the-prize/media/post/noel-pearson-s-2010-john-button-oration-nights-when-i-dream-of-a-better-world-moving-from-the-centre-left-to-the-radical-centre-of-australian-politics>.

Peterson, N 2010, 'Other people's lives: secular assimilation, culture and ungovernability', in *Culture crisis: anthropology and politics in Aboriginal Australia*, eds J Altman & M Hinkson, UNSW Press, Sydney, pp. 248–58

Povinelli, E 2006, 'Finding Bwudjut: common land, private profit, divergent objects', in *Moving anthropology: critical Indigenous studies*, eds T Lea, E Kowal & G Cowlishaw, Charles Darwin University Press, Darwin, pp. 147–66.

—— 2010, 'Indigenous politics in late liberalism', in *Culture crisis: anthropology and politics in Aboriginal Australia*, eds J Altman & M Hinkson, UNSW Press, Sydney, pp. 17–31.

Pratt, A 2005, *Practising reconciliation? The politics of reconciliation in the Australian parliament, 1991–2000*, Department of Parliamentary Services, Canberra.

Prout, S 2011, 'Indigenous wellbeing frameworks in Australia and the quest for quantification', *Social Indicators Research* (online first) 2011, DOI: 10.1007/s11205-011-9905-7 (viewed 19 June 2012).

Raftery, J 2006, *Not part of the public*, Wakefield Press, Adelaide.

Read, P 1981, *The Stolen Generations: the removal of Aboriginal children in New South Wales 1883 to 1969*, NSW Ministry for Aboriginal Affairs, Sydney.

—— 1999, *A rape of the soul so profound*, Allen & Unwin, Sydney.

—— 2003, 'How many separated Aboriginal children?' *Australian Journal of Politics and History*, vol. 49, no. 2, pp. 155–63.

Reconciliation Australia 2011, 'New race relations barometer released: where is the love?' media release, 14 February.

Reilly, A, Behrendt, L, Williams, G, McCausland, R & McMillan, M 2007, 'The promise of regional governance for Aboriginal and Torres Strait Islander communities' *Ngiya: Talk the Law*, vol. 1, pp. 126–66.

Ritter, D 2009, *Contesting native title: from controversy to consensus in the struggle over Indigenous land rights*, Allen & Unwin, Sydney.

—— 2010, 'The ideological foundations of arguments about native title', *Australian Journal of Political Science*, vol. 45, no. 2, pp. 191–207.

Rowley, CD 1971, *Outcasts in White Australia*, Penguin, Ringwood.

Rowse, T 1978, *Australian liberalism and national character*, Kibble Books, Malmesbury.

—— 1988, 'From houses to households? The Aboriginal Development Commission and economic adaptation by Alice Springs town campers', in *Aborigines and the state in Australia*, special issue of *Social Analysis*, no. 24, ed. J Beckett, pp. 50–65

—— 1996, '"Past has merit" — Minister' (a review of G. Partington *Hasluck versus Coombs*), *Meanjin*, vol. 55, no. 4, pp. 614–29.

—— 1998, 'The modesty of the State: Hasluck and the anthropological critics of assimilation', in *Paul Hasluck in Australian History*, eds K Saunders & CT Stannage, University of Queensland Press, Brisbane, pp. 119–32.

—— 1999, The collector as outsider: TGH Strehlow as 'public intellectual', Occasional Paper 2, Strehlow Research Centre, Darwin, pp. 61–120.

—— 2000, *Obliged to be difficult: Nugget Coombs' legacy in Indigenous affairs*, Cambridge University Press, Melbourne.

—— 2002, *Nugget Coombs: a reforming life*, Cambridge University Press, Melbourne.

—— 2005a, 'The social science of assimilation 1947–66', in *Contesting assimilation*, ed. T Rowse, API Network, Perth, pp. 151–68.

—— 2005b, 'The Indigenous sector', in *Culture, economy and governance in Aboriginal Australia: Proceedings of a Workshop of the Academy of Social Sciences*, eds D Austin-Broos & G Macdonald, Sydney University Press, Sydney, pp. 207–24.

—— 2006, 'The public occasions of Indigenous selves', *Aboriginal History*, no. 30, pp. 187–207.

—— 2007, 'Lands of confusion' (review article on H Hughes, *Lands of Shame*), *Australian Policy Online*, viewed 29 November 2011, <http://www.sisr.net/apo/rowse.pdf>.

—— 2009, 'The Reconciliation Barometer and the Indigenous imaginary', *Australian Policy Online*, viewed 29 November 2011, <http://apo.org.au/research/reconciliation-barometer-and-indigenous-imaginary>.

—— 2010, 'Knowing and not knowing: the Ngarrindjeri dilemma', *Life Writing*, vol. 7, no. 3, pp. 245–58.

—— 2011, 'Debating the categories of remote Indigenous sociality', *Alternatives: global, local, political*, vol. 36, no. 1, pp. 39–47.

Rowse, T & Smith, L 2010, 'The limits of "elimination" in the politics of population', *Australian Historical Studies*, vol. 41, no. 1, pp. 90–106.

Sanders, W 2002, 'Adapting to circumstance: the 2001 Census in the Alice Springs town camps', in *Making sense of the Census: observations of the 2001 enumeration in remote Aboriginal Australia*, eds DF Martin, F Morphy, WG Sanders & J Taylor, CAEPR Research Monograph no. 22, ANU ePress, Canberra, pp. 77–93.

—— 2004, *Thinking about Indigenous community governance*, CAEPR Discussion Paper 262, Centre for Aboriginal Economic Policy Research, Australian National University, Canberra.

—— 2007, 'A vast improvement: The 2006 enumeration in the Alice Springs town camps', in *Agency, contingency and Census process: Observations of the 2006 Indigenous Enumeration Strategy in remote Aboriginal Australia*, ed. F. Morphy, CAEPR Research Monograph no. 28, ANU ePress, Canberra, pp. 21–31.

—— 2008, 'Regionalism that respects localism: the Anmatjere Community Government Council and beyond', eds J Hunt, D Smith, S Garling and W Sanders *Contested Governance: culture power and institutions in Indigenous Australia*, CAEPR Research Monograph no. 29, ANU ePress, Canberra, pp. 283–309

Smith, B 2008, 'Regenerating governance on Kaanju homelands', in *Contested governance: culture, power and institutions in Indigenous Australia*, eds J Hunt, D Smith, S Garling & W Sanders, CAEPR Research Monograph no. 29, ANU ePress, Canberra, pp. 153–73.

Smith, D 2002, *Jurisdictional devolution: towards an effective model for Indigenous community self-determination*, CAEPR Discussion Paper 233, Centre for Aboriginal Economic Policy Research, Australian National University, Canberra.

—— 2007, 'Networked governance: issues of process, policy and power in a West Arnhem Land region initiative', *Ngiya: Talk the Law*, vol. 1, pp. 24–52.

—— 2008, 'Cultures of governance and the governance of culture: transforming and containing Indigenous institutions in West Arnhem Land', in *Contested governance: culture, power and institutions in Indigenous Australia*, eds J Hunt, D Smith, S Garling & W Sanders, CAEPR Research Monograph no. 29, ANU ePress, Canberra, pp. 75–111.

Smith, L 1980, *The Aboriginal population of Australia*, ANU Press, Canberra.

Stanner, WEH 1970, 'Foreword', in *Aboriginal advancement to integration*, ed. HP Schapper, ANU Press, Canberra, pp. vii–viii.

Stolper, D & Hammond, J 2010, *2010 Reconciliation Barometer: a report prepared for Reconciliation Australia*, Reconciliation Australia, Canberra, viewed 26 March 2012, <http://www.reconciliation.org.au/home/resources/australian-reconciliation-barometer>.

Strehlow, TGH 1947, *Aranda traditions*, Melbourne University Press, Melbourne.

—— 1956, *The sustaining ideals of Australian Aboriginal societies*, Aborigines Advancement League (South Australia), Adelaide.

—— 1958, *Dark and white Australians*, Riall Bros, Melbourne.

—— 1961, *Nomads in No-Man's land*, Specialty Printers, Adelaide.

—— 1965, 'Some comments from Mr TGH Strehlow, Reader in Australian Linguistics, University of Adelaide', in Legislative Council of the Northern Territory, *Report of the Select Committee on the Native and Historical Objects and Areas Preservation Ordinance 1955–60*, Appendix II, Commonwealth Government Printer, Darwin, pp. 8–9.

—— 1969, 'Review of DJ Mulvaney *The Prehistory of Australia*', *Australian Book Review*, vol. 8, no. 10, p. 211.

—— 1971a, Letter to WC Wentworth, 7 July, Strehlow Research Centre, Alice Springs, annual correspondence files.

—— 1971b, Letter to Chairman of Council, AIAS, 9 March, Strehlow Research Centre, Alice Springs, annual correspondence files.

—— 1971c, Letter to RM Berndt, 20 April, Strehlow Research Centre, Alice Springs, annual correspondence files.

—— 1973, Letter to D Freeman, 3 July, Strehlow Research Centre, Alice Springs, annual correspondence files.

—— 1974a, Letter to HC Coombs, 2 February, Strehlow Research Centre, Alice Springs, annual correspondence files.

—— 1974b, Letter to Drake, 29 March, Strehlow Research Centre, Alice Springs, annual correspondence files.

—— 1986, 'Review of the aims and achievements of the Australian Institute of Aboriginal Studies, Canberra, during the first decade of its establishment, 1961–71 (part one)', *Strehlow Research Foundation Pamphlet*, vol. 9, no. 4, pp. 1–4.

—— 1987a, 'Review of the aims and achievements of the Australian Institute of Aboriginal Studies, Canberra, during the first decade of its establishment, 1961–71 (part two)', *Strehlow Research Foundation Pamphlet*, vol. 10, no. 1, pp. 1–4.

—— 1987b, 'Review of the aims and achievements of the Australian Institute of Aboriginal Studies, Canberra, during the first decade of its establishment, 1961–71 (part three)', *Strehlow Research Foundation Pamphlet*, vol. 10, no. 2, pp. 1–3.

Strelein, L 2006, *Compromised jurisprudence: native title cases since Mabo*, Aboriginal Studies Press, Canberra.

Sullivan, P 2011, *Belonging together: dealing with the politics of disenchantment in Australian policy*, Aboriginal Studies Press, Canberra.

Sutton, P 2005, 'Rage, reason and the honourable cause: a reply to Cowlishaw', *Australian Aboriginal Studies*, no. 2, pp. 35–43.

—— 2009, *The politics of suffering*, Melbourne University Publishing, Melbourne.

Swansson, J 2010, *Analysing key characteristics in Indigenous corporate failure*, Research Paper, Office of the Registrar of Indigenous Corporations, Canberra, viewed 26 March 2012, <http://www.orac.gov.au/content.aspx?content=publications/otherReports.htm&menu=publications&class=publications&selected=Other%20reports>.

Taylor, J 2002, 'The context for observation', in *Making sense of the Census: observations of the 2001 enumeration in remote Aboriginal Australia*, eds DF Martin, F Morphy, WG Sanders & J Taylor, CAEPR Research Monograph no. 22, ANU ePress, Canberra, pp. 1–11.

—— 2007, 'Whose Census? Institutional constraints on the Indigenous Enumeration Strategy at Wadeye', in *Agency, contingency and Census process: observations of the 2006 Indigenous Enumeration Strategy in remote Aboriginal Australia*, ed. F Morphy, CAEPR Research Monograph no. 28, ANU ePress, Canberra, pp. 55–71.

—— 2009, 'Data mining: Indigenous peoples, applied demography and the resource extraction industry', in *Power, culture and economy: Indigenous Australians and mining*, eds

REFERENCES

J Altman & D Martin, CAEPR Research Monograph no. 30, ANU ePress, Canberra, pp. 51–72.

Thorburn, K 2007a, 'What sort of town is Fitzroy Crossing? Logistical and boundary problems of the 2006 enumeration in the southern Kimberley', in *Agency, Contingency and Census Process*, ed. F Morphy, CAEPR Research Monograph no. 28, ANU ePress, Canberra, pp. 73–85.

—— 2007b, 'Managing dilemmas in Indigenous community-based organisations: viewing a spectrum of ways through the prism of accountability', *Ngiya: Talk the Law*, vol. 1, pp. 2–23.

—— 2008 ' Mapping expectation around a "governance review" exercise of a Western Kimberley organisation', in *Contested governance: culture, power and institutions in Indigenous Australia*, eds J Hunt, D Smith, S Garling & W Sanders, CAEPR Research Monograph no. 29 ANU ePress, Canberra, pp. 331–50.

Warin, J 2007, *Remote Aboriginal communities: why the trade in girls and other human rights abuses remains hidden*, Occasional Paper, The Bennelong Society, Sydney.

Weiner, JF 2006, 'Eliciting customary law', *The Asia Pacific Journal of Anthropology*, vol. 7, no. 1, pp. 15–25.

Wilson, D 1998, *The cost of crossing bridges*, Small Poppies Publishing, Mitcham, Vic.

Windschuttle, K 2009, *The fabrication of Australian history vol 3: The Stolen Generations, 1881–2008*, Macleay Press, Sydney.

Wise, T 1985, *The self-made anthropologist: a life of AP Elkin*, George Allen & Unwin, Sydney.

Yates, A 2009, 'The bush food industry and poverty alleviation in Central Australia', *Dialogue*, vol. 28, no. 2, pp. 47–56.

Index

Aboriginal Advancement Council (WA) 2
Aboriginal Arts Board 55
Aboriginal Community Controlled Health Organisation (ACCHO) 133, 134, 135
Aboriginal heritage protection 52–5
Aboriginal and Torres Strait Islander Commission (ATSIC) 117, 121, 124
Aboriginal and Torres Strait Islander Social Justice Commissioner (ATSISJC) 131–2
African Americans 149–51
Ah Kit, John 23, 190
alcohol and substance use 26, 132, 153, 155, 160, 163, 166, 167, 168, 169, 177, 190, 192, 208
Alice Springs 45, 49, 139
anthropology and anthropologists x, xvi, xvii, xx, 13, 14, 23, 31–5, 37, 38, 39, 44, 45, 46, 50, 51, 68, 102, 108–9, 114, 116, 146, 161, 162, 181, 184, 185, 191 *and see* Abbie, AA 72–3, 74, 76; Berndt CH 39, 41, 64–5; Berndt, RM 39, 40, 50, 53, 64–5; Durkheim, Emile xvi, 40–1; Elkin, AP x, xvi, xx, 38–41, 43–4; Fox, Robin 181; Freeman, Derek 55; Geddes, WR 50; Stanner, WEH 46–8, 50, 82, 184–6; Strehlow, TGH xvi, xx, 45–61; Sutton, Peter ix, 160–72, 189–90, 194, 197
assimilation policy ix, x, xvi, xx, 5, 16, 17, 22, 24, 31, 32, 33, 35, 37, 38, 39, 40, 41, 42, 43, 44, 45, 47, 48, 57, 67, 68, 68, 104, 127, 150, 163, 169, 181, 186, 187, 195, 219, 220
AusAID 131

Australian Institute of Aboriginal Studies (AIAS) 50–5
Australian Labor Party vii, 46, 78, 154
Australian Law Reform Commission 18–19, 21, 25
Australian National University (ANU) 46, 50, 55, 179, 184
Australian and New Zealand Association for the Advancement of Science (ANZAAS) 31, 38, 39, 185, 187
Australian Securities and Investments Commission (ASIC) 129

Barnes, CE 16–7
Bawaninga Aboriginal Corporation (BAC) 113
Bennelong Society 134
'Big Men' xvii, 133–7
Bjelke-Petersen, Johannes x
Blackburn, Justice 17–8, 23, 68
Borrie, W 9–10
Bourke viii, 83, 84
Brough, Mal 188
Burke, JT 50
Busbridge, DL 69–70, 75, 77–8

Calma, Tom 132, 136, 157
Canada 19, 78, 224
capacity (Indigenous political) xvi–xvii, xix–xx, 17, 22–3, 31, 38, 58–60, 68, 71–3, 107–8, 111, 121, 132, 181, 182, 183–5, 186, 187, 188, 201, 203, 209–10, 215
see also 'Big Men'; leadership
Castan, Ron 157

INDEX

Centre for Aboriginal Economic Policy Research (CAEPR) 12, 115
Charles Darwin University 173
Cherbourg 87
citizenship x, 7, 22, 42, 43, 71, 104, 148, 149, 150
common law 18–20, 24, 59, 144–5
Community Development Employment Projects (CDEP) 14, 15, 16, 101, 103, 113, 121, 123, 128, 133, 177, 179, 195, 197
Community Housing and Infrastructure Program (CHIP) 121
conservation of nature 64, 75–6, 158–9
Constitution of Australia vii, 7, 46, 193
Coolbaroo League 22
Coombs, Herbert Cole ix, xi, xvi, xviii, xix, xx, 45–9, 51, 53, 55–61, 130, 134, 139, 174–197
Cooper, William 126–7
Cootamundra Home for Girls 91
Copland, Mark 86–91
Council for Aboriginal Affairs (CAA) ix, 46–8, 58–9
Council of Australian Governments (COAG) 131, 196, 198
Crawford, RM 50
cultural relativism 161–5
culture
  adaptation 57–60, 108–9, 113–4, 125
  loss xvi, 26, 53–7, 165, 191
  persistence of difference xi, xx, 3–4, 16–17, 27, 37–8, 41, 59–60, 68, 104–9, 114, 116–7, 120, 159, 161, 174, 188–9, 204
  see also capacity, Indigenous political; cultural relativism; customary law; 'dysfunction'; family; 'group life'; socialisation
customary law xv, 4, 17–21, 23, 24–7, 113, 116, 130, 145, 165

Darwin, Charles (perspective on human history) 180–3, 192
Democrats (party) vii
Department of Aboriginal Affairs 63, 64 (SA); 179, 185 (Commonwealth).
Department of Finance 131
Department of Social Security 44
Dexter, Barrie 48, 95, 185–6
Dillon, Michael xi, 124

disadvantage, public perceptions of 205–8
Dix, Warwick 54
Dodson, Mick 95, 125–7
Dodson, Patrick 7
Dunstan, Donald xvi, xx, 18, 62–5, 68–9, 71–9
'dysfunction' (of Aboriginal communities) ix, 23, 31, 102, 160, 167, 190, 192, 218

education viii, x, 5, 9, 10, 22, 34, 60, 70, 73, 92, 106, 125, 131–2, 135, 136, 149, 157, 170, 177, 179, 187, 193, 198, 206, 208, 215
Evans, BF 70, 77

family (structure and process) 11–14, 39, 40, 153, 161, 166–7, 190
Federal Council for the Advancement of Aborigines and Torres Strait Islanders (FCAATSI) 22
Fenner, Frank 50
Foundation for Aboriginal Affairs 22
Fraser government xvii, 164, 179

Gerard 78
Gorton government 48, 95
Greens Party vii, 158
Griffith University 86
governance
  as accountability structures and processes 24, 115, 117, 120–2, 131, 143
  as knowledge production 173–6
'group life' x, xvi, xx, 13, 17–18, 22, 24, 32, 34, 38–44, 45, 125

Hasluck, Paul ix, x, xv, xvi, 31–44, 47, 163, 176, 187, 195, 197
Herron, John 157
High Court of Australia vii, 18, 19, 21, 144, 145, 179
History, significant re-interpretations of xvii, 86–93, 146–9, 163–70
Holt government 46
homelands 129, 133, 135–9, 178, 184, 188, 193
Howard, John (and government of) vii, xvii, xix, 5–6, 81, 93, 105, 115, 128, 134, 139, 156, 157, 165, 177, 188, 233
Howson, Peter 134
Hughes, Helen ix, xvii, 128–139, 176–8
Hughes, L 74

Human Rights and Equal Opportunity
  Commission (HREOC) 81–4, 86,
  87, 97

Indigenous Coordination Centre
  (ICC) 131
Indigenous Land Use Agreement
  (ILUA) 21
Indigenous sector 101–4
individual agency and responsibility x,
  xvi, 35–6, 39–41, 42, 44, 78–9, 125,
  179, 204, 208, 209, 210–12
  see also personal experience
International Labour Organization (ILO)
  5, 69
Israel 78

Johnson, Martin 80

Keating, Paul vii, 156, 179
Killoran, Pat x
Kinchela Home for Aboriginal Boys 91
Kruger, Alec 82–3
Kurungal Inc 112–3

Lake Tyers 67
land rights vii–xii, xvi, xvii, 17–19, 23,
  44, 46, 48, 55, 62–5, 67–8, 71, 74, 77,
  103, 119, 133–4, 137, 150, 163, 179,
  185–6, 195
Langton, Marcia ix, 164, 191, 230
Lawton, GH 50
leadership (Indigenous) ix, xvii, 5, 16, 17,
  24, 47, 48, 102, 111, 112, 113, 117, 118,
  120, 125, 126, 127, 128, 135, 137, 149,
  152, 156, 157, 198, 204, 210
  see also 'Big Men'
legislation xvii
  Aboriginal Affairs Act (SA) 1962 66, 72
  *Aboriginal Councils and Associations (Cth)
    Act 1976* 105, 115
  Aboriginal Land Rights (Cth) Act 1976
    68, 133, 134
  Aboriginal Land Trust Act (SA) 1966 xvi,
    62–79
  Aborigines Protection Act (NSW) 1909 92
  *Aborigines and Torres Strait Islander
    (Corporation) (Cth) Act 2006* 105,
    110, 115
  Native Title Act 1993 vii, x, 18, 20, 179
'liberal consensus' xi, xviii, 160, 163–170

Liberal Party of Australia vii, 156
liberalism x, xvi, 7, 20–1, 31, 40–2, 67,
  130, 146, 148, 149–50, 154, 157, 161,
  165, 168, 181, 187–8, 197, 220
local government x, 17, 23, 101, 103,
  122–4, 130, 133, 135, 138
'localism' 116–9
Long, Jeremy 47
Lutheran Church xi, 151–3

Mabo (judgment) vii
Mabo, Eddie Jnr 23
Male–female relationships 25–7, 151–2
Manne, Robert 85
middle class xvii, 135–6, 139, 155–6, 158
missions and missionaries x, 22
moral community x–xi, 211–12
  Coombs' view 193–4
  Hasluck's view 33
  Pearson's view 146–7, 157, 159
  public perceptions xi, 202, 205,
    210, 213
Murdoch University 23

native title vii, x, 18–21, 24, 116, 117, 126,
  144–5, 150, 156, 179, 225
Native Title Representative Body
  (NTRB) 24, 118
neo-liberalism 136, 154–5, 189
New Zealand 6, 19, 224
Ngarrindjeri 150
Northern Territory x, xvi, 4, 8, 10, 12, 17,
  18, 23, 25, 35, 45, 46, 47, 52, 68, 77, 80,
  119, 126, 130, 136, 139, 179, 191
  Emergency Intervention x, xvii, xx,
    157, 165, 233
  Land Councils 133–5, 185–6
  local government 122–3, 124
  Stolen Generations in 82–5

Office of Aboriginal Affairs (OAA) 47
Office of the Registrar of Aboriginal/
  Indigenous Corporations (ORAC/
  ORIC) 102, 105–110, 128–9
One People of Australia League
  (OPAL) 22

Pearson, GG 71, 73
Pearson, Noel ix, x–xi, xviii, xx, 6, 19,
  20, 143–159, 164–6, 187

INDEX

'peoples' and 'people-hood' viii, 16–26, 31–2, 34–5, 62, 76–9, 81, 92, 94–7, 143, 203, 215
  see also culture; land rights; leadership
personal experience (significance of) xi, xviii, 48–9, 52–3, 55–56, 156–7, 161–2, 170–2, 204, 214
  see also individual agency and responsibility
Playford, Sir Thomas 73–4, 78
Point McLeay 73, 77
Point Pearce 73, 74, 75, 77
Polanyi, Karl 146
'populations'
  as concept viii, 10–16, 82, 95
  Australian Bureau of Statistics (ABS) 9, 11, 16
  National Aboriginal and Torres Strait Islander Survey (NATSIS) 84–5, 93
  statistics (official) xix, 5–6, 8–16, 95, 196–8, 202

Queensland x, 8, 22, 25, 85, 86, 87, 89, 90, 93, 122, 123, 124, 126, 130, 136, 139, 153, 164
Queensland Council for the Advancement of Aborigines and Torres Strait Islanders (QCAATSI) 22
Quirke, PH 63

racism and racial discrimination xi, 47, 146, 149, 153, 156, 162, 163, 207, 211–12
Recognition of Indigenous Australians vii, viii, xii, xv, 3–4, 6, 7, 8, 16–21, 24–5, 67, 68, 77, 95, 113, 116, 129, 144, 145, 186, 201, 203, 225
  see also 'peoples'; 'populations'
reconciliation xii, 162, 171–2, 203
Reconciliation Australia 201–2
Reconciliation Barometer xii, 201–16
remote Aboriginal communities x, xi, xviii, 10–11, 13–15, 23, 25, 33–4, 46, 62–3, 67, 76, 101, 122–6, 129–30, 133, 135, 137–8, 148–51, 170–2, 174–9, 184–5, 187, 189, 192, 194–5, 197, 231, 232
  and see Amata 53; Anmatjere Community Government 119; Aranda (Arrernte) 45, 49, 53; Balgo 110; Cape York 146, 154, 158, 162; Central Australia 45, 47, 49, 53, 56, 119, 173, 185; Ernabella 53; Finke Siding 53;

Fitzroy Crossing 10; Granite Downs 64; Hope Vale xi, xviii, 151–3; Indulkana 64; Jawoyn 114; Jay Creek 45; Kimberley region 179; Maningrida 138; Musgrave Park 63, 64, 79; Mutitjulu 138; North West Reserve viii, 62–6, 68, 70–9; Oodnadatta 65; Palm Island 138; Pitjantjatjara 53, 132; Rembarrnga 114–5; Wadeye 10, 113–4, 131, 138, 178; Warburton 138; Warlpiri 80; Windidda 109–10; Yalata 63, 71–2; Yirrkala 58, 184,–5; Yolngu 14, 16–17, 111, 184–6
reserves 34, 67–8
  see also remote Aboriginal communities, North-West Reserve
Ride, WDL 54
Rotary 134, 184
Rowley, C D 22, 47
Royal Commission into Aboriginal Deaths in Custody 25

self-determination ix, x, xi, xvi, xviii, xix, 17, 22, 31, 45, 47, 48, 58, 96, 101, 104, 109, 112–14, 116–17, 120, 122, 124, 127, 179, 183, 188
service delivery (to Aboriginal communities) viii, x, xi, 24, 43, 44, 64, 94, 101, 103, 104, 107, 115, 117, 118, 120, 121–7, 129, 133–5, 138, 148, 161, 163–4, 166, 170, 198, 208
Shannon, H 72, 73
Shared Responsibility Agreements (SRA) 131–2
social justice,(contested meaning)vii–viii, xii, 162
  Closing the Gap xii, xx, 5–6, 9–10, 13, 16, 143, 195–8, 202, 205
socialisation (of Aboriginal children) 94, 161, 166–8, 170, 176, 178, 187, 191–2, 195, 231
Society for Aboriginal Civilization (SAC) 55
South Australia viii, xvi, 8, 11, 18, 53, 62–79, 130, 136, 139, 185
South Australian Museum 53
Soviet Union 133
Steering Committee for the Review of Government Service Provision (SCRGSP) 10, 198
Stolen Generations xvi, 26, 80–98

Tangentyere Council 11
Tent Embassy vii
terra nullius ix
Trendall, AD 50
Tybingoompa, Gladys 162

United Nations (UN) 5
United States of America 78
University of Adelaide 45, 46, 50, 53, 58
University of Sydney 151

Vickery, FJ 70, 77, 78

Wearing, AS 74
Wentworth, William Charles 48
Westbury, Neil xi, 124
Western Australia 8, 9, 11, 25, 54, 59, 77, 122, 123–4, 130, 136, 139
Whitlam government 47
Windschuttle, Keith 87, 90–3, 146
women (as agents and/or victims) 25–7
Woodward, Edward 18, 48, 185
work 14–16, 173–5
Wyles, WA 63

Yates, Peter 173–5